MANAGING RELIGIOUS DIVERSITY IN THE OTTOMAN EMPIRE

Edinburgh Studies on the Ottoman Empire
Series Editor: Kent F. Schull

Published and forthcoming titles

The Ottoman Canon and the Construction of Arabic and Turkish Literatures
C. Ceyhun Arslan

Migrating Texts: Circulating Translations around the Ottoman Mediterranean
Edited by Marilyn Booth

Ottoman Translations: Circulating Texts from Bombay to Paris
Edited by Marilyn Booth and Claire Savina

Death and Life in the Ottoman Palace: Revelations of the Sultan Abdülhamid I Tomb
Douglas Scott Brookes

Ottoman Sunnism: New Perspectives
Edited by Vefa Erginbaş

Ethnic Cleansing in Western Anatolia, 1912–1923: Ottoman Officials and the Local Christian Population
Umit Eser

Jews and Palestinians in the Late Ottoman Era, 1908–1914: Claiming the Homeland
Louis A. Fishman

Governing Migration in the Late Ottoman Empire
Ella Fratantuono

Spiritual Vernacular of the Early Ottoman Frontier: The Yazıcıoğlu Family
Carlos Grenier

The Politics of Armenian Migration to North America, 1885–1915: Sojourners, Smugglers and Dubious Citizens
David Gutman

The Kizilbash-Alevis in Ottoman Anatolia: Sufism, Politics and Community
Ayfer Karakaya-Stump

Çemberlitaş Hamami in Istanbul: The Biographical Memoir of a Turkish Bath
Nina Macaraig

Hagia Sophia in the Long Nineteenth Century
Edited by Emily Neumeier and Benjamin Anderson

The Kurdish Nobility in the Ottoman Empire: Loyalty, Autonomy and Privilege
Nilay Özok-Gündoğan

Armenians and Land Disputes in the Ottoman Empire, 1850–1914
Mehmet Polatel

Nineteenth-Century Local Governance in Ottoman Bulgaria: Politics in Provincial Councils
Safa Saraçoğlu

Prisons in the Late Ottoman Empire: Microcosms of Modernity
Kent F. Schull

Ruler Visibility and Popular Belonging in the Ottoman Empire
Darin Stephanov

Managing Religious Diversity in the Ottoman Empire: Experiences of Istanbul Armenians in the Nineteenth Century
Masayuki Ueno

The North Caucasus Borderland: Between Muscovy and the Ottoman Empire, 1555–1605
Murat Yaşar

Children and Childhood in the Ottoman Empire: From the 14th to the 20th Centuries
Edited by Gülay Yılmaz and Fruma Zachs

edinburghuniversitypress.com/series/esoe

MANAGING RELIGIOUS DIVERSITY IN THE OTTOMAN EMPIRE

EXPERIENCES OF ISTANBUL ARMENIANS IN THE NINETEENTH CENTURY

Masayuki Ueno

EDINBURGH
University Press

Edinburgh University Press is one of the leading university presses in the UK. Publishing new research in the arts and humanities, EUP connects people and ideas to inspire creative thinking, open new perspectives and shape the world we live in. For more information, visit www.edinburghuniversitypress.com.

Edinburgh University Press Ltd
13 Infirmary Street, Edinburgh EH1 1LT

First published in hardback by Edinburgh University Press 2025

Typeset in Jaghbuni by
Cheshire Typesetting Ltd, Cuddington, Cheshire
Printed and bound in the UK using 100% renewable electricity by
CPI Group (UK) Ltd

A CIP record for this book is available from the British Library

ISBN 978 1 3995 4261 6 (hardback)
ISBN 978 1 3995 4262 3 (paperback)
ISBN 978 1 3995 4263 0 (webready PDF)
ISBN 978 1 3995 4264 7 (epub)

Contents

Preface

I first came across the term '*millet* system' when I attended a world history class as a high school student in Japan in the 1990s and learned about the Ottoman Empire. At the time, I had no idea that this analytical framework regarding the Ottoman Empire's treatment of non-Muslims would attract my future scholarly interest. Nor could I have imagined that what appeared in a high school textbook was already controversial among scholars. When I began graduate studies in Ottoman history in 2002, little was understood about the Ottoman Empire's treatment of non-Muslims. Since then, I have devoted myself to examining how the Ottoman Empire tried to become a modern state with subjects who were diverse in terms of religious and cultural backgrounds. This book is a product of research that I have been working on since graduate school.

This book's main goal is to respond to the recent resurgence of interest among Ottomanist scholars in the empire's arrangements with non-Muslims and the *millet* system by examining the words and deeds of the lay and ecclesiastical elites of Istanbul Armenians and Muslim state officials in the nineteenth century. As such, this book does not deal with the experience of Armenians in the eastern provinces, who constituted the majority of Ottoman Armenians, or with the massacres and genocide in the last decades of the empire. Excellent studies already exist on these topics. However, this book does contribute to our understanding of Ottoman Armenian history by examining the political and social profiles of the Armenians in Istanbul. Although Istanbul was home to the largest Armenian community in the Ottoman period, the catastrophe during World War I and the subsequent circumstances greatly reduced the size of Istanbul's Armenian community. This book sheds light on aspects of the Armenian experience in Istanbul that are often overlooked from the perspectives of Turkish and Armenian nationalisms.

Preface

Many people have supported me since I started graduate school. I would like to acknowledge a few of them here. First and foremost, I would like to express my deepest gratitude to Kayoko Hayashi, my undergraduate advisor, who welcomed me into the study of Ottoman history and who has guided me directly and indirectly for a long time since. An ingenious and sincere scholar, she played a major role in shaping my attitude towards Ottoman scholarship. I am profoundly indebted to my graduate advisor, Tadashi Suzuki, for his sensible, tender and patient guidance. I would also like to thank Cemal Kafadar for allowing me to do post-doctoral research at Harvard University. Special acknowledgement is also due to Jun Akiba, Hiroyuki Ogasawara, Nobuyoshi Fujinami and Madoka Morita for their insight, generosity and hospitality.

I owe much to my colleagues in the Department of History at Osaka Metropolitan University (formerly Osaka City University) for their intellectual stimulation. The joint research project I undertook with one of them, Takashi Tsukada, allowed me to spend a year at Yale University. I am also thankful to Daniel Botsman and Alan Mikhail for their help with this project. I would like to acknowledge the support of Yaşar Tolga Cora, thanks to whom I was able to devote a year to research at Boğaziçi University after the pandemic.

I benefited a great deal from archives and libraries in Japan, Turkey, Armenia and the United States. I am indebted to many staff members of the Ottoman Archives of the Turkish Presidency (formerly the Prime Ministry). The late Patriarch Mesrop Mutafian not only taught me the basics of Western Armenian but also gave me special permission to use the Library of the Armenian Patriarchate of Istanbul, which was in the process of being organised. Its librarian, Helda Aynayüz, found many periodicals and books in the library for me. I also benefited from Atatürk Library, the Centre for Islamic Studies, Boğaziçi University Library, Matenadaran, Armenian Academy of Sciences Library, Armenian National Library and Harvard University and Yale University Libraries.

Chapters 3, 5 and 6 include several rewritten sections from four of my previous articles: '"For the Fatherland and the State": Armenians Negotiate the Tanzimat Reforms', *International Journal of Middle East Studies* 45, no. 1 (2013): 93–109; 'Religious in Form, Political in Content?: Privileges of Ottoman Non-Muslims in the Nineteenth Century', *Journal of the Economic and Social History of the Orient* 59, no. 3 (2016): 408–41; 'Empire as a Career: Hagop Grjigian or an Armenian in the Ottoman Bureaucracy', *Memoirs of the Research Department of the Toyo Bunko* 76 (2018): 57–80; 'In Pursuit of Laicized Urban Administration: The *Muhtar* System in Istanbul and Ottoman Attitudes toward Non-Muslim

Religious Authorities in the Nineteenth Century', *International Journal of Middle East Studies* 54, no. 2 (2022): 302–18.

I am grateful to the Heiwa Nakajima Foundation and the Japan Society for the Promotion of Science (Grant Numbers 25884054, 15K16846, 19K01021, 20KK0266 and 23K00870) for their financial support.

I would like to thank Kent F. Schull, the series editor, the advisory board, the anonymous reviewers and Rachel Bridgewater, the senior commissioning editor, for their constructive comments and criticisms and for seeing the value in publishing this book.

Finally, and most importantly, I would like to express my love and appreciation to my wife, Manami Ueno, who was always my greatest emotional support, intellectual inspiration and source of motivation while writing this book. The greatest blessing of my research career was meeting and building a relationship with someone of her integrity and intelligence.

Note on Transliteration and Dates

Western Armenian and Eastern Armenian have been transliterated according to the Library of Congress transliteration system. Turkish in Armenian script has been transliterated according to the same rule for bibliographic information and according to the orthography of modern Turkish in the text of this book. Ottoman Turkish has been transliterated according to the modern orthography. I use English spellings whenever they are widely recognised (e.g., Istanbul, ulama). I use conventional spellings for Armenian and Turkish proper names for increased readability. In place of dates using the Hijri, Rumi and Julian calendars, I have provided converted dates using the Gregorian calendar.

Introduction: Ottoman Armenians, Multireligious Empire and Politicisation of Religion

In 1852, a significant dispute erupted between Russia and France over Christian holy places in Ottoman Palestine. In this dispute, the Russians demanded that the Ottoman Empire sign an agreement guaranteeing privileges for Orthodox Christian Ottoman subjects. High-ranking Ottoman officials responded by asserting that the empire already guaranteed religious privileges to its non-Muslim subjects and had done so of its own accord, refusing to submit to Russian demands. While the Russians had referred to privileges in general, Ottoman officials added the adjectives 'religious' and 'ecclesiastical' during their negotiations with the Russian envoy. The Ottomans' response did not satisfy the Russians, whose troops subsequently marched on Walachia and Moldavia in July 1853. With the odds of battle poised against the Ottomans, Britain and France entered the war on their side in an effort to maintain the European balance of power, which reversed the outcome of the conflict.[1] The Crimean War ended following the Treaty of Paris in March 1856 and the Reform Edict of February in the same year, which pronounced the equality of Muslim and non-Muslim Ottoman subjects. These events overshadowed the Ottoman government's earlier edict issued on the eve of the war, publicly guaranteeing the same religious privileges for non-Muslims, which would be later repeated in the Reform Edict.[2]

In the nineteenth century, many countries addressed the principle of equality in crafting their new regimes, with varying answers to the question of 'equality for whom?' reflecting their social configurations. The Ottomans deemed the form of inequality most in need of correction was neither that of the social class for free people nor of slavery and serfdom but rather the religious inequality favouring Muslims over non-Muslims. The abolition of this type of inequality marked a significant milestone in the empire's long history, as this fundamental principle had persisted for more than 1,000 years throughout various Muslim dynasties since the Prophet Muhammad's lifetime. Thus, researchers viewed the promise of equality in the Reform Edict as the first step towards creating an Ottoman nation undifferentiated by religion and united under the principle of universal citizenship, identifying this new policy of integration as Ottomanism. Meanwhile, scholars failed to recognise that the guarantee of religious privileges during the same decade was a novelty in the empire's long history, viewing its repetition in the Reform Edict as a remnant of early modern arrangements for non-Muslims, terming it as an incongruity, as incomplete and as lukewarm.[3] Nevertheless, the guarantee of religious privileges was not temporary but was later embedded in the empire's legal regime; both equality and religious privileges were eventually enshrined in the Ottoman Constitution of 1876.[4] Thereafter, the preservation of religious privileges remained a contentious topic of negotiation between the state and non-Muslims until the nascent Republic of Turkey rejected this Ottoman legacy in 1923.

What, then, were the religious privileges granted to non-Muslims, and why did the Ottoman Empire repeatedly guarantee these privileges? As this book will argue, these religious privileges were the inventive products of the Ottoman statesmen's inclination to institutionalise the statuses of non-Muslim clerical bodies while creating the new regime. By doing so, they – without overtly infringing non-Muslims' freedoms in practising their own religion – aimed at reducing the influence of non-Muslim clergymen to merely religious affairs, thus keeping them under control. Contrary to how this expression may sound, their main objective was not to strengthen and utilise the influence of clergymen to rule over non-Muslim subjects but to lessen the non-Muslims' area of activity as a community. Accordingly, they used this new term to collectively describe the favours and exemptions that Ottoman sultans granted to the top echelons of non-Muslim religious hierarchies.

The Ottoman Turkish term *imtiyazat* (plural; singular *imtiyaz*), meaning privileges, originates from Arabic and derives from the concept of separating and distinguishing. For Ottomanist scholars, the first association is often with the commercial and legal favours that Ottoman sultans granted to European visitors, commonly known as capitulation.[5] Contrary to general belief, however, capitulation was not referred to as *imtiyazat* in Ottoman documents until the nineteenth century. In recent years, scholarship on Ottoman foreign relations has witnessed the development of research on its legal regimes, examining the Ottoman responses to and influence on the development of the Eurocentric international order.[6] This line of research has revealed that the Ottoman Empire originally referred to capitulation as *müsaade* (favour) and replaced this traditional terminology with *imtiyazat* at the turn of the nineteenth century. Around the same time, the empire also began using the same term to describe the territorial autonomy and benefits granted to non-Muslim clergymen.[7] The fact that all these were related to areas where Ottoman sovereignty was limited in relation to the European Great Powers suggests that the Ottoman Empire, in confrontation with the Eurocentric legal regime, used this new term as a tool to incorporate these carved-out areas into the configuration of the modern sovereign state and to restructure its early modern organisation of diversity.[8] Among the three types of privileges recognised by the Ottoman Empire in the nineteenth century, religious privileges symbolise the Ottoman approach towards non-Muslim clergymen in the face of possible foreign intervention and reflect how the empire struggled to manage its populace's religious diversity while pursuing the civil integration of individuals under the principle of equality.

However, the use of the term 'privileges' did not solely reflect the top-down Ottoman initiative. Non-Muslims adapted this framework for their own purposes, with the aim to safeguard – and even broaden – their communities' rights and exemptions. As the empire sought to more narrowly define the privileges accorded to non-Muslim religious authorities, Armenian elites in Istanbul (among others) tested and pushed back the new imperial parameters. In negotiations between non-Muslim communities and the state, 'religious privileges' emerged as a key term concerning their collective rights. This book reconstructs the efforts made by both Ottoman officials and Armenian elites in their political agendas and the places where they negotiated or came into conflict. It elucidates how the development of the institutional framework for arrangements between the Ottoman state and non-Muslims was a product of their negotiations and addresses a renewed interest among Ottomanist scholars in this subject, formerly known as the *millet* system.

Thus, while acknowledging the significance of the international situation surrounding the Ottoman Empire, this book will avoid a common view that emphasises the influence of foreign intervention when investigating the evolving treatment of non-Muslims. Instead, it will prioritise the experiences of Ottomans – especially Armenians, who were the empire's second-largest non-Muslim denominational group – when considering the new framework's transformative and constitutive influence on their political, social and cultural lives. Both lay and ecclesiastical Armenian elites in Istanbul, who gathered in the city's Patriarchate (their most important clerical body in the empire), eagerly and promptly responded to the changes implemented by the empire in its approach to non-Muslim clerical bodies. The deep ties of Armenian elites with the Ottoman regime compelled them to depend on its institutional framework to navigate this period of drastic change. By examining their experiences, which have not received adequate attention in Ottoman historiography, this book explores the strategies adopted by Ottoman Armenians to find a secure place in the multireligious empire, both as individuals and as members of an ethnoreligious community.

A Multireligious Empire

Around the year 1300, the Ottomans began as a small principality in northwestern Anatolia. Over the following centuries, they gradually expanded their realm into the Balkans, the remainder of Anatolia and the eastern and southern Mediterranean. This territorial expansion was accompanied by the incorporation of the religiously, ethnically and linguistically diverse populations inhabiting these newly acquired lands. Among these populaces were Christians and Jews of various ethnic backgrounds. Present in the Balkans were mainly Slavic- and Greek-speaking Orthodox Christians with whom Muslims intermingled, especially in urban areas. In Western and Northern Anatolia, Greek Orthodox Christians coexisted with Turkish Muslims, while in what is now Eastern Anatolia, a sizeable number of Armenian Christians shared the region with the more numerous Kurdish and Turkish Muslims. In the eastern and southern Mediterranean, small communities of various Christian denominations resided alongside the predominantly Arabic-speaking Muslim populace. Furthermore, a substantial number of Jews, after being expelled from the Iberian Peninsula, joined their coreligionists in Ottoman territory.

While some Christians and Jews adopted the religion of the ruling dynasty and became assimilated Muslims, the imperial policy, in general, was not assimilative.[9] The Ottoman authorities, inheriting the approach of earlier Islamic dynasties towards *dhimmi*s – non-Muslims under the protection of a Muslim polity – allowed non-Muslim subjects to practise their own faiths and maintain their own religious organisations as long as they paid the necessary tributes and adhered to the restrictions on their social and religious lives. The rising prominence of Islamic legitimacy in the sixteenth century led to the exclusion of non-Muslims from political and military positions and the formalisation of their treatment; nevertheless, Orthodox Christians, Armenians, Jews and others were generally able to maintain their religious affiliations. In the late nineteenth century, the descendants of the members of these non-dominant religious groups comprised approximately 30 per cent of the empire's population.[10] It was the religious diversity of the populace rather than its multiethnic nature that characterised Ottoman society. The state's arrangements with its non-Muslim subjects thus garnered early attention from scholars, giving rise to the theory of the *millet* system.

In 1937, Alford Carleton wrote a PhD dissertation titled 'The Millet System for the Government of Minorities in the Ottoman Empire' at Hartford Seminary, Connecticut.[11] Harry Charles Luke and Arnold J. Toynbee had already used the term 'millet system' to describe the Ottoman treatment of non-Muslims in 1925 and 1927, respectively, shortly after the collapse of the empire.[12] However, Carleton's dissertation marked the first in-depth analysis of the subject that employed the term. His work traced the concept of the nation across the history of the Near East, focusing on the *millet*, which, he argued, had undergone a semantic shift from religion and religious community to nation. Carleton's research primarily drew from works written in Western languages published during the final century of the Ottoman Empire and was founded on his personal experiences as a Protestant missionary in Adana and Mardin in Turkey and Aleppo in Syria, where he worked after graduating from college in 1924 until his return to the United States in 1936. He incorporated into his writings the belief – also held by nineteenth-century Ottomans and foreign observers – that by appointing the Orthodox Christian and Armenian patriarchs in Istanbul and tacitly recognising the Jewish chief rabbi after the conquest of the city, Mehmet II assigned them responsibility for the affairs of their respective religious communities.[13]

Drawing on Carleton's work, H. A. R. Gibb and Harold Bowen promoted the same interpretation in their 1957 book *Islamic Society and the West*, which introduced Carleton's argument on the *millet* system to a broader audience. In this system, the Ottoman Empire organised its non-Muslim subjects into three *millet*s or religious communities, namely, Orthodox Christians, Armenians and Jews, and gave the religious head of each community, based in Istanbul, the authority to form a centralised community and autonomously administer the affairs of their coreligionists throughout the empire. This arrangement, which helped the state govern religiously diverse subjects, was consistently in place from the mid-fifteenth century, following the conquest of Constantinople, to the early twentieth century, when the empire collapsed.[14] The *millet* system came to be widely understood as a symbol of Ottoman tolerance towards non-dominant religious groups, and this understanding was then exported back to the Turkish academic community.[15] It also led historians to view Ottoman society as a collection of autonomous and distinct religious groups, with minimal interaction between members of different sects. However, since Benjamin Braude cast doubt on this prevailing view in 1982, revisionist scholarship has extensively explored state and non-Muslim arrangements.[16]

One significant historiographical development lies in the examination of Ottoman treatment of the Orthodox Church in general and the patriarch of Istanbul in particular. Research has indicated that patriarchal power and jurisdiction were relatively restricted in the early years of Ottoman rule but expanded in subsequent periods, especially during the eighteenth century. Additionally, historians have identified how the empire incorporated Christian prelates into its own administration through a tax farming system: the government granted favours and exemptions to prelates in exchange for tributes, hoping to profit financially from the ecclesiastical networks and properties of the Church. Thus, the state viewed the highest-ranking Orthodox clerics not as powerful administrators of communal autonomy but as an effective means of collecting revenue.[17] Elif Bayraktar Tellan conducted an assessment of the eighteenth-century expansion of the rights granted to the Patriarchate of Istanbul by investigating Ottoman documents. She surmised that behind this development was the rise of lay notables who actively involved themselves in Orthodox Church affairs along with the necessity for the Church to soundly handle the challenges presented by Catholic missionaries.[18]

Revisionist scholarship seems to have acquired enough weight to 'put to rest the *millet* system explanation for Ottoman governance of non-Muslims'.[19] However, while studies of Orthodox Christians have significantly altered our understanding of the state's arrangements with non-Muslims, studies of other non-Muslim groups have not made a comparable contribution, making it difficult to obtain a more comprehensive view of the development of the Ottoman arrangements that twentieth-century researchers had termed the *millet* system. Another challenge is the common focus among researchers on the intervention of the European Great Powers when examining changes in the nineteenth century.[20] Therefore, the primary focus of this book is to address these problems and expand readers' understanding of the arrangements between the state and non-Muslims by exploring how the Ottoman treatment of non-Muslim religious authorities changed as the empire transitioned into a modern state, with a focus on the Armenians as my main point of analysis, along with comparative references to the case of the Orthodox Christians.

The Armenians developed a distinct church organisation headed by a catholicos and a religious tradition that depended on the classical form of the Armenian language from late antiquity. Consequently, the Church provided the Armenians with a long-standing sense of group cohesiveness without a corresponding independent political identity under the Sassanids, the Byzantines and multiple Muslim dynasties. However, the Armenian Church lost its unity over the course of history. When the Ottomans conquered Constantinople in 1453, four religious authorities were present: the catholicoi of Echmiadzin, Sis and Aghtamar and the patriarch of Jerusalem. Nevertheless, each was situated outside what was then Ottoman territory. The Ottomans permitted the Armenians to preserve their ecclesiastical peculiarities as they incorporated Armenians and, ultimately, three of these religious authorities by the early sixteenth century. Furthermore, the Ottomans allowed the Armenians to have a prelate in the new imperial capital following the conquest and, by the second quarter of the sixteenth century, granted this role the title of patriarch.[21]

In their discussion of the charters that sultans granted to Orthodox Christian patriarchs, Çolak and Bayraktar Tellan asserted that the Orthodox Church should be called an Ottoman institution, suggesting that the role of the state should be considered in the analysis of the patriarchates rather than dividing the political history of the Ottoman Empire from the experiences of non-Muslim communities.[22] This proposal applies more to the case of the Armenian Patriarchate of Istanbul, given its creation by the Ottomans, its lack of an ecclesiastical basis for its authority and prestige, and its resulting reliance on Ottoman state support. This book explores how the Armenian Patriarchate rose to become the Armenians' most important representative to the government, how this institution was incorporated into Ottoman governance and how the patriarchs interacted with the Ottoman regime. It will also provide an account of how, from an intra-communal perspective, the patriarchate functioned as a venue for political discussion (including the politics of the Armenian Church) among the lay and ecclesiastical elites of Istanbul's Armenian community.

In their recent books, Richard E. Antaramian and Talin Suciyan used Armenian and Armeno-Turkish (that is, Turkish in Armenian script) sources to discuss the activities and roles of Armenian clergymen and their Istanbul Patriarchate, focusing on their involvement with Armenians in the provinces in the mid-nineteenth century. They also discussed the relationship between the state and non-Muslim clergymen, suggesting that the Ottoman government preferred to use non-Muslim clergymen to centralise the empire and gather information about the provinces. From this perspective, Antaramian argued that the Armenian clergymen actively cooperated with the centralisation of the empire, which, in turn, dismantled their local networks and weakened their power.[23] However, these scholars' understanding of the state's approach to non-Muslim clergymen does not align with the information available in the Ottoman archives.

Indeed, the resources available to Ottoman Muslim statesmen in the nineteenth century were limited, and they were sometimes compelled to use the networks of non-Muslim clergymen. However, as Jack Fairey showed, by 1840, they had already developed a cautious attitude towards clergymen, seeing them as a factor in the intervention of European powers.[24] As this book shows, in the nineteenth century, when stabilising relations with the European powers was paramount to the survival of the empire, Muslim statesmen were not willing to allow the influence of the clergymen to grow by tolerating their role in the centralisation of the empire but sought to limit their activities and keep them under control. Religious privileges, the focus of this book, were key to understanding their approach to non-Muslim religious authorities.

Ottoman arrangements with non-Muslim religious authorities can be divided into three stages.[25] The first stage was from the early Ottoman period to the late seventeenth century, during which the Ottomans focused more on financial gain from the church networks and did not necessarily seek to grant greater power to the clergymen. The second stage was from the late seventeenth century to the early nineteenth century, during which the financial aspect remained as an institutional framework but dealing with the Catholic issue became more important. This required the Ottoman government to strengthen the authority of the patriarchates. In the third stage, from the mid-nineteenth century, the Ottoman government increasingly saw the clergymen as a nuisance that could provide a pretext for foreign intervention and sought to bring them under control.

This book begins by discussing the transition from the first to the second stage. Chapter 1 analyses the process of the rise of the Armenian Patriarchate of Istanbul, which paralleled that of the Patriarchate of Orthodox Christians, and examines how the patriarchate acquired a particular role for itself in Ottoman governance in the late seventeenth and eighteenth centuries. Accordingly, this book aligns itself with recent trends in Ottoman historiography that perceive Ottoman modernity as a product of long-term, internal transformations that took place in the seventeenth and eighteenth centuries as different types of power holders, including janissaries, ulamas and local notables, participated in Ottoman governance.[26]

Later chapters will extensively cover the transition to the third stage and the subsequent developments that occurred in the nineteenth century. In this century, two primary trends influenced the relationship between the Ottoman state and non-Muslim religious authorities. First, the state increased the centralisation of political authority, which, on the one hand, tremendously reinforced its intervention in society with the intent to strengthen its control over the society's diverse aspects, and, on the other hand, negatively affected the status of power holders who had participated in imperial governance.[27] Second, the cultural developments among Armenians expanded the space for their communal activities within the multireligious empire, leading their lay and ecclesiastical elites, who gathered in and around the Patriarchate of Istanbul, to reinforce their intervention in affairs concerning Armenians. These trends eventually led to disagreements between state officials and Armenian elites over the jurisdiction of non-Muslim religious authorities. Although Ottoman statesmen could not simply abolish the privileged status of non-Muslim religious authorities, they did not leave them untouched; they turned to forging new arrangements between the state and non-Muslims by relying more on individual lay elites and curtailing the scope of clerical and communal activity. Amidst these developments, the focal point was the interpretation of the religious privileges that the government guaranteed for non-Muslims.

Armenians in the Ottoman Empire

The region known as the Armenian Highlands, stretching along the southern face of the Caucasus Mountains and between Anatolia and the Iranian Plateau, was the native soil of the Armenians. In the first half of the sixteenth century, the Safavid and Ottoman states came into conflict over the region and eventually incorporated its eastern and western parts, respectively, into their empires. During the same period, the Mediterranean region of Cilicia, which had been the territory of the Armenian Kingdom in the late medieval period and was still home to many Armenians, was also incorporated into the Ottoman realm. Consequently, most of the Armenian population in the world fell under Ottoman rule.

In the late sixteenth and early seventeenth centuries, numerous Armenians were threatened by the turmoil caused by rebellions. Consequently, many emigrated from the western Armenian Highlands to Thrace, Western Anatolia and Istanbul, where they joined the small groups of their coreligionists who had settled there earlier. In the subsequent centuries, similar waves of Armenian migrants continued due to the poor economic and social conditions at home, contributing to the growth of their communities and culture in the western part of the Ottoman Empire.[28] This migration further dispersed Armenians across the empire, leading them to settle throughout Anatolia and in some cities in the Balkan and Arab provinces, where they formed small communities. A salient exception was Istanbul, which continued to attract Armenian immigrants and migrant workers in the seventeenth and eighteenth centuries, evolving into the largest concentration of Armenians in the empire, comprising 15 to 20 per cent of the city's population.[29] Their prominence in the capital exceeded their numerical representation due to their success in international commerce and their financial role as *sarrafs* (financiers) within the empire's primary tax collection system.[30] The remarkable presence of Armenians in Istanbul and their close interaction with the city's Muslims was evidenced by a negative comment made by Fazlizade Ali, a Muslim preacher, in 1740. Expressing discomfort over the influence of non-Muslims on their Muslim neighbours, he particularly criticised Armenians and claimed:

> the Armenian infidels, who are called the *reᶜāyā* of this city, have been favoured to such an extent, and that they meddle in everything and that they come to every business and to chosen houses and noble places and that the community of Muḥammad is in need of those low and mean people.[31]

In the nineteenth century, while the eastern part of the Armenian Highlands and its population were incorporated into the Russian Empire, the western part (now Eastern Anatolia) remained under Ottoman rule and formed its eastern provinces. Most Ottoman Armenians resided in this region, a sizeable number of whom engaged in artisanal businesses, including goldsmithing, blacksmithing, rug-making and cloth-making, particularly in cities and towns. However, the majority of Armenians here were indigent peasants living in rural areas under the threat of violence from Kurdish tribal groups. The desperate situation in the region led to a continuous outflow of temporary and permanent migrant labourers from the eastern provinces to the imperial capital, where the Armenian community had become their religious and cultural centre within the empire. After the Kurdish migrant porters, who had engaged in goods distribution in Istanbul under the protection of the Janissary corps, lost this role because of the abolishment of the corps in 1826, Armenian migrants took their place. Consequently, this shift further increased the influx of Armenian immigrants into Istanbul in subsequent decades.[32]

In nineteenth-century Istanbul, while most Armenians belonged to a modest artisanal class, some elites emerged as influential figures of community administration and significant financial supporters of community institutions. Among these elites were financiers and technical experts in the first half of the century, while state officials and doctors gained prominence in the latter half. In addition to their personal interests, they were deeply committed to the development of the Armenian community in Istanbul, centred around the patriarchate. As will be discussed in Chapters 2 and 3, Armenian elites in Istanbul enthusiastically advanced the reforms of their community administration, adopting the term 'constitution' to describe their community regulations and institutionalising a communal deliberative assembly resembling a parliament. Meanwhile, although they considered the eastern provinces as their fatherland (*hayrenik'*), calling it Armenia (*Hayasdan*), they had little concern for the situation of their coreligionists in that region until the 1860s.

Recent scholarship on the eastern provinces (or the Ottoman East) has challenged the dominant Istanbul-centric historiography of nineteenth-century reforms. These studies revealed a significant gap between the political intentions of the central government and the implementation of reforms on the ground.[33] These discussions, along with research focused on reforms in other localities, have criticised the traditional understanding, which regarded the reforms as a largely top-down state project. The emerging perspective directs attention to developments in different locales and expands the scope of understanding to encompass diverse interpretations of and responses to reforms from local actors, unexpected consequences and the reorganisation of power relations at a local level.[34] As a part of this trend, studies on the rise of Armenian notables in the provinces, transregional clerical activities and Armenians' interactions with local Muslims and Protestant missionaries have immensely advanced our understanding of the nineteenth-century history of Ottoman Armenians. This novel line of research, along with examinations of other groups, has markedly contributed to bridging the historical gap between the Ottoman Empire and the experiences of the diverse groups under its rule, which have generally otherwise been analysed within the national histories of each group.

While studies focusing on provincial Armenians have made profound contributions, a tendency in some recent studies has been to downplay the agency of the Armenians in Istanbul or view them as obedient collaborators in the government's centralising reforms.[35] Although this book's focus on the Armenians of Istanbul primarily concerns elucidating the change in the empire's institutional dealings with non-Muslims, it also aims to address the limited understanding of their political and social profiles. This book achieves this by examining how they interacted with the state and challenged its reforms by going beyond the expectations of Muslim statesmen, as was the case in the provinces. Considering that Istanbul was the political, religious and cultural centre of the Ottoman Armenians in the nineteenth century, boasting the largest concentrated Armenian population in the empire and acknowledging the interactions between the Armenians of Istanbul and their provincial counterparts, their experiences warrant separate attention in understanding Ottoman Armenian history. This book seeks to update our understanding of their history, which, despite significant advancements in Ottoman studies in recent decades, is still discussed based on publications from the 1980s and earlier.[36]

Some scholars have delved into the roles of lay Armenian elites in Istanbul in the administration of the Armenian community and its reforms, while others have explored their political careers to reconstruct their involvement in specific Ottoman political circles.[37] However, the association between the positions of Armenian elites in Ottoman political society and the roles within the Armenian community has not received sufficient attention. In the nineteenth-century Ottoman Empire, Armenian elites in Istanbul, among the largest non-Muslim groups, were notably advanced in implementing community reforms.[38] Many of those leading these reforms were also members of the Ottoman bureaucracy and actively participated in state reforms. After the Ottoman government opened state bureaucracy to non-Muslims in 1856 as part of a project to achieve equality between Muslims and non-Muslims, Armenians became the most prominent non-Muslim community occupying bureaucratic roles.[39] This prominence can be attributed, in part, to Orthodox Christians, the largest non-Muslim community, pursuing an alternative route for upward mobility. They established dominance in international trade in the late eighteenth century, as well as in finance by the mid-nineteenth century. Consequently, Armenians as a group experienced a reduction in power and influence in those sectors.[40] The remaining avenue for upward mobility was thus entering state bureaucracy, a route likely facilitated by the fluency in Turkish among Armenian males.[41]

Hence, like their religious elites, the lay Armenian elites of Istanbul were characterised by their integration into Ottoman governance. A thorough assessment of this phenomenon necessitates close attention to their connections with Muslim political elites while examining their profiles and involvement in communal politics. It should be noted that this embeddedness, while limiting their choices, does not imply mere obedience as agents of Muslim state officials and sultans. Armenian elites in Istanbul followed their own discretion based on their positions in both Ottoman political society and the Armenian community, as well as their goal of improving the position of their community (from their own perspective) within the multireligious configuration of the empire. Stories of Armenian elites in Istanbul reveal pivotal moments in which they strategically involved the state in their communal politics and negotiated with Muslim officials about their communal rights. Concurrently, Muslim officials and sultans interacted with them, addressing delicate political matters related to non-Muslims.

As Armenian elites were deeply enmeshed in the multireligious Ottoman society, they closely monitored the actions and statuses of the other religious communities within the empire. According to Julia Phillips Cohen, Jews in the late Ottoman Empire perceived themselves as receiving less esteem than other non-Muslim groups and aspired to be acknowledged by the Ottoman government in a manner similar to that of other non-Muslims.[42] The relative position among non-Muslim communities was of no small concern to Istanbul Armenians. This underscores that understanding the functioning of the multireligious Ottoman Empire requires consideration not only of the vertical relationships between the state and specific groups but also of the horizontal and relative relationships between the diverse communities under the same rule. Hence, while the bulk of this book is devoted to discussion of Armenian lay and ecclesiastical elites, it also takes into account the situations of other religious groups.

I conclude my analysis in the final decades of the nineteenth century, during which established rules for negotiation between the state and the Armenians underwent a transformation as violence emerged as an alternative tool. This change was instigated by the Armenian revolutionary parties that vied with the Armenian elites in Istanbul to represent the Armenian community at large. A comprehensive understanding of the period that followed due to this shift requires a different perspective, but this topic falls beyond the scope of this book.

Religion and Politics

When Ottoman officials decided to guarantee privileges for non-Muslims in 1853, they added the adjective 'religious' to limit the extent of privileges available to non-Muslims. This facilitated the development of an approach wherein a distinct area of activity existed, allowing members of non-Muslim groups to make decisions at their discretion. This area was separate from the jurisdiction of the state, prompting Ottoman actors to adopt the terms 'religion' and 'religious' to describe the non-Muslim sphere of authority and 'politics' and 'political' for the state's jurisdiction. This book explores how these actors contributed to shaping the idea that religion constituted a distinct sphere of human society. It closely examines the separation of the spheres of religion and politics in their discussions, as well as the difficulties in drawing a clear line between them. Accordingly, this book draws upon studies that have explored the historicity of the concept of 'religion' and highlighted its connotations, which are rooted in the Christian, particularly the Protestant, experience in Western Europe. These discussions explore concepts often juxtaposed with what is 'religious' and, consequently, help define it by delineating what it is not; such terms include 'secular' or sometimes 'political'.[43]

In discussions among Ottomanists and Armenologists regarding whether nineteenth-century Ottoman reforms were secularising, whether the government aimed to secularise non-Muslim communities and whether the history of Ottoman Armenians in the nineteenth century could even be characterised as a process of secularisation, the historicity of the concepts of the religious and the secular has not always been duly considered.[44] While other researchers have highlighted the drawbacks of employing these binary terms for the nineteenth-century reforms,[45] this book delves into how and why Ottoman political actors themselves invoked this distinction in their use of the terms 'religion'/'religious' and 'politics'/'political'. Therefore, the significance of this dichotomy for the late Ottoman Empire extends beyond the relationship between politics and Islam, as suggested by researchers in Ottoman and Turkish studies, and should be expanded to include the state's relationship with non-Muslim religions.[46]

The Russian treatment of non-dominant religious groups is also relevant for understanding why Ottoman actors incorporated religious rhetoric into their negotiations. Paul Werth argued that the rhetoric accompanying the term 'religious' held strategic importance for non-dominant religious groups resisting state intervention in their communal affairs in the nineteenth century. Meanwhile, the term 'political' was employed by the state to curb undesirable actions by these non-dominant groups.[47] Similarly, Ottoman actors utilised 'religion'/'religious' and 'politics'/'political', asserting that while religious affairs fell under the jurisdiction of non-Muslim religious authorities and were exempt from state intervention, political affairs were within the domain of the state. Similar to the Russian case, no attempt was made to precisely specify what was considered primarily religious. Consequently, the definition of this binary became a battleground determining the extent to which members of each non-Muslim group could make decisions at their discretion.

This book contends that this distinction only gained increased significance for nineteenth-century non-Muslims as state authorities heightened their intervention in society while attempting to establish a new regime. As a result, non-Muslim elites were compelled to defend and possibly expand their sphere of influence. Simultaneously, Muslim state officials, seeking to avoid explicitly denying the historical rights of non-Muslims, aimed to reinforce state sovereignty by confining the arena where non-Muslims could act to affairs that they deemed simply religious. Keeping non-Muslim groups under control was crucial for Ottoman state officials facing political interventions by the European Great Powers on behalf of Ottoman Christians during this period. This necessity prompted the government to establish a new institutional framework for arrangements between the state and non-Muslims, as well as to localise the religious affairs of non-Muslims, which were not always bound by existing political borders; the Ottoman Armenians held ties with the Catholicosate of Echmiadzin, the highest religious authority of the Armenian Church, under Russian rule. Understandably, this state of affairs troubled the political elites of the Ottoman Empire.

The Ottoman Empire was not alone in developing an institutional framework for non-dominant religious groups during this period. The most prominent example was the case of the Russian Empire, referred to by scholars as a confessional state or multiconfessional establishment. In this system, the Russian Empire formulated statutes governing the communal affairs of non-Orthodox Christian groups and the selection of their religious functionaries, incorporating them into the legal system of the empire. As part of this initiative, the Russians established a new hierarchical structure of religious functionaries for Muslim subjects, who comprised the largest non-Orthodox group. Similarly, France, as part of the *système des cultes reconnus*, created a system of consistories for the Jews, an organisation based in Paris responsible for managing their communal affairs. The Austro-Hungarian Empire established its own confessional administration for the newly incorporated Bosnian Muslims, a *Reis-ul-ulema*ship and a council of ulamas.[48]

Behind the developments in the Russian and Austro-Hungarian empires lay the politicisation of religion, in which the Ottoman monarch became increasingly involved. Asserting his spiritual ties with all Muslims, even those outside his empire as caliph, this claim gained strength in the late eighteenth century when the empire lost its territory on the northern shore of the Black Sea, home to a large Muslim population.[49] The incorporation of this region and part of the Polish–Lithuanian Commonwealth significantly increased the number of Muslims, Catholics and Jews under the Russian Empire's rule; this shift prompted the Russians to institutionalise the treatment of non-dominant religious groups. Thus, the politicisation of religion and the institutionalisation of the arrangements between the state and non-dominant religious groups were two sides of the same coin. They exhibited interactive development in both Russia and the Ottoman Empire as political borders gained increasing importance, demonstrating the desire of the ruling circles of both empires to situate their own non-dominant religious groups within their legal framework and to limit the influence of foreign religious and/or political authorities.

Sources and Composition

This book focuses on the words and deeds of the lay and ecclesiastical elites of Istanbul Armenians and Muslim state officials, especially as these were used in negotiations over the jurisdictional scope granted to non-Muslim religious authorities. These words and deeds can be found in Ottoman archival documents, Armenian newspaper articles and the minutes of the Armenian communal assembly.

The variety of these materials and their combination are crucial for our discussion. The most important source for this book comprises the unpublished documents in the Turkish Presidency Archives in Istanbul, written in Ottoman Turkish from the seventeenth to nineteenth centuries. Thorough research of these documents, whose absence has prolonged the discussion about the *millet* system in the field of Ottoman studies, forms the basis for my arguments. Ottoman documents reflect formal communications and justifications used by state officials. Documents submitted by the Armenian Patriarchate to the government help us understand how Armenian elites engaged with the state. Additionally, this book uses Armenian newspapers published in nineteenth-century Istanbul. These newspapers express Armenians' understandings of their claims and their responses to state policies, and also report on negotiations between Muslim statesmen and Armenian elites, many of which were limited to spoken and informal exchanges and, thus, not recorded in official documents. As will be discussed later, some Muslim state officials preferred to negotiate with non-Muslims in non-public ways to avoid the attention of the European Great Powers. In addition, given that most documents held by the Ministry of Justice and Religious Affairs (which had jurisdiction over non-Muslim religious affairs) were lost in a fire, the great part of correspondence between the government and non-Muslim religious authorities after the mid-nineteenth century has been lost.[50] These shortcomings increase the importance of newspapers for any investigation into the state–Armenian negotiations.

Contemporary newspapers and the printed minutes of the Armenians' communal assembly demonstrate that the dichotomy between the religious and the political was not only used in negotiations with state authorities but frequently appeared in discussions among Armenians as well, suggesting that this shared public sphere enabled the formation of intra-communal discourse, further facilitated by the growth of Armenian journalism in this period.[51] Within the Ottoman Empire, each major religious group had its own set of media outlets, which circulated mainly within that group. It was during the latter half of the nineteenth century that newspapers and magazines first began to saturate Ottoman society, opening venues of public discussion for several groups in the empire. The Armenian community published newspapers not only in Armenian but also in Turkish in Armenian script (Armeno-Turkish). The latter was used because while the Armenians had their own language and unique alphabet, many – especially those living outside eastern Ottoman provinces – had acquired fluency in Turkish. Some had done so while keeping hold of their own linguistic culture, but others had not.[52] Of particular importance for this book are two newspapers published in Istanbul: *Masis*, the semi-official newspaper of the Armenian Patriarchate (published in Armenian), and *Manzume-i Efkar* (published in Armeno-Turkish), which opposed the Patriarchate and *Masis*. A contemporary American Protestant missionary considered *Manzume-i Efkar* to be the 'most influential' publication among Armenians.[53]

In examining Armeno-Turkish materials, researchers have exhibited a strong preference for literary materials and translations with cultural influence, resulting in closer attention to inter-communal relations within the multilingual Ottoman society.[54] This has caused a neglect of newspapers, which were both politically and socially significant media within the Armenian community. Although these Armeno-Turkish newspapers were an important part of Armenian communal history, especially in the 1860s and 1870s, the historiography of Ottoman Armenians has largely ignored them. In addition to my use of Ottoman archival documents and Armenian materials, my heavy reliance on non-literary Armeno-Turkish sources, especially newspapers, is a distinguishing feature.

This book progresses chronologically. Chapter 1 discusses the status of the Armenian patriarchs of Istanbul and the patriarchate's rise by investigating the charters of investiture granted to them in the seventeenth and eighteenth centuries. I will question why the rise of the patriarchal position occurred and how Armenian prelates obtained additional rights from the Ottoman government. Chapter 2 addresses the first half of the nineteenth century and explores the creation of an institutional basis for lay participation in community administration and concomitant discussion of the separation between clergy and lay jurisdictions, splitting the religious from the secular. Chapter 3 follows the shift in the Ottoman treatment of non-Muslims in the 1850s, closely examining official guarantees of religious privileges and the promise of equality expressed in the Reform Edict. I argue that these promises encouraged Armenian elites in Istanbul to expand their sphere of influence, leading to the creation of the Armenian National Constitution.

Chapters 4 and 5, which cover 1863 to 1878, investigate a new set of terminology – that of privileges, religion and politics – adopted by Istanbul Armenians and Ottoman state officials. Chapter 4 focuses on the transimperial connections of the politics of the Armenian Church and argues that Armenian ecclesiastical affairs took on political meaning for the upper echelons of the Ottoman Empire due to the existence of the Catholicosate of Echmiadzin under Russian rule. Chapter 5 directs attention to domestic affairs and demonstrates that guarantees of religious privileges allowed Armenians to negotiate with the Ottoman government to determine the scope of their communal jurisdiction. This incorporates an examination of these negotiations, paying close attention to the foundations that the actors put forward for their arguments. Chapter 6 deals with the first half of the reign of Abdülhamit II (r. 1876–1909) and considers continuity and change in relation to the earlier period. As part of this, it analyses the Privileges Question, as the issue of the exceptions made for non-Muslims was termed in the 1880s and 1890s, and investigates the movements of Orthodox Christians and Armenians.

Notes

1. Jack Fairey, *The Great Powers and Orthodox Christendom: The Crisis over the Eastern Church in the Era of the Crimean War* (Basingstoke: Palgrave Macmillan, 2015), chap. 5.
2. The edict was addressed to non-Muslim religious authorities in Istanbul and delivered to the embassies of the European Great Powers. BOA, A.AMD 45/61 (6 June 1853).
3. Roderic H. Davison, *Reform in the Ottoman Empire 1856–1876* (Princeton: Princeton University Press, 1963; repr. New York: Gordian Press, 1973), chap. 2; Kemal H. Karpat, '*Millet*s and Nationality: The Roots of the Incongruity of Nation and State in the Post-Ottoman Era', in *Christians and Jews in the Ottoman Empire: The Functioning of a Plural Society*, ed. Benjamin Braude and Bernard Lewis, vol. 1 (New York: Holmes & Meier Publishers, 1982), 141–69.
4. *Kanun-ı Esasi* (Istanbul: Karabet Matbaası, 1908/9), 8.
5. Halil İnalcık, 'İmtiyazat, Osmanlı Dönemi', in *Türkiye Diyanet Vakfı İslam Ansiklopedisi* vol. 22 (Istanbul: Türkiye Diyanet Vakfı, 2000), 245–52.
6. On the capitulations in the early modern period, see Maurits H. van den Boogert, *The Capitulations and the Ottoman Legal System: Qadis, Consuls and* Beratlıs *in the 18th Century* (Leiden: Brill, 2005); Edhem Eldem, 'Capitulations and Western Trade', in *The Cambridge History of Turkey*, vol. 3, ed. Suraiya N. Faroqhi (Cambridge: Cambridge University Press, 2006), 281–335. Among the recent works on the development of Ottoman legal frameworks in the nineteenth and early twentieth centuries are Nobuyoshi Fujinami, 'Between Sovereignty and Suzerainty: History of the Ottoman Privileged Provinces', in *A World History of Suzerainty: A Modern History of East and West Asia and Translated Concepts*, ed. Takashi Okamoto (Tokyo: Toyo Bunko, 2019), 41–69; Nobuyoshi Fujinami, 'The Ecumenical Patriarchate in the Age of Ottoman Suzerainty', in *A World History of Suzerainty*, 241–70; Nobuyoshi Fujinami, 'Georgios Streit on Crete: International Law, Greece, and the

Ottoman Empire', *Journal of Modern Greek Studies* 34 (2016): 321–42; Nobuyoshi Fujinami, 'The First Ottoman History of International Law', *Turcica* 48 (2017): 245–70; Elektra Kostopoulou, 'Armed Negotiations: The Institutionalization of the Late Ottoman Locality', *Comparative Studies of South Asia, Africa and the Middle East* 33, no. 3 (2013): 295–309; Lâle Can, 'The Protection Question: Central Asians and Extraterritoriality in the Late Ottoman Empire', *International Journal of Middle East Studies* 48, no. 4 (2016): 679–99; Umut Özsu, 'The Ottoman Empire, the Origins of Extraterritoriality, and International Legal Theory', in *The Oxford Handbook of the Theory of International Law*, ed. Anne Orford and Florian Hoffmann (Oxford: Oxford University Press, 2016), 123–37; Will Hanley, *Identifying with Nationality: Europeans, Ottomans, and Egyptians in Alexandria* (New York: Columbia University Press, 2017); Aimee M. Genell, 'Autonomous Provinces and the Problem of "Semi-Sovereignty" in European International Law', *Journal of Balkan and Near Eastern Studies* 18, no. 6 (2016): 533–49; Sarah Abrevaya Stein, *Extraterritorial Dreams: European Citizenship, Sephardi Jews, and the Ottoman Twentieth Century* (Chicago: The University of Chicago Press, 2016). See also the contributions in the special issues of *Oriente Moderno* 83, no. 3 (2003), *Journal of the History of International Law* 18, no. 1 (2016) and *Journal of the Ottoman and Turkish Studies Association* 3, no. 2 (2016).

7. Fujinami, 'Sovereignty and Suzerainty'; Fujinami, 'Ecumenical Patriarchate'. Scholars have rarely analysed the historicity of the Ottoman term 'privileges'. Cahit Külekçi, for example, used it in the title of his recent book and simply described as privileges any kind of benefits that the Ottoman Empire granted to non-Muslims. *İmtiyâzlar Bağlamında Osmanlı Devleti'nde Ermeniler* (Istanbul: Dün Bugün Yarın Yayınları, 2017).
8. Some researchers use the legal pluralism framework to discuss the early modern organisation of diversity in the Ottoman Empire. Karen Barkey, 'Aspects of Legal Pluralism in the Ottoman Empire', in *Legal Pluralism and Empires, 1500–1850*, ed. Lauren Benton and Richard J. Ross (New York: New York University Press, 2013), 83–107; Timur Kuran, *The Long Divergence: How Islamic Law Held Back the Middle East* (Princeton: Princeton University Press, 2011), chap. 9. The careful remarks of Nobuyoshi Fujinami are instructive. 'Legal Pluralism for Whose Sake? Ottoman Law, Greek Jurists, and Religious Privileges', *Byzantine and Modern Greek Studies*. Advance online publication. doi: 10.1017/byz.2023.22
9. Karen Barkey analyses the Ottoman model of imperial diversity and multiculturalism in *Empire of Difference: The Ottomans in Comparative Perspective* (Cambridge: Cambridge University Press, 2008).
10. Kemal H. Karpat, *Ottoman Population 1830–1914: Demographic and Social Characteristics* (Madison: The University of Wisconsin Press, 1985), 148–9.

    This book uses 'non-dominant religious groups' to reserve the term 'minority' for the legal status of the post-WWI era.

11. Alford Carleton, 'The Millet System for the Government of Minorities in the Ottoman Empire' (PhD diss., Hartford Seminary, 1937). Carleton published a summary of his dissertation in 1938. Alford Carleton, 'Near Eastern Aspects of the Problem of Church and State', *The Moslem World* 28 (1938): 279–84.
12. Harry Charles Luke, *Mosul and Its Minorities* (London: M. Hopkinson & Company, 1925), 64; Arnold J. Toynbee, *Turkey* (New York: Scribner, 1927), 113.
13. Documents confirm that among the Ottomans, Cevdet Pasha and Harutyun Dadian viewed the history of Ottoman non-Muslims in a manner similar to the later argument of the *millet* system. BOA, Y.EE 38/69 (5 March 1892), 9/7 (June 1900). Interestingly, both were involved in the Privileges Question in the late nineteenth century, which will be discussed in Chapter 6.
14. H. A. R. Gibb and Harold Bowen, *Islamic Society and the West: A Study of the Impact of Western Civilization on Moslem Culture in the Near East*, vol. 1, part 2 (London: Oxford University Press, 1957), chap. 14.
15. Will Kymlicka, *Multicultural Citizenship: A Liberal Theory of Minority Rights* (Oxford: Clarendon Press, 1995), chap. 8; Chantal Mouffe, *On the Political* (London: Routledge, 2005), 123; Bilal Eryılmaz, *Osmanlı Devletinde Gayrimüslim Teb'anın Yönetimi* (Istanbul: Risale, 1990); Bilal Eryılmaz, *Osmanlı Devleti'nde Millet Sistemi* (Istanbul: Ağaç Yayıncılık, 1992); Cevdet Küçük, 'Osmanlı Yönetiminde Gayrimüslimler ve "Millet Sistemi"', in *Söğüt II Osmanlı Sempozyumu (Eylül 1985, Söğüt)* (Ankara: Ertuğrul Gazi'yi Anma ve Söğüt Şenliği Vakfı, 1986), 61–86; Cevdet Küçük, 'Osmanlı İmparatorluğu'nda "Millet Sistemi" ve Tanzimat', in *Mustafa Reşid Paşa ve Dönemi Semineri Bildiriler Ankara, 13–14 Mart 1985* (Ankara: Türk Tarih Kurumu Basımevi, 1987), 13–23.
16. Benjamin Braude, 'Foundation Myths of the Millet System', in *Christians and Jews*, vol. 1, 69–88; Kevork B. Bardakjian, 'The Rise of the Armenian Patriarchate of Constantinople', in *Christians and Jews*, vol. 1, 89–100; Paraskevas Konortas, 'From Tâ'ife to Millet: Ottoman Terms for the Ottoman Greek Orthodox Community', in *Ottoman Greeks in the Age of Nationalism: Politics, Economy, and Society in the Nineteenth Century*, ed. Dimitri Gondicas and Charles Issawi (Princeton: The Darwin Press, 1999), 169–79; Bruce Masters, *Christians and Jews in the Ottoman Arab World: The Roots of Sectarianism* (Cambridge: Cambridge University Press, 2001); Molly Greene, *The Edinburgh History of the Greeks, 1453 to 1768: The Ottoman Empire* (Edinburgh: Edinburgh University Press, 2015). For recent works on the *millet* system and Ottoman non-Muslims in the early modern period, see Eleni Gara, 'Conceptualizing Interreligious Relations in the Ottoman Empire: The Early Modern Centuries', *Acta Poloniae Historica* 116 (2017): 57–91; Antonis Hadjikyriacou, 'Beyond the *Millet* Debate: Communal Representation in Pre-Tanzimat-Era Cyprus', in *Political Thought and Practice in the Ottoman Empire: Halcyon Days in Crete IX A Symposium held in Rethymno 9–11 January 2015*, ed. Marinos Sariyannis (Rethymno: Crete

University Press, 2019), 71–96. For recent discussions about the meanings of the term *millet*, see Yusuf Ziya Karabıçak, 'Ottoman Attempts to Define the Rebels during the Greek War of Independence', *Studia Islamica* 114, no. 3 (2019): 316–54; Nikos Sigalas, '"And Every Language that Has Been Voiced Became a *Millet*": A Genealogy of the Late Ottoman *Millet*', *Die Welt des Islams* 62, no. 3–4 (2022): 325–59; Markus Dressler, 'Tracing the Nationalisation of *Millet* in the Late Ottoman Period: A Conceptual History Approach', *Die Welt des Islams* 62, no. 3–4 (2022): 360–88. See also Maurits H. van den Boogert, 'Millets: Past and Present', in *Religious Minorities in the Middle East: Domination, Self-Empowerment, Accommodation*, ed. Anne Sofie Roald and Anh Nga Longva (Leiden: Brill, 2012), 27–45; Vjeran Kursar, 'Non-Muslim Communal Divisions and Identities in the Early Modern Ottoman Balkans and the *Millet* System Theory', in *Power and Influence in South-Eastern Europe: 16th–19th Century*, ed. Maria Baramova, Plamen Mitev, Ivan Parvev and Vania Racheva (Zürich: Lit, 2013), 97–108.

17. Halil Inalcık, 'The Status of the Greek Orthodox Patriarch under the Ottomans', *Turcica* 21-23 (1991): 407–36; Macit Kenanoğlu, *Osmanlı Millet Sistemi: Mit ve Gerçek* (Istanbul: Klasik, 2004); Tom Papademetriou, *Render unto the Sultan: Power, Authority, and the Greek Orthodox Church in the Early Ottoman Centuries* (Oxford: Oxford University Press, 2015).
18. Elif Bayraktar Tellan, 'The Patriarch and the Sultan: The Struggle for Authority and the Quest for Order in the Eighteenth-century Ottoman Empire' (PhD diss., Bilkent University, 2011); Hasan Çolak, *The Orthodox Church in the Early Modern Middle East: Relations between the Ottoman Central Administration and the Patriarchates of Antioch, Jerusalem and Alexandria* (Ankara: Türk Tarih Kurumu, 2015); Hasan Çolak and Elif Bayraktar-Tellan, *The Orthodox Church as an Ottoman Institution: A Study of Early Modern Patriarchal Berats* (Istanbul: Isis Press, 2019). See also Yusuf Ziya Karabıçak, 'Local Patriots and Ecumenical Ottomans: The Orthodox Patriarchate of Constantinople in the Ottoman Configuration of Power, 1768–1828' (PhD diss., McGill University, 2020).
19. Yaron Ayalon, 'Rethinking Rabbinical Leadership in Ottoman Jewish Communities', *Jewish Quarterly Review* 107, no. 3 (2017): 325. Some researchers prefer to keep using '*millet* system' for certain arrangements between the state and non-Muslims either as a sign of its emergence in the later history of the empire or by loosely defining it as the entirety of the arrangements between them. Among the more recent examples, see Bruce Masters, 'The Millet Wars in Aleppo, 1726–1821: An Ottoman Perspective', in *Aleppo and Its Hinterland in the Ottoman Period/Alep et sa province à l'époque ottomane*, ed. Stefan Winter and Mafalda Ade (Leiden: Brill, 2019), 130–51; Barkey, *Empire of Difference*, chap. 4; Karen Barkey and George Gavrillis, 'The Ottoman Millet System: Non-Territorial Autonomy and Its Contemporary Legacy', *Ethnopolitics* 15, no. 1 (2016): 24–42. For criticism of Barkey's argument, see Gara, 'Conceptualizing Interreligious Relations', 68–9.

20. Fairey, *The Great Powers*; Denis Vovchenko, *Containing Balkan Nationalism: Imperial Russia and Ottoman Christians, 1856–1914* (New York: Oxford University Press, 2016); Lora Gerd, *Russian Policy in the Orthodox East: The Patriarchate of Constantinople (1878–1914)* (Berlin: De Gruyter, 2014).
21. Hayg Bērbērean, 'G. Bolsoy Hay Badriark'ut'ean Himnargut'iwně', *Hantēs Amsōreay* 78, no. 7–9 (1964): 337–50; no. 10–12: 497–510; Bardakjian, 'Armenian Patriarchate of Constantinople'; Markus Rahn, *Die Entstehung des Armenischen Patriarchats von Konstantinopel* (Hamburg: Lit, 2002).
22. Çolak and Bayraktar-Tellan, *Orthodox Church*.
23. Richard E. Antaramian, *Brokers of Faith, Brokers of Empire: Armenians and the Politics of Reform in the Ottoman Empire* (Stanford: Stanford University Press, 2020); Talin Suciyan, *Outcasting Armenians: Tanzimat of the Provinces* (Syracuse: Syracuse University Press, 2023). Dzovinar Derderian, in her recent article discussing the limits of the Istanbul Patriarchate's authority, followed Antaramian's argument. 'Orders and Disorders of Marriage, Church, and Empire in Mid-Nineteenth-Century Ottoman Armenia', *International Journal of Middle East Studies* 56, no. 1 (2024): 77. Ramazan Erhan Güllü's work provides a considerable amount of information available from the Ottoman archives about the history of the Armenian Patriarchate from 1878 to 1923, but his book lacks analytical discussion. *Ermeni Sorunu ve İstanbul Ermeni Patrikhanesi (1878–1923)* (Ankara: Türk Tarih Kurumu, 2015).
24. Fairey, *The Great Powers*, chap. 3.
25. It could be argued that the 1820s and 1830s, between the second and the third stages, should be considered as another stage. During this period, the Ottoman government actively used non-Muslim religious authorities in Istanbul to enhance security in the imperial capital. Masayuki Ueno, 'In Pursuit of Laicized Urban Administration: The *Muhtar* System in Istanbul and Ottoman Attitudes toward Non-Muslim Religious Authorities in the Nineteenth Century', *International Journal of Middle East Studies* 54, no. 2 (2022): 307–8.
26. Among the major contributions are Rifa'at Abou-El-Hajj, *Formation of the Modern State: The Ottoman Empire, Sixteenth to Eighteenth Centuries* (Syracuse: Syracuse University Press, 2005); Baki Tezcan, *The Second Ottoman Empire: Political and Social Transformation in the Early Modern World* (Cambridge: Cambridge University Press, 2010); Ali Yaycioglu, *Partners of the Empire: The Crisis of the Ottoman Order in the Age of Revolutions* (Stanford: Stanford University Press, 2016).
27. For the shift of the state–society relationship in the late eighteenth century, see Betül Başaran, *Selim III, Social Control and Policing in Istanbul at the End of the Eighteenth Century: Between Crisis and Order* (Leiden: Brill, 2014).
28. Henry R. Shapiro, *The Rise of the Western Armenian Diaspora in the Early Modern Ottoman Empire: From Refugee Crisis to Renaissance* (Edinburgh:

Edinburgh University Press, 2022), chaps 2, 3. See also Polina Ivanova, 'Armenians in Urban Order and Disorder of Seventeenth-Century Istanbul', *Journal of the Ottoman and Turkish Studies Association* 4, no. 2 (2017): 239–60; Eunjeong Yi, 'Interreligious Relations in 17th Century Istanbul in the Light of Immigration and Demographic Change', *Radovi* 51, no. 1 (2019): 117–43.

29. According to the census data of the late nineteenth century, Armenians made up 17 per cent of Istanbul's population. Karpat, *Ottoman Population*, 148–9.
30. Hagop Levon Barsoumian, 'The Armenian *Amira* Class of Istanbul' (PhD diss., Columbia University, 1980); İsmail Hakkı Kadı, *Ottoman and Dutch Merchants in the Eighteenth Century: Competition and Cooperation in Ankara, Izmir, and Amsterdam* (Leiden: Brill, 2012).
31. Marlene Kurz, *Ways to Heaven, Gates to Hell: Fażlīzāde ʿAli's Struggle with the Diversity of Ottoman Islam* (Berlin: EB-Verlag, 2011), 33.
32. Donald Quataert, 'Labor Policies and Politics in the Ottoman Empire: Porters and the Sublime Porte, 1826–1896', in *Humanist and Scholar: Essays in Honor of Andreas Tietze*, ed. Heath W. Lowry and Donald Quataert (Istanbul: The Isis Press, 1993), 62–5; Florian Riedler, 'Armenian Labor Migration to Istanbul and the Migration Crisis of the 1890s', in *The City in the Ottoman Empire: Migration and the Making of Urban Modernity*, ed. Ulrike Freitag, Malte Fuhrmann, Nora Lafi and Florian Riedler (London: Routledge, 2011), 160–76.
33. Yaşar Tolga Cora, Dzovinar Derderian and Ali Sipahi eds, *The Ottoman East in the Nineteenth Century: Societies, Identities and Politics* (London: I. B. Tauris, 2016); Yaşar Tolga Cora, 'Transforming Erzurum/Karin: The Social and Economic History of a Multi-ethnic Ottoman City in the Nineteenth Century' (PhD diss., The University of Chicago, 2016); Yaşar Tolga Cora, 'Why was Pastırmacı Khachatur Efendi Killed?: The Life of an Ottoman-Armenian Elite in Mid-19th-Century Erzurum/Karin', in *Ottoman Armenians: Life, Culture, Society* 1, ed. Vahé Tachjian (Berlin: A Houshamadyan Publication, 2014), 64–87; Nilay Özok-Gündoğan, 'Ruling the Periphery, Governing the Land: The Making of the Modern Ottoman State in Kurdistan, 1840–70', *Comparative Studies of South Asia, Africa and the Middle East* 34, no. 1 (2014): 160–75; Nilay Özok-Gündoğan, *The Kurdish Nobility in the Ottoman Empire: Loyalty, Autonomy and Privilege* (Edinburgh: Edinburgh University Press, 2022); Owen Miller, 'Sasun 1894: Mountains, Missionaries and Massacres at the End of the Ottoman Empire' (PhD diss., Columbia University, 2015); Owen Miller, '"Back to the Homeland" (Tebi Yergir): Or, how Peasants Became Revolutionaries in Muş', *Journal of the Ottoman and Turkish Studies Association* 4, no. 2 (2017): 287–308; Ali Sipahi, 'At Arm's Length: Historical Ethnography of Proximity in Harput' (PhD diss., University of Michigan, 2015); Antaramian, *Brokers of Faith*; Dzovinar Derderian, 'Mapping the Fatherland: Artzvi Vaspurakan's Reforms through the Memory of the Past', in *Ottoman Armenians*, 144–69; Dzovinar Derderian,

'Nation-Making and the Language of Colonialism: Voices from Ottoman Van in Armenian Print Media and Handwritten Petitions (1820s to 1870s)' (PhD diss., University of Michigan, 2019); Edip Gölbaşı, 'The Official Conceptualization of the Anti-Armenian Riots of 1895–1897: Bureaucratic Terminology, Official Ottoman Narrative, and Discourses of Revolutionary Provocation', *Études arméniennes contemporaines* 10 (2017): 33–62; Brad Ronald Dennis, 'Explaining Coexistence and Conflict in Eastern Anatolia 1800–1878' (PhD diss., University of Utah 2015). These achievements have substantially contributed to a better understanding of the massacres in the 1890s and the genocide in the 1910s. Besides these studies of the eastern provinces, Chris Gratien has dealt with the environmental history of Cilicia, where a relatively large number of Armenians lived, in his remarkable book, *The Unsettled Plain: An Environmental History of the Late Ottoman Frontier* (Stanford: Stanford University Press, 2022). Suciyan investigated Armenians' petitions from all over Anatolia. *Outcasting Armenians*. 'The Ottoman East' is a term recently proposed to draw more attention to this relatively neglected region, which stretches 'roughly south of the Black Sea Coast, north of the Levant and east of the centre of the Anatolian plateau'. Cora, Derderian and Sipahi, *The Ottoman East*, 1–2.

34. Among the publications on the application of reforms in the provinces are Marc Aymes, *Un grand progrès sur le papier: Histoire provinciale des réformes ottomanes à Chypre au XIXe siècle* (Leuven: Peeters, 2010); Milen Petrov, 'Everyday Forms of Compliance: Subaltern Commentaries on Ottoman Reform, 1864–1868', *Comparative Studies in Society and History* 46, no. 4 (2004): 730–59; Milen Petrov, 'Tanzimat for the Countryside: Midhat Paşa and the Vilayet of Danube, 1864–1868' (PhD diss., Princeton University, 2006); Yonca Köksal, 'Imperial Center and Local Groups: Tanzimat Reforms in the Provinces of Edirne and Ankara', *New Perspectives on Turkey* 27 (2002): 107–38. On the case of Orthodox Christians in Anatolia, see Ayşe Ozil, *Orthodox Christians in the Late Ottoman Empire: A Study of Communal Relations* (London: Routledge, 2013).
35. Suciyan, *Outcasting Armenians*, 26–32; Antaramian, *Brokers of Faith*, 4–7.
36. While older studies have undoubtedly made important contributions, it should be noted that their information is not always reliable, as sometimes they repeat errors from late nineteenth- and early twentieth-century chronicles.
37. Vartan Artinian, *The Armenian Constitutional System in the Ottoman Empire 1839–1863: A Study of Its Historical Development* (Istanbul: n.p., 1988); Barsoumian, 'Armenian *Amira* Class'; Onnik Jamgocyan, 'Les finances de l'Empire ottoman et les financiers de Constantinople (1732–1853)' (PhD diss., Université de Paris I, 1988); Anahide Ter Minassian, 'A Family of Armenian Amiras: The Dadians', *Armenian Review* 45, no. 3 (1992): 1–16; Y. G. Çark, *Türk Devleti Hizmetinde Ermeniler, 1453–1953* (Istanbul: Yeni Matbaa, 1953); Pars Tuğlacı, *The Role of the Balian Family in Ottoman Architecture* (Istanbul: Yeni Çığır Bookstore, 1990); Pars Tuğlacı, *The*

Role of the Dadian Family in Ottoman Social, Economic and Political Life (Istanbul: Pars Yayın, 1993); Sezai Balcı, ‘Bir Osmanlı-Ermeni Aydın ve Bürokratı: Sahak Abro (1825–1900)’, in *Osmanlı Siyasal ve Sosyal Hayatında Ermeniler*, ed. İbrahim Erdal and Ahmet Karaçavuş (Istanbul: IQ Kültür Sanat, 2009), 105–38.

38. There are numerous publications on Armenians’ community reforms and the end product, the Armenian National Constitution. See, for example, Arshag A. Albōyajean, ‘Azkayin Sahmanatrut‘iwnĕ: Ir Dzakumĕ ew Girar̩ut‘iwnĕ’, in *1910 Ĕntartsag Ōrats‘oyts‘ S. P‘rgchean Hiwantanots‘i Hayots‘* (Istanbul: Dbakrut‘iwn H. Madt‘ēosean, 1910), 76–528; Artinian, *Armenian Constitutional System*; Masayuki Ueno, ‘The First Draft of the Armenian Millet Constitution’, *Annals of Japan Association for Middle East Studies* 23 (2007): 213–51; Murat Bebiroğlu, *Tanzimat’tan II. Meşrutiyet’e Ermeni Nizamnameleri* (Istanbul: Orhan Matbaacılık, 2003); Albert Khar̩atyan, ‘Arevmtahayeri Azgayin “Sahmanadrut‘yunĕ” (1860–1863)’, *Patma-Banasirakan Handes* 136 (1992): 51–66; Albert Khar̩atyan, ‘Dardzyal Arevmtahayeri Azgayin Sahmanadrut‘yan Masin’, *Patma-Banasirakan Handes* 178 (2008): 81–92; Aylin Koçunyan, ‘Nizâmnâme-i Millet-i Ermeniyân Anayasa Mıydı?’ *Toplumsal Tarih* 216 (2011): 46–52; Aylin Koçunyan, ‘Long Live Sultan Abdülaziz, Long Live the Nation, Long Live the Constitution…’, in *Constitutionalism, Legitimacy, and Power: Nineteenth-Century Experiences*, ed. Kelly L. Grotke and Markus J. Prutsch (Oxford: Oxford University Press, 2014), 189–210; Antaramian, *Brokers of Faith*; Suciyan, *Outcasting Armenians*; Canan Seyfeli, *İstanbul Ermeni Patrikliği (Kuruluşu ve Tarihten Günümüze İdari Yapısı)* (Ankara: Aziz Andaç Yayınları, 2005); Arus Yumul, ‘Osmanlı’nın İlk Anayasası’, *Toplum ve Bilim* 83 (1999/2000): 338–51. On the parallel communal reforms and similar regulations of Orthodox Christians and Jews, see Davison, *Reform in the Ottoman Empire*, chap. 4; Gülnihâl Bozkurt, *Alman-İngiliz Belgelerinin ve Siyasî Gelişmelerin Işığı Altında Gayrimüslim Osmanlı Vatandaşlarının Hukukî Durumu (1839–1914)* (Ankara: Türk Tarih Kurumu Basımevi, 1989); Aylin Koçunyan, *Negotiating the Ottoman Constitution 1839–1876* (Paris: Peeters, 2018), 104–48; Fairey, *The Great Powers*; Ilan Karmi, *The Jewish Community of Istanbul in the Nineteenth Century: Social, Legal and Administrative Transformations* (Istanbul: Isis Press, 1996); Aron Rodrigue, ‘The Beginnings of Westernization and Community Reform Among Istanbul’s Jewry, 1854–1865’, in *The Jews of the Ottoman Empire*, ed. Avigdor Levy (Princeton: Darwin Press, 1994), 439–56.

39. Gülden Sarıyıldız, *Sicill-i Ahvâl Komisyonu’nun Kuruluşu ve İşlevi (1879–1909)* (Istanbul: Der Yayınları, 2004), 151–63.

40. Dimitrios Stamatopoulos, ‘From Millets to Minorities in the 19th-Century Ottoman Empire: An Ambiguous Modernization’, in *Citizenship in Historical Perspective*, ed. Steven G. Ellis, Guðmundur Hálfdanarson and Ann Katherine Isaacs (Pisa: Pisa University Press, 2006), 258–65.

41. Masayuki Ueno, 'One Script, Two Languages: Garabed Panosian and his Armeno-Turkish Newspapers in the Nineteenth-Century Ottoman Empire', *Middle Eastern Studies* 52, no. 4 (2016): 612.
42. Julia Phillips Cohen, *Becoming Ottomans: Sephardi Jews and Imperial Citizenship in the Modern Era* (Oxford: Oxford University Press, 2014), 26–30.
43. Talal Asad, *Genealogies of Religion: Discipline and Reasons of Power in Christianity and Islam* (Baltimore: Johns Hopkins University Press, 1993); Talal Asad, *Formations of the Secular: Christianity, Islam, Modernity* (Stanford: Stanford University Press, 2003); Junichi Isomae, *Kindai Nihon no Shukyo Gensetsu to sono Keihu: Shukyo, Kokka, Shinto* (Tokyo: Iwanami Shoten, 2003); Derek R. Peterson and Darren R. Walhof eds. *The Invention of Religion: Rethinking Belief in Politics and History* (New Brunswick, NJ: Rutgers University Press, 2002).
44. Selçuk Akşin Somel, *The Modernization of Public Education in the Ottoman Empire 1839–1908: Islamization, Autocracy and Discipline* (Leiden: Brill, 2001), 13; Selçuk Akşin Somel, 'Osmanlı Reform Çağında Osmanlıcılık Düşüncesi (1839–1913)', in *Cumhuriyet'e Devreden Düşünce Mirası: Tanzimat ve Meşrutiyet'in Birikimi*, ed. Mehmet Ö. Alkan (Istanbul: İletişim Yayınları, 2001), 90; Ussama Makdisi, *The Culture of Sectarianism: Community, History, and Violence in Nineteenth-Century Ottoman Lebanon* (Berkeley: University of California Press, 2000), 10, 60; Artinian, *Armenian Constitutional System*, 1; Anahide Ter Minassian, 'Sociétés de culture, écoles et presse arméniennes à l'époque d'Abd-ul-hamid II', *Revue du monde arménien moderne et contemporain* 3 (1997): 12; Pamela J. Young, 'Knowledge, Nation, and the Curriculum: Ottoman Armenian Education (1853–1915)' (PhD diss., University of Michigan, 2001), 19–20, 53; Antaramian, *Brokers of Faith*, 7.
45. Benjamin C. Fortna, *Imperial Classroom: Islam, the State, and Education in the Late Ottoman Empire* (Oxford: Oxford University Press, 2002), 2, 4, 17–18, 93–5; Avi Rubin, *Ottoman* Nizamiye *Courts: Law and Modernity* (New York: Palgrave Macmillan, 2011).
46. The seminal work by Niyazi Berkes presents a typical example: *The Development of Secularism in Turkey* (Montreal: McGill University Press, 1964; repr. New York: Routledge, 1998). See also Erik-Jan Zürcher, 'Ottoman Sources of Kemalist Thought', in *Late Ottoman Society: The Intellectual Legacy*, ed. Elisabeth Özdalga (London: RoutledgeCurzon, 2005), 16–18; Masami Arai, *Isuramu to Kindaika: Kyowakoku Toruko no Kuto* (Tokyo: Kodansha, 2013). Julia Phillips Cohen's discussion on the state's mobilisation of Islam and the responses of Ottoman Jews is instructive. 'Between Civic and Islamic Ottomanism: Jewish Imperial Citizenship in the Hamidian Era', *International Journal of Middle East Studies* 44, no. 2 (2012): 237–55.
47. Paul W. Werth, *The Tsar's Foreign Faiths: Toleration and the Fate of Religious Freedom in Imperial Russia* (Oxford: Oxford University Press, 2014), 67–9, 108–9.

48. Robert Crews, 'Empire and the Confessional State: Islam and Religious Politics in Nineteenth-Century Russia', *The American Historical Review* 108, no. 1 (2003): 50–83; Werth, *Tsar's Foreign Faiths*; Paula E. Hyman, *The Jews of Modern France* (Berkeley: University of California Press, 1998); Akio Matsushima, *Reihai no Jiyu to Naporeon: Konin Shukyo Taisei no Seiritsu* (Tokyo: Yamakawa Shuppansha, 2010); Daisuke Yoneoka, 'Hapusuburuku Teikokuka Bosunia niokeru Isuramu Tochi to sono Hanno: Reisu uru Urema Shoku wo Megutte', *Shirin* 94, no. 2 (2011): 89–107. Since the publication of Selim Deringil's seminal work, most researchers in Ottoman studies have been mindful of the Ottoman participation in international trends. *The Well-Protected Domains: Ideology and the Legitimation of Power in the Ottoman Empire 1876–1909* (London: I. B. Tauris, 1998); Jun Akiba, 'Preliminaries to a Comparative History of the Russian and Ottoman Empires: Perspectives from Ottoman Studies', in *Imperiology: From Empirical Knowledge to Discussing the Russian Empire*, ed. Kimitaka Matsuzato (Sapporo: Slavic Research Center, 2007), 33–47. Russian historians have noted the parallel development in the Ottoman Empire in their treatment of non-dominant religious groups during the nineteenth century. For example, see Robert Crews, *For Prophet and Tsar: Islam and Empire in Russia and Central Asia* (Cambridge, MA: Harvard University Press, 2006), 354–5.
49. Selim Deringil, 'Legitimacy Structures in the Ottoman State: The Reign of Abdülhamid II (1876–1909)', *International Journal of Middle East Studies* 23, no. 3 (1991): 345–59; Deringil, *The Well-Protected Domains*. On the connection between religious protection and autonomy, see Kostopoulou, 'Armed Negotiations', 302–3.
50. Fatmagül Demirel, *Adliye Nezareti: Kuruluşu ve Faaliyetleri (1876–1914)* (Istanbul: Boğaziçi Üniversitesi Yayınevi, 2008), 227–8.
51. In this regard, the discussion about the public sphere after the Young Turk Revolution is useful. See Bedross Der Matossian, *Shattered Dreams of Revolution: From Liberty to Violence in the Late Ottoman Empire* (Stanford: Stanford University Press, 2014), chap. 1.
52. For the use of Turkish language by Armenians, see Ueno, 'One Script, Two Languages', 607–8.
53. ABCFM, Reel 584, No. 317, Memorandum concerning the newspapers of Constantinople. The document does not contain a date but was in a file from the early 1870s.
54. Ueno, 'One Script, Two Languages', 605–6.

1

Cooperation against the Religion of the Pope

When the Ottoman Empire incorporated a large number of Christians and Jews under its rule in the course of territorial expansion, it took over the traditions of preceding Muslim dynasties and allowed non-Muslim subjects to practise their own religion as *dhimmi*s. This was accompanied by allowing their clerical bodies, which were indispensable for practising religion, to continue to exist; Christians and Jews could form local communities around their clerical and lay leaders and live in the empire as both members of their own religious community and a multireligious society.[1] Moreover, the empire went further in its relationship with Christians: at their request, it made separate arrangements with their prelates and guaranteed their status through granting them charters of investiture in exchange for the payment of tribute. These arrangements enabled the empire not only to fulfil the Islamic requirement of treating *dhimmi*s justly but also to gain an extra source of income. Obtaining imperial backing, meanwhile, allowed the high clergy of the Christian groups, especially the Orthodox Christians and the Armenians, to preserve their positions and hierarchical church organisations, whose lower-status members helped shape the religious and communal lives of commoners at the local level, administered charitable organisations, provided religious guidance to their flocks and reconciled disputes within their community.[2] This chapter examines the understudied arrangements between the empire and the Armenian patriarchs of Istanbul in the seventeenth and eighteenth centuries in comparison to the case of Orthodox Christians.[3]

Recently, Ottoman scholars have emphasised that the restructuring in the seventeenth and eighteenth centuries allowed different types of power holders to participate in imperial governance.[4] Molly Greene has proposed further development for this realm of study, which has until now focused primarily on the Muslim members of the empire, arguing that the transition that expanded the number of 'people who were able to claim a role in imperial governance' potentially included Christian clergy. She has further suggested that the rise of the Orthodox Christian Patriarchate of Istanbul should be understood in the context of this trend.[5] Until the seventeenth century, the patriarchate had limited geographical jurisdiction and only qualified power. In the early eighteenth century, however, reforms of the tax system catalysed the rise of the patriarchate's power. Thanks to larger financial contributions to the imperial treasury, the patriarchate began to expand its geographic jurisdiction at the expense of other patriarchates of the Orthodox Church, extracting additional rights from the government and considerably improving its status vis-à-vis state officials and the confessional community.[6]

As I will discuss in this chapter, Armenian prelates in Istanbul also succeeded in improving the position of their patriarch at the turn of the eighteenth century. They achieved this not by offering a larger financial contribution to the government but by finding opportunities to have greater involvement in imperial governance. Until the late seventeenth century, the Armenian Patriarchate of Istanbul was not a very important position either for the empire or for ordinary Armenians. However, it gained importance at the end of the seventeenth century when the empire found it necessary to rely on the networks of Christian clergymen in their struggle against the propagation activity of Catholic missionaries and the conversion of Ottoman Christian subjects to Catholicism. This shift helped strengthen the authority of the Istanbul Patriarchate and increased its exclusive power in Armenian religious affairs. In the first and second sections of this chapter, I analyse the charters of investiture granted to the Armenian patriarchs in the seventeenth and eighteenth centuries and discuss how the empire changed the status of the Armenian patriarchs of Istanbul. The third and fourth sections are devoted to a discussion of the reasons behind this change and its implications.

The Ottomans and the Armenian Church

After the conquest of Constantinople, the Ottomans preserved the position of Orthodox Christian patriarch of the city and appointed Gennadios as the patriarch. They also appointed Hovagim as the Armenian prelate of Istanbul and, by the second quarter of the sixteenth century, allowed the holder of this position to use the title of patriarch.[7] The Ottomans extended a special favour to these two non-Muslim groups that had much larger populations than others by allowing them to have high clerical position in the imperial capital. Nevertheless, the authority and geographical jurisdiction of Armenian patriarchs remained restricted until the end of the sixteenth century; in the eyes of Armenian Christians, their patriarchate did not have an ecclesiastical basis for authority or prestige.

The first step in the rise of the Armenian Patriarchate came with the influx of the Armenian population to Istanbul and other western parts of the empire at the turn of the seventeenth century. Henry Shapiro convincingly demonstrates that the unrest in Anatolia caused by the Celali revolts triggered the mass migration of Armenians from the eastern regions of the Ottoman Empire to Thrace, Istanbul and Western Anatolia from the end of the sixteenth century to the beginning of the seventeenth. This influx tremendously increased the Armenian population in those areas and led to the development of Armenian culture in the region and the rise of the Armenian Patriarchate of Istanbul, which had been a 'regional obscurity' before then.[8] During its rise, factional rivalries arose with it and continued throughout the seventeenth century, resulting in frequent changes in patriarch and instability in the administration of communal affairs, including situations in which several clerics cooperatively shouldered the role of patriarch, a Catholic convert ascended to the position and laymen assumed patriarchal duties during years of vacancy.[9]

How, then, did the Ottoman government deal with the Armenian patriarchs of Istanbul? According to the *millet* system explanation, the Ottomans used the patriarchs of Istanbul to govern Christian subjects by granting them autonomous and monopolistic power over all their coreligionists in the empire since the mid-fifteenth century.[10] Challenging this view, Tom Papademetriou has recently argued that Ottoman arrangements with the Orthodox Christian patriarchs of Istanbul were based on the framework of the tax farming system and that the foremost expectation that the Ottomans had was not that the patriarchs would become powerful administrators of communal autonomy but that they would pay tribute from the money they collected through their ecclesiastical networks.[11] This argument helps to explain the Ottoman arrangements with Armenian patriarchs in the seventeenth century. The charters of investiture that Ottoman sultans granted them suggest that while the ruling circles of the empire expected financial gain from the patriarch's ecclesiastical networks, they did not give patriarchs too many responsibilities in imperial governance.

Although charters granted to Armenian patriarchs before the early eighteenth century were rare, during my archival research I located copies of charters from 1618, 1641, 1682 and 1698. These four copies contained similar stipulations with some minor changes.[12] In a manner similar to what they had done with the Orthodox Christians, the Ottomans imposed the payment of tribute on the Armenians: 100,000 *akçe* was imposed on the patriarch at the moment of appointment and at renewal, and an annual tribute was also charged.[13] In exchange, the empire recognised the rights of the patriarchs, including those related to the appointment and dismissal of clergymen, superintendence over marriage, ownership of church property and collection of church offerings.

The charters of Armenian patriarchs prove that the empire had no intention of making them powerful community administrators. These documents include references to the involvement of Muslim officials and local judges in their business, which demonstrates that the charters assigned rights to the addressee while at the same time they tempered official power over Armenians. For example, among the eleven clauses of the 1618 charter, three referred to this type of involvement.[14] One clause regards the inheritance of clergymen and allowed the patriarch to seize any inheritance totalling less than 5,000 *akçe*. However, it also stipulates that officials are to confiscate it if it amounts to a larger sum, preventing clergymen from accumulating excessive wealth. Another clause relates to the involvement of sharia court judges in the collection of church offerings. This stipulation, which helped to smooth the collection of offerings, also served to prevent them from hoarding wealth. Moreover, a clause in this document mandates that Armenians use sharia courts: 'No one other than the patriarch should not interfere in issues that occur between Armenians in relation with the religion, but a lawsuit should be brought to the sharia court judges of the region when a problem related to sharia arises'. Although no indication is given of which problems were related to the Armenian religion and which were related to sharia, this stipulation clearly assumes that Armenian recourse to Muslim judges should not be an unusual or irregular act.

The limited scope of the power of the Armenian patriarch in the seventeenth century can also be observed in the geographical extent of his jurisdiction. According to the charter of investiture granted to the patriarch in 1618, this included Istanbul, Galata, the Balkans (*Rumeli*), Üsküdar, Bursa, Kütahya, Sivas, Tokat, Kayseri, Trabzon, Ankara and Caffa.[15] Although several cities had been added to the list by 1682, the extent of this jurisdiction, broadly conceived, was largely the same: Istanbul, the Balkans and Western and Central Anatolia.[16] This reflects that the empire did not approve the authority of Istanbul's patriarchs over Armenians in the eastern Ottoman provinces, where the majority of Ottoman Armenians lived.

The regions outside of the jurisdiction of the Istanbul patriarchs were under the jurisdiction of other religious authorities of the Armenian Church: south-central Anatolia was under the jurisdiction of the Sis Catholicosate, the Arab provinces were under the Jerusalem Patriarchate and the eastern

Ottoman provinces were under the jurisdiction of the Echmiadzin Catholicosate, which was then under Safavid rule.[17] A petition submitted by the Armenians of the province of Erzurum clearly stated that monks in the monasteries of that province were subordinate to the Echmiadzin Catholicosate.[18] The limited authority of the Istanbul patriarch included limits to his control over clergymen. Because the Armenian population in the eastern provinces did not fall under the jurisdiction of the religious authorities under Ottoman rule, they could choose how to request appointments for their clergymen, either through provincial officials and sharia court judges or by directly petitioning the central government. Additionally, they sometimes asked the Istanbul patriarch to mediate their petitions.[19] Thus, the ruling circles of the empire, in general, did not expect much from the Armenian Patriarchate of Istanbul in the seventeenth century and even allowed the religious authorities living outside their empire's territory to have spiritual jurisdiction over Ottoman subjects.

Few records remain on the relationship between the Echmiadzin Catholicosate and the Ottoman government in the sixteenth and seventeenth centuries, but we can confirm that the catholicosate did not refrain from directly communicating with foreign political authorities, and the Ottoman government did not attempt to sever the tie between their subjects and this foreign religious authority. In 1667, the empire promulgated an edict that recognised the right of the catholicos to distribute holy oil to the Ottoman Armenians in exchange for a payment of tribute. This document refers to the charters of investiture that the Ottoman Empire granted to the catholicos.[20] In 1713, the new candidate for the catholicosate directly petitioned the Ottoman government, requesting the issuance of a charter of investiture in exchange for a payment of 6,800 *akçe*.[21] Ecclesiastical tax farming networks could therefore extend even beyond the borders of the empire.

The Eighteenth Century

A clear shift is observable in the charters of investiture granted to the Armenian patriarchs of Istanbul in the eighteenth century; the Ottomans opted to confer additional powers on them and reinforce their authority in their relationships both with fellow clergymen and with Muslim officials and judges. Thus, the Istanbul Armenian Patriarchate saw an elevation in its position in the same period as that of the Orthodox Christians.

A comparison of the 1682 and 1698 charters demonstrates that the geographical authority of the patriarchate expanded in the late seventeenth century: Sis and the rest of Anatolia (*sair vilayet-i Anadolu*) were added to the list of sites under its jurisdiction in 1698.[22] In the early eighteenth century – in contrast to the charters of the Orthodox Christian patriarchs, which continued to include a lengthy list of place names – the Ottoman bureaucracy used a simplified means of describing this territory, writing that the patriarch had jurisdiction over Istanbul, the Balkans, Anatolia and their environs.[23]

Documents from the late seventeenth and early eighteenth centuries demonstrate that this change in description led to further substantial expansions of the patriarchate's territory. First, Istanbul's patriarchs began to claim jurisdiction over Armenians in the eastern provinces. These claims sometimes provoked friction between local Armenians and the patriarchs of Istanbul in the early eighteenth century. Because Ottoman bureaucracy usually relied on precedents, Armenians in the east justified their claims by referring to historical practices.[24] Nevertheless, the expansion continued, and scribes began to describe the eastern areas, such as Erzurum, Diyarbakır and Van, as being under the jurisdiction of the Istanbul Patriarchate.[25] Along with this expansion, patriarchs also petitioned the government to revive the prelate position in monasteries that had been left vacant in Kars, Ergani, Erzurum and Van.[26] Furthermore, although the Catholicosate of Sis was still given authority over south-central Anatolia and northern Syria, it was placed under the jurisdiction of the Istanbul Patriarchate towards the end of the seventeenth century.[27] This required the catholicosate to correspond with the government through the mediation of the Istanbul Patriarchate. Ottoman bureaucracy also placed the Catholicosate of Echmiadzin under the Istanbul Patriarchate in the same manner.[28] The collapse of the Safavids and the temporary incorporation into Ottoman territory in the 1720s and 1730s likely strengthened the Echmiadzin Catholicosate's reliance on the central Ottoman government.

The treatment of these two catholicosates remained limited to administrative questions and did not result in a change in ecclesiastical hierarchy, in which catholicoi were higher than the second-highest position of patriarch. The right to ordain bishops and produce holy oil were still reserved to the catholicoi, following the tradition of the Armenian Church, and the Istanbul Patriarchate was forced to rely on the Echmiadzin Catholicosate in these matters.[29] In the 1880s, high-ranking Ottoman official Ahmet Cevdet Pasha wrote that although all Armenians were supposed to refer to the Istanbul patriarch for recourse in their relationship with the Sublime Porte, the Sis catholicos regarded the Istanbul patriarch as merely 'our resident representative [*kapu-kethüdamız*] who delivers our petitions to the Sublime Porte'.[30] Nevertheless, the jurisdictional expansion gave the Istanbul patriarchs an advantage in their relationships with the two catholicosates. In the late eighteenth century, Simeon Yerevantsi, the Echmiadzin catholicos from 1763 to 1780, complained that the catholicosate was forced to petition the

Ottoman government through the mediation of the Istanbul Patriarchate, and that the patriarchs neglected to pass on petitions that were not in accordance with their own interests. Moreover, he claimed that the Istanbul Patriarchate charged the catholicosate additional amounts when it mediated the tribute payments of the Echmiadzin Catholicosate to the Ottoman government.[31] The change in administrative jurisdiction clearly had a heavy impact on the power balance between the religious authorities of the Armenian Church, allowing the Istanbul Patriarchate greater influence.

Although the patriarchal authority to appoint and dismiss clergy had been included in the charters since the seventeenth century, the further monopoly on the appointment and dismissal of prelates was established by a new restriction that was added to the charter regarding the involvement of Muslim judges in the appointment of Armenian clergymen: 'The position of prelate [*marhasa*] should not be given to anyone by a request from a judge or a petition if no request stamped by the patriarch is submitted'.[32] With the exception of individuals under the jurisdiction of the Jerusalem Patriarchate, all Armenian prelates in the empire and the catholicos of Echmiadzin were required (in principle) to obtain their charters of investiture from the Ottoman government through the mediation of the Istanbul patriarchs. The eighteenth-century charters also granted the patriarchs the exclusive right to punish clergymen who acted against their religion and to investigate the activities of priests and monks.

Elif Bayraktar Tellan shows that behind the rise of the Orthodox Christian Patriarchate in the eighteenth century was the financial expectation that the Ottomans had from this clerical institution.[33] This does not apply, however, to the case of the Armenian Patriarchate; although the Armenian patriarchs of Istanbul were still required to pay an annual tribute of 140,000 *akçe* to the government, in the eighteenth century, Ottoman bureaucracy stopped including the stipulations on the collection of church offerings that had been observed in the seventeenth-century charters.[34] This tendency marks a striking contrast with the changes observed in the charters of Orthodox Christian patriarchs over the same period, in which additional clauses were added on the collection of church offerings.[35] The total amounts of an annual tribute paid by the two patriarchs to the Ottoman treasury were also strikingly different. The Orthodox Christians paid 1,200,000 *akçe* a year in 1714, which was doubled to 2,400,000 *akçe* in 1716.[36] Meanwhile, the amount imposed on Armenians remained 140,000 *akçe* until the early nineteenth century, despite the inflation of the Ottoman currency and the expansion of the Armenian Patriarchate's territory. Financial profitability was clearly not a major concern for the Ottomans at this point in their relationships to the Armenian patriarchs.

Meanwhile, references to the involvement of Muslim officials and judges were largely eliminated from the charters of the Armenian patriarchs by 1716. Together with the removal of the stipulations for collection of church offerings, all reference to the involvement of judges in the collection process disappears. The charters also stopped requiring Armenians to use sharia courts. The confiscation of clergymen's inheritance was conducted by the patriarch or his agents, and state officials were prohibited from interfering. Complaints from Armenians suggest that this prohibition was put into place to prevent officials from illegally seizing church property alongside deceased clergy's estates.[37]

One clause in the 1716 charter stipulated the following:

> Officials and others should neither interfere in nor harm, without reason, churches, monasteries, sites of pilgrimage that they [Armenians] have had since old times, things that have belonged or related to them since old times, the practices that they have had heretofore according to their false religion or the repair of monasteries and churches conducted under an imperial decree in the manner as once was within the scope of sharia.[38]

This clause requires special attention because, in addition to specific prohibitions, it allows the holder of the charter to request redress for any violation of the principle of non-interference in Armenians' religious affairs. The Orthodox Christian Patriarchate also benefited from this change in the charter of Armenian patriarchs, and a prohibition of interference in religious affairs was added to their charter in 1725.[39]

In a charter of an Armenian patriarch from 1730, twelve new clauses appear, and the length of the document almost doubles. Eight more clauses were added in 1752.[40] These new additions reinforced the autonomy of the Armenian patriarchs in their relationship with Muslim officials and judges; half of the clauses added in the 1730 charter prohibit officials, judges and other authorities from disturbing the Armenians in general or the patriarch in particular. For instance, officials were prohibited from disturbing the riding animals and attendants of the patriarch. Muslim judges were prohibited from forcing Armenian clergymen to bury Armenians who had been married outside their church. A prohibition of forced conversions to Islam was also put in place.

The Religion of the Pope

What prompted Ottoman ruling circles to change their attitude towards Armenian patriarchs, to grant them greater autonomy in their religious affairs and relationships with local officials and judges and to give them greater control over their fellow clergymen? As noted above, there appears to be no question of financial profitability. The rise of the *amira*, a class of lay Armenian notables, has been proposed as the reason for this expansion, but this is not a sufficient answer. Although the *amira* may have contributed to the further expansion of patriarchal authority in later periods, this change in the patriarchal charters began before the rise of the *amira*, which did not occur until the mid-eighteenth century.[41]

A document dated 1714 suggests that the reason for this change was the threat of a spread of Catholicism among Armenians.[42] The Armenians in the province of Erzurum petitioned the government to appoint one Apraham as the abbot of a local monastery in the place of the man sent by the Istanbul patriarch, calling the latter oppressive. Moreover, they offered an additional payment of tribute in exchange for the appointment of their desired candidate. Ottoman bureaucrats found that this position was 'not included in the charter of investiture' granted to the patriarch, and that there had been precedents in which the abbot was appointed through the request of sharia court judges or locals' direct petition. Thus, the request to appoint Apraham was granted. The patriarch protested this decision, claiming that local prelates should be appointed through his request, and that Apraham was 'acting in accordance with the religion of the Franks', that is, Catholicism. This claim successfully reversed the previous decision. The government cancelled Apraham's appointment and granted a charter of investiture to the clergyman that the Istanbul patriarch had chosen on the condition that he would neither become Catholic nor oppress his flock. Here, the patriarch of Istanbul was acting as the supervisor of the religious beliefs of local prelates. As noted above, the patriarch's consent eventually became an unconditional requirement for the appointment of local prelates in the charter of 1730.

As Catholics in sixteenth-century Western Europe began to renew their interest in foreign missions, the Ottoman Empire – Europe's closest non-Christian neighbour and the protector of the most notable Christian holy sites – did not go overlooked. Catholic missionaries became active in Ottoman territory in the early seventeenth century.[43] Muslims in the Ottoman Empire were reluctant to listen, and the missionaries did not risk proselytising to them to avoid retribution from the Ottoman government. Instead, their main target was Christians of other denominations. In 1627, Pope Urban VIII founded the Collegium Urbanum in the Sacred Congregation for the Propagation of the Faith in Rome to educate missionaries. The papacy invited Christians from the Ottoman Empire, including Armenians, to the college. After completing their training, students were dispatched back to their homelands to proselytise to their former coreligionists.[44] Unlike the Orthodox Christians, Armenians in the Ottoman Empire did not have a well-established church organisation. This lack allowed the missionaries to have greater success among them.[45]

The Ottoman ruling circles changed their attitude towards Catholic missionary activity in the empire by the end of the seventeenth century. Before then, they had expressed little concern about Catholic missionaries, so long as they did not proselytise to Muslims. The failure of the Siege of Vienna in 1683 and the subsequent war with the Holy League of 1684 (which had been proposed and blessed by Pope Innocent XI) did not promptly change the situation. However, Ottoman ruling circles were alarmed by the 1694 Venetian invasion of the island of Chios, where Catholic Ottoman subjects resided. After the island was retaken by the Ottomans in 1695, they began to look at Catholic clerics with a more sceptical eye. The empire ordered that the Catholic churches of Chios be destroyed.[46] Three of them were converted into mosques.[47] According to an edict issued in 1695, which is available in English translation, İbrahim Pasha warned of the seditious behaviour of 'Frank' priests at Chios, whom the edict describes as 'Agents of the Roman Pope' and 'Spies in our Empire'. It further ordered officials to ensure that the Ottoman subjects who had converted to Catholicism return to their original faiths and to prohibit Catholic clerics from performing seditious activities.[48]

An anti-Catholic faction within the Armenian community considered this event the perfect opportunity to obtain support from the Ottoman authorities in their fight against Catholic converts and sympathisers. In 1697 and 1698, Armenians in Istanbul petitioned the government, condemning both Catholic missionaries and Armenians who had converted to Catholicism.[49] The choice of words in these petitions suggests that the petitioners were fully aware of the political significance of the 1695 edict. Converts were described as those who had 'abandoned their old rites and followed the religion of the pope'. Moreover, the Armenian petitioners referred to the treason and sedition of the 'Franks' of Chios who followed the pope, writing that monks who had been sent by the papacy were travelling from province to province to convert Orthodox Christians, Armenians and other Ottoman Christian groups to Catholicism.

In the seventeenth and eighteenth centuries, Catholicism was generally called the 'religion of the Franks' (*ayin-i Frenk*) in Ottoman documents, but the documents written from the 1690s to the 1710s also included another expression, 'religion of the pope' (*papa milleti/papa dini*).[50] The unconventional use of this term in the above petition was likely to draw attention to the connection of this religion to a foreign religious authority. The Armenians requested that the previous order be reinstated, warning that these Catholic missionary activities were causing trouble. The government responded positively.

Due to the pope's support of the Habsburgs in the recent war and the following Venetian invasion of Chios, anti-Catholic sentiment was running high in Ottoman ruling circles, which created an atmosphere in which 'confessional and political loyalties were fused as one'.[51] Another Armenian petition, likely submitted in the early 1700s, reflects this convergence of political and religious allegiances.[52] Six clergymen accused Minas, the incumbent Armenian patriarch of Jerusalem, of Catholicism. Their accusation stated that the patriarch had urged the clergy to convert to Catholicism and 'pray for the Frankish Pope', when they were 'praying for our sultans of the Ottoman dynasty (*al-i Osman padişahımız*), according to our old rite'. The government began an investigation and ended with the dismissal of the patriarch from his position.

The edict issued in 1701 more clearly illustrates the change in the government's attitude towards Catholic missionaries.[53] In this edict, which was delivered to regions of the empire where Catholic conversion was known to have occurred, the sultan declared that missionaries who belonged 'to the religion of the pope' were causing disturbances with their proselytisation and thus 'were not within my imperial satisfaction', prohibited them from continuing and ordered the punishment of Catholic converts among the Armenians, Syriac Christians and other non-Muslims if they did not return to their original faiths. This edict is remarkable for the breadth of its prohibition of Catholic missionaries in the Ottoman realm. Similar edicts were issued in a more comprehensive form in the same month and again the next year, ordering the punishment of the Orthodox Christians, Armenians and other non-Muslims who had converted to Catholicism.[54]

Cesare Santus has shown that some of the impetus for the anti-Catholic trend at the turn of the eighteenth century came from the influence of Feyzullah Efendi, a notorious *şeyhülislam* (the mufti of Istanbul and the head of the Ottoman Islamic hierarchy) who enjoyed a close connection with the reigning sultan, Mustafa II. Santus notes that Feyzullah summoned Avedik, an Armenian clergyman from Erzurum, to be patriarch of Istanbul. The two knew each other from living in Erzurum, where Avedik had opposed the Catholic missionaries, leading to French diplomatic intervention on behalf of the missionaries and his imprisonment.[55] In the petition requesting his appointment to the Patriarchate of Istanbul, Avedik stated that the Armenians in Istanbul were in favour of making him patriarch because he had successfully returned Armenians who converted to Catholicism back to the flock during his time at Erzurum.[56] It is not clear whether Istanbul Armenians actually called for Avedik's appointment to the patriarchate, but his petition suggests that the ability to cope with the conversion problem was a criterion in the decision of whether a clergyman was suitable for the position. This perspective is supported by the treatment of another Armenian patriarch, Melkiseteg, who was deposed and sentenced to prison in 1701 because of his tolerance towards Catholic converts.[57]

In this political context, able clergymen who were unsympathetic to Catholicism were an asset to Armenian society in Istanbul. In 1709, when Armenian notables requested the issuance of a charter of investiture addressed to Sahag, the new candidate for the patriarchate, they stated that he had no relationship with the Catholics as part of their argument of his suitability for the position. Moreover, they swore that they would accept punishment if Sahag were to have any relationships with Catholics or ever act in a way that followed Catholic rite.[58] Whether the Ottoman government demanded that the Armenian notables make this oath or they did so of their own accord remains unclear, but distance from Catholicism was clearly considered a requirement for patriarchal candidates.

Although researchers have aptly identified a connection with anti-Catholic policies in the actions of Feyzullah and Avedik,[59] the state of affairs following the Edirne Incident of 1703 (in which the janissaries and their supporters killed Feyzullah and ousted Mustafa II from power) and the French abduction of Avedik in 1706 suggests that both Ottoman ruling circles and Armenian patriarchs maintained a negative attitude towards Catholic missionary activities and the conversion of Ottoman subjects. As has been discussed above, the accusation that an abbot was a secret Catholic was considered sufficient to remove him from his position in Erzurum in 1714. In 1722, Hovhannes Golod, the Armenian patriarch of Istanbul, petitioned the government to revoke the charter of investiture they had granted the prelate of the Maronite Christians of Aleppo.[60] According to his petition, the Maronites had secretly worshipped before their prelates were granted a charter, and now they had somehow obtained one. The Maronites publicly announced the granting of the charter in the multireligious commercial city of Aleppo, interpreting it as official recognition of their group, and this caused a disturbance. Golod maintained that the Maronites were converted Syriac Christians and belonged to the 'religion of the Franks'. He requested the cancellation of the charter. The government decided that no further charters be issued to Maronite prelates. He also asked the government to issue an imperial decree to punish the converts in 1723 and 1739.[61] The government accommodated these requests. According to Bruce Masters, Orthodox Christians in 1720s Aleppo also saw the shift in the central government's attitude towards the

Catholics as an opportunity. However, local political alliances continued to prevent the Orthodox Christians from dominating the Catholics.[62]

Expansion of Patriarchal Authority

After the disastrous war with the Holy League revealed the weaknesses of the Ottoman military, Ottoman ruling circles worked to block the further expansion of Catholicism among its subjects using domestic measures. They were generally unable to take a hard line towards the Catholics because doing so would invite protest from France, the empire's most important ally, for violating its capitulation.[63] They therefore had to rely on the ecclesiastical networks of non-Catholic Christians and, to make this easier, they allowed the growth of patriarchal authority. The treatment of the Armenian Patriarchate of Istanbul was even more important for two reasons: first, the patriarchate lacked an ecclesiastical basis for its authority and was highly dependent on the support of the Ottoman state, and second, Catholic conversion was most common among Armenians.

This change in the government's attitude allowed the anti-Catholic faction among the Armenians to dominate the moderates and purge Catholic converts and sympathisers during the first decade of the eighteenth century: numerous converts were sentenced to the galleys, one well-known cleric was sentenced to death by hanging and Mkhitar Sevastatsi – who was a prominent Armenian Catholic cleric – was forced to flee Ottoman territory with his disciples.[64] Moreover, the new Ottoman policy encouraged the Armenians to request more rights in their patriarchs' charters, especially those related to the patriarchal power to control the activities of Armenian clerics. There were many Catholic converts and sympathisers in the latter group, and some converted clerics were wandering from province to province to propagate their new faith to their former coreligionists.[65] The case of Erzurum demonstrates that some Armenian Catholic clerics had obtained positions in local churches. This situation likely prompted the central government to favour the idea of a monopoly of control over Armenian clergy by the Istanbul patriarch. As has been noted, the additions to the 1716 charter granted the patriarch the right to punish clergymen who were acting outside the Armenian religion and prohibited others from interfering in this punishment. The charters issued after 1730 added to this power that of detaining clergymen, which was allowed only to the patriarchs and their agents, so far as the sharia courts found necessary. The charter issued in 1752 granted the patriarch and his agents the right to investigate 'priests and monks living in churches and monasteries in the protected [Ottoman] domains', preventing the government's involvement in the treatment of

Armenian clergy.[66] In 1780, when an Armenian patriarch requested the renewal of the edict that declared his unique right to request the appointment of local prelates from the government, he supported his argument with an allusion to the threatening spread of Catholicism, claiming that in some provinces clergymen were acting outside of the Armenian rite and conducting 'another rite' in Armenian churches.[67]

In contrast to the eighteenth-century charters of investiture for the Orthodox Christian patriarchs of Istanbul, those granted to the Armenian patriarchs of Istanbul included specific mentions of Catholics.[68] Among the several clauses added in 1752, one prevented officials from transferring churches and monasteries from the 'hands of genuine Armenian subjects' to 'seditious people who follow another religion and are called Catholics'. Another prohibited officials from treating 'genuine Armenian subjects' unfavourably because of offences committed by 'Catholics who follow another religion' or 'seditious people of that kind'.[69] These two clauses, which had no direct parallel in the charters of Orthodox patriarchs, emphasised the necessity of differentiating the Armenians belonging to the Armenian Church from those who had converted to Catholicism, to the detriment of the latter. Here, it should be noted, bureaucrats employed the new term 'Catholic' instead of the more conventionally used 'religion of the Franks'.

The geographical expansion of the patriarchate was essential for enabling the functioning of patriarchal surveillance over the clergy. Armenian conversions to Catholicism were relatively common in Erzurum, which had been under the jurisdiction of the Catholicosate of Echmiadzin until the early eighteenth century and whose prelates could be appointed through the mediation of local sharia court judges or governors.[70] In 1776, the Ottoman government allowed the establishment of a new prelateship in Mardin, responding to a petition from the Armenian patriarch, who wrote that a Catholic Armenian cleric was propagating the 'religion of the Franks' to the 'genuine Armenian subjects' of that area.[71]

Muslim ruling circles must have realised that they were incapable of determining whether a Christian cleric had a proclivity towards Catholicism. A document dated 1782 clearly demonstrates that officials had to rely on the Christian clergy to make this assessment. After the patriarch of the Syriac Christians died, they requested the appointment of a new candidate through the mediation of the governor of Baghdad. On this occasion, the government asked the Armenian patriarch of Istanbul to investigate whether the candidate was Catholic and found that suspicion to be well-founded. The government then administratively subordinated the Syriac Christians to the Armenian Patriarchate of Istanbul, determining that thereafter the request for appointment of Syriac patriarchs must be delivered by Armenian patriarchs, who were expected to scrutinise whether candidates were Catholic.[72]

For the hierarchy of the Armenian Church to have absolute authority to conduct surveillance over the religious creed followed by its flock and clergymen, Muslim officials and judges had to refrain from interfering in ecclesiastical business, especially in religious matters. Therefore, as noted, the expansion of patriarchal authority included the exclusion of Muslim officials, judges and imams from meddling in the religious affairs of Armenians. For example, the lack of exclusive supervision over marriage restricted Armenian clergymen from adopting an adamant policy towards the marriages of individuals who did not follow the religious rules of the Church, such as those who converted to Catholicism. Although they might have had other reasons for desiring exclusive supervision over marriage, the Armenian patriarchs referred to the threat of conversion as a justification for demanding it. In 1759, the Armenian patriarch requested that the government prohibit local imams in Istanbul from marrying Armenians outside of their rite, because the fact that they did so was causing Armenians to abandon their 'old rite', and the 'imams of Muslim neighbourhoods have nothing to do with the marriage of infidels'. Because the request was in accord with the text of the patriarchal charter, the government approved it.[73]

The growing challenge of Catholic missionaries in their communities led Armenian clergy to focus on the necessity of religious instruction. Adopting the strategies used by Catholic missionaries, the Armenian clergy printed and distributed religious and linguistic materials, which led to an increase in religious works printed in Armenian script in Istanbul.[74] Ottoman documents attest to the growing concern about religious indoctrination among Armenian clergymen in the second half of the eighteenth century. Beginning in the 1750s and with increasing frequency in the 1770s, the Armenian Patriarchate requested that the central government prevent local officials from interfering in the religious indoctrination conducted by Armenian priests in diverse localities.[75] The fact that these cases were brought from numerous places with relatively small Armenian populations suggests that higher clergy were cautioning local priests about the necessity of religious indoctrination and causing it to spread to places where this activity had been neglected. In turn, this novelty invited the attention of local Muslims. The patriarchs, however, successfully argued before the government that interference in religious indoctrination was an interference in the practice of religion and therefore against their charters of investiture.

Conclusion

In the eighteenth century, the Armenians of Istanbul were blessed by the emergence of three outstanding patriarchs. Each held his position for more than twenty years, which was much longer than any of their predecessors in the seventeenth century. Foremost among the three was Hovhannes Golod, to whom scholars have attributed the rise of the patriarchate and its subsequent era of stability.[76] This chapter has suggested that this rise was a product of their participation in imperial governance.

At the turn of the eighteenth century, the Ottoman Empire adopted a negative attitude towards Catholic missionaries and their conversion of its subjects. This shift allowed the anti-Catholic faction among the Armenians to develop dominance over Catholic sympathisers and forced them to find clergymen who were unsympathetic to Catholics and capable of coping with the problem of conversion. This shift in attitude in ruling circles also increased the political usefulness of the patriarchs, allowing them to extract additional rights from the government, which in turn expanded the Istanbul Patriarchate's geographical authority to cover all imperial territory (except for the Arab lands) and boosted its authority in two significant ways. First, new clauses added to the charters allowed the patriarchs stricter control over their clergy, granting them a monopoly on the right to appoint, dismiss and punish clerics throughout the expanded jurisdiction. Second, the patriarchs gained greater autonomy from Muslim officials and judges in many aspects of their role. In principle, the religious affairs of Armenians were put under the exclusive supervision of the Istanbul patriarchs.

The lack of surviving charters of investiture granted to the Orthodox Patriarchate of Istanbul in the seventeenth century has limited the ability of scholars to determine when and how the rise of the patriarchate began. The Armenian case shows that the rise of the Armenian Patriarchate of Istanbul began at the turn of the eighteenth century in conjunction with the ruling circles' changing attitude towards Catholic conversion, and it is likely that similar circumstances, together with their financial contribution, prompted the rise of the Orthodox Patriarchate. The example of non-interference in religious affairs suggests that, in some cases, Orthodox Christians extracted additional rights from the empire, using the benefits gained by the Armenian Patriarchate as a precedent.

It should be noted that although government support certainly contributed to the growth of the power of the Armenian Patriarchate of Istanbul, the patriarchate still had only limited control over the provincial Armenians. As the case of Orthodox Christians in Aleppo suggests,[77] in the eighteenth century, the central government lacked the power to ensure that patriarchs' rights were not violated in the provinces, where local power holders were largely in control. The centralisation of the Armenian community remained mostly an administrative question for the Armenians in the eastern provinces who had recently been incorporated into the jurisdiction of the Istanbul Patriarchate. As will be discussed in the next chapter, only in the 1840s did Istanbul Armenians begin serious intervention in the affairs of the eastern provinces.

Notes

1. For non-Muslim communities in the early modern period, see Ayalon, 'Rethinking Rabbinical Leadership'.
2. Papademetriou, *Render unto the Sultan*; Çolak and Bayraktar-Tellan, *Orthodox Church.*
3. The pioneering 1982 article by Kevork Bardakjian addressed the rise of the Armenian Patriarchate, but he limited his discussion to the expansion of the geographical jurisdiction and kept his investigation to Armenian narrative sources, emphasising the initiative of Armenians in this process. See 'Armenian Patriarchate of Constantinople'.
4. Tezcan, *The Second Ottoman Empire*; Yaycioglu, *Partners of the Empire.*
5. Greene, *History of the Greeks*, 181.
6. Bayraktar Tellan, 'Patriarch and the Sultan', chap. 3.
7. For the early history of the Armenian Patriarchate, see Bērbērean, 'G. Bolsoy Hay'; Rahn, *Entstehung des Armenischen Patriarchats.*
8. Shapiro, *Western Armenian Diaspora*, 129–31.
9. Albert Khaṛatyan, *Kostandnupolsi Hay Gaght'ōjakhě (XV–XVII Darer)* (Erevan: Erevani Hamalsarani Hratarakch'ut'yun, 2007), chap. 2.
10. Gibb and Bowen, *Islamic Society*, chap. 14.
11. Papademetriou, *Render unto the Sultan*, chaps 3, 4.
12. İŞS, İstanbul Mahkemesi 3, 90a; BOA, MŞH. ŞSC.d 7298 (Rodoscuk 1587), p. 107; 6574 (Manisa 154), pp. 29–30; 6293 (Kütahya 1), 115a–115b; Ayşe Özkan, '1587 Numaralı Rodoscuk (Tekfurdağı) Şer'iyye Sicilinin Transkripsiyonu ve Değerlendirilmesi' (Master's thesis, Sakarya University, 2019), 277–9; Hediye Önderoğlu, '154 Numaralı Manisa Şer'iyye Sicili'nin Transkripsiyon ve Değerlendirmesi (1095–1096/1684–1685)' (Master's thesis, Celal Bayar University, 2015), 267–8; Ekrem Güngör, '1 Numaralı Kütahya Şer'iyye Sicili (II. Bölüm) Transkripsiyonu ve Kritiği' (Master's thesis, Dumlupınar University, 2006), 307–8. Although there are some major differences between the oldest and the remaining three, and minor differences between the later three, the contents of these four are relatively similar when compared to those from the eighteenth century.
13. References to annual tribute can be found in the 1641 charter. Ottoman documents from the late seventeenth century indicate that the amount was

140,000 *akçe*. BOA, İE.ML 29/2840 (20 December 1689); MŞH. ŞSC.d 6293, 115a–115b.
14. İŞS, İstanbul Mahkemesi 3, 90a.
15. Ibid.
16. BOA, MŞH. ŞSC.d 6574, pp. 29–30.
17. On the Sis Catholicosate and the Jerusalem Patriarchate during the Ottoman period, see Avedis K. Sanjian, *The Armenian Communities in Syria under Ottoman Dominion* (Cambridge, MA: Harvard University Press, 1965); Yavuz Ercan, *Kudüs Ermeni Patrikhanesi* (Ankara: Türk Tarih Kurumu Basımevi, 1988). References to the Catholicosate of Aghtamar are seldom found in Ottoman documents. The jurisdiction of this catholicosate was limited to the island of Aghtamar and some villages around Lake Van.
18. BOA, D.PSK 1/93 (23 April 1688).
19. For example, BOA, İE.DH 15/1387, no. 3 (18 April 1696); D.PSK 2/21 (17 September 1701); 5/17 (17 August 1714).
20. İŞS, Bab Mahkemesi 3, 129b; Simeōn Erewants'i, *Jambr* (Vagharshapat: Tparan Srboy Kat'ughike Ējmiatsni, 1873), 24–5.
21. BOA, C.ADL 5/293 (16 January 1713).
22. İŞS, İstanbul Mahkemesi 3, 90a; BOA, MŞH. ŞSC.d 6574, pp. 29–30; 6293, 115a–115b.
23. BOA, KK.d 2542-1, p. 19; 2542-8, 84b–85a; 2542-6, 20b–21a.
24. BOA, D.PSK 2/21; 5/17.
25. BOA, D.PSK 1/135 (1 May 1693); 2/60 (6 April 1702); KK.d 2542-1, p. 42 (7 January 1718); 2542-1, pp. 145–6 (14 January 1723). Ottoman documents on the appointment of local prelates usually indicated whether that prelateship was under the jurisdiction of the Istanbul Patriarchate by writing 'included in the patriarchate' (*patrikliğine dahil*).
26. BOA, KK.d 2542-1, pp. 42; 2542-1, p. 68 (29 March 1719); 2542-3, p. 166 (3 July 1742).
27. BOA, İE.DH 4/353 (13 April 1696); 15/1387 (19 December 1695).
28. In 1757, the catholicosate was described as under the jurisdiction of the Istanbul Patriarchate in an Ottoman document. BOA, KK.d 2542-28, p. 55 (18 May 1757). The incorporation of the catholicosate is likely the change that Erevantsi mentions, which occurred when an Ottoman Armenian was appointed as catholicos in 1726. See Erewants'i, *Jambr*, 235–7. Some have implied that İzmir and Baghdad were not incorporated into the jurisdiction of the Istanbul Patriarchate in the eighteenth century but remained under the jurisdiction of the Echmiadzin Catholicosate until its Russian incorporation in the nineteenth century. See Bardakjian, 'Armenian Patriarchate of Constantinople', 96. Although I could not find information about Baghdad, I have confirmed that İzmir was under the jurisdiction of the Istanbul Patriarchate in the early eighteenth century and thereafter transferred to the jurisdiction of Echmiadzin Catholicosate in 1761. See BOA, KK.d 2542-28, p. 109 (3 October 1761).

29. Malachia Ormanian, *L'Église arménienne: Son histoire, sa doctrine, son régime, sa discipline, sa liturgie, sa littérature, son présent* (Paris: Ernest Leroux, 1910), 105.
30. Cevdet Paşa, *Tezâkir 21–39*, ed. Cavid Baysun, 2nd ed. (Ankara: Türk Tarih Kurumu Basımevi, 1986), 238. According to a report on the status of Syriac Christians – presumably written by Cevdet Pasha – they also considered the Armenian patriarch of Istanbul to be the resident representative. BOA, Y.EE 38/69 (5 March 1892).
31. Erewants'i, *Jambr*, 235–7.
32. BOA, KK.d 2542-8, 84b–85a.
33. Bayraktar Tellan, 'Patriarch and the Sultan', chap. 3.
34. BOA, KK.d 2542-1, p. 19.
35. Çolak and Bayraktar-Tellan, *Orthodox Church*, 79–90, 94–8, 111–29, 133–48.
36. Bayraktar Tellan, 'Patriarch and the Sultan', 167.
37. BOA, KK.d 2542-28, pp. 62–3 (5 October 1757).
38. BOA, KK.d 2542-1, p. 19.
39. Çolak and Bayraktar-Tellan, *Orthodox Church*, 98.
40. BOA, KK.d 2542-8, 84b–85a; KK.d 2542-6, 20b–21a.
41. For the rise of the *amiras*, see Barsoumian, 'Armenian *Amira* Class', chap. 2.
42. BOA, D.PSK 5/17 (17 August 1714); KK.d 2542, 36a.
43. For the Catholics in the Ottoman Empire, see Charles A. Frazee, *Catholics and Sultans: The Church and the Ottoman Empire 1453–1923* (London: Cambridge University Press, 1983); Guillaume Aral, 'La Juridiction du Saint-Siege de Rome sur les Armeniens Catholiques (XVIIe–XIXe siècle)' (PhD diss., Université de Nice, 2001).
44. Aral, 'Juridiction du Saint-Siege', 152–64; Frazee, *Catholics and Sultans*, 73–83, 90–2, 178.
45. Frazee, *Catholics and Sultans*, 178. According to Frazee, there were 8,000 Armenian Catholics in Istanbul by 1700. Likewise, Paolo Girardelli has claimed that Armenian Catholics in mid-eighteenth-century Istanbul numbered in the thousands, proving that most of the worshippers at Catholic churches in Istanbul were Armenians. See 'Architecture, Identity, and Liminality: On the Use and Meaning of Catholic Spaces in Late Ottoman Istanbul', *Muqarnas* 22 (2005): 246–52, 257–8.
46. BOA, A.DVNSMHM.d. 106, p. 191, no. 736 (23 June–2 July 1695).
47. Muzaffer Özgüleş, 'A Missing Royal Mosque in Istanbul that Islamized a Catholic Space: The Galata New Mosque', *Muqarnas* 34 (2017): 167.
48. Cesare Santus, 'Sheikh ül-islam Feyzullah Efendi and the Armenian Patriarch Awetik': A Case of Entangled Confessional Disciplining?', in *Entangled Confessionalizations? Dialogic Perspectives on the Politics of Piety and Community-Building in the Ottoman Empire, 15th–18th Centuries*, ed. Tijana Krstić and Derin Terzioğlu (Piscataway: Gorgias Press, 2022), 237–8; Aubry de La Motraye, *Travels through Europe, Asia, and into Part of Africa*, vol. 1 (London: printed for the Author, 1723), 393–4.

49. BOA, A.DVNSMHM.d 110, p. 28, no. 157 (22–31 May 1697); 110, p. 438, no. 1941 (11–20 May 1698).
50. The term *papa milleti* is relatively well known among Ottomanist researchers interested in non-Muslims because Ahmet Refik Altınay introduced the aforementioned document into his compilation of sources on social life in Istanbul. See *Hicrî On İkinci Asırda İstanbul Hayatı (1100–1200)* (Istanbul: Enderun Kitabevi, 1988), 21–2. Diplomatic documents used a variety of expressions to refer to Catholicism. Radu Dipratu, *Regulating Non-Muslim Communities in the Seventeenth-Century Ottoman Empire: Catholics and Capitulations* (London: Routledge, 2022), 49, 90, 95, 97, 98.
51. Sebouh David Aslanian, 'The "Great Schism" of 1773: Venice and the Founding of the Armenian Community in Trieste', in *Reflections of Armenian Identity in History and Historiography*, ed. Houri Berberian and Touraj Daryaee ([Irvine]: UCI Jordan Center for Persian Studies, 2018), 90.
52. Ensar Köse, 'Bir Hayalin Peşinde Yüz Yıl: Kudüs ve İstanbul Ermeni Patrikliğini Birleştirme Çabaları (1650–1750)', *Tarih Dergisi* 63 (2016): 58–9; BOA, AE.SMST.II 139/15427 (no date).
53. BOA, A.DVNSMHM.d 111, p. 626, nos. 2204–11 (18–27 July 1701).
54. BOA, A.DVNSMHM.d 111, p. 631, nos. 2224–31 (18–27 July 1701); 112, p. 309, nos. 1095–109.
55. Santus, 'Sheikh ül-islam Feyzullah Efendi'.
56. BOA, D.PSK 2/48 (7 March 1702).
57. BOA, A.DVNSMHM.d 111, p. 645, no, 2291 (16–25 August 1701).
58. BOA, D.PSK 4/41 (11 January 1709); KK.d 2542, 34a (11 January 1709).
59. Ensar Köse, 'İstanbul Ermeni Patrikliği'nin Osmanlı Hükümeti'yle Münasebetlerine Tesir Eden Dinamikler (18. Yüzyılın İlk Yarısı)', *Osmanlı Medeniyeti Araştırmaları Dergisi* 3, no. 5 (2017): 13; Santus, 'Sheikh ül-islam Feyzullah Efendi'; Frazee, *Catholics and Sultans*, 179.
60. BOA, AE.SAMD.III 208/20085 (26 December 1722); KK.d 2542-1, p. 149 (26 December 1722).
61. BOA, İE.DH 34/2955 (29 January–6 February 1723); KK.d 2542-3, p. 76 (24 May 1739).
62. Masters, 'Millet Wars', 137–8. Although this article is informative about the influence of Catholicism and local politics in Aleppo, the author seems to have overemphasised the importance of this city in the pan-imperial shift in the relationship between the state and non-Muslims and underestimated the initiative of the state.
63. For example, when an Armenian patriarch petitioned the government to prohibit the Armenians' visits to the Catholic Churches of the Franks, a scribe confirmed that there was no mention of this issue in the capitulation granted to the French king. BOA, AE.SMHD.I 105/7493 (25 February 1744). Also see, BOA, AE.SMST.III 305/24346 (28 November 1761).
64. Frazee, *Catholics and Sultans*, 178–81; Aslanian, 'Great Schism', 88–93. According to Fariba Zarinebaf, several dozen Armenians were sent to the

galleys. *Mediterranean Encounters: Trade and Pluralism in Early Modern Galata* (Oakland: University of California Press, 2018), 260.

65. For example, see BOA, A.DVNSMHM.d 117, p. 51, no. 211 (3–12 December 1710).
66. BOA, KK.d 2542-8, 84b–85a; 2542-6, 20b–21a.
67. BOA, KK.d 2542-30, pp. 5–6 (14 October 1780).
68. Although Çolak and Bayraktar-Tellan have emphasised the influence of Catholicism behind the change in the charters of investiture granted to Orthodox Christian patriarchs, direct reference to the Catholics was quite rare. The only exception the authors introduce seems to be the charter granted to the patriarch of Alexandria in 1758. See *Orthodox Church*, 50–1, 166–7.
69. BOA, KK.d 2542-6, 20b–21a.
70. This does not mean that being outside the jurisdiction of Istanbul caused Catholic conversion among Armenians. The list of the cities where conversion was more frequently observed suggests that those in the centres of international trade were more likely to convert due to their contact with Western Christianity. For the conversion of Armenians to Catholicism in Erzurum, see Henry R. Shapiro, 'Falling Out of Love with the Franks: The Life and Writings of an Armenian Catholic Diplomat in the Service of Late Safavid Persia', *Iranian Studies* 54, no. 3–4 (2021): 573–603.
71. BOA, KK.d 2542-29, p. 87 (25 November 1776).
72. BOA, KK.d 2542-30, p. 32 (14 August 1782). Although the literature has indicated that in the early modern period, the Ottoman government allowed Syriac Christians to use the holy sites in Palestine as the 'dependent' of the Armenian Patriarchate of Jerusalem, and although the Syriac Christians had an official relationship with the Armenian Patriarchate of Istanbul in the nineteenth century, when and why the latter relationship began has been controversial. Henry Clements, 'Documenting Community in the Late Ottoman Empire', *International Journal of Middle East Studies* 51, no. 3 (2019): 429–31; İbrahim Özcoşar, 'Osmanlı Taşrasında Bir Patriklik: Yakubî Süryani Patrikliği', *Avrasya İncelemeleri Dergisi* 7, no. 2 (2018): 168–72.
73. BOA, KK.d 2542-28, p. 79 (28 February 1759).
74. For example, a catechism published in 1740 included elementary instruction in Armenian script. *Ayppenaran ew K'risdonēagan* (Istanbul: n.p., 1740). Baghdasar published a book of religious instruction in Armeno-Turkish. See *Grt'ut'iwn K'risdonēagan* (Istanbul: n.p., 1742). On the activities of Armenian Catholics, see Sebouh David Aslanian, '"Prepared in the Language of the Hagarites": Abbot Mkhitar's 1727 Armeno-Turkish Grammar of Modern Western Armenian', *Journal of the Society for Armenian Studies* 25 (2016): 54–86. For the relationship between the spread of printing and confessional rivalry among Armenians, see Sebouh David Aslanian, *Early Modernity and Mobility: Port Cities and Printers across the Armenian Diaspora, 1512–1800* (New Haven: Yale University Press, 2023).

75. For example, BOA, KK.d 2542-28, p. 73 (24 August 1758, Kirmasti), p. 80 (16 April 1759, Köstence); 2542-29, p. 61 (21 February 1775, İslimye), p. 76 (14 September 1775, Edincik), p. 100 (9 December 1777, Larende).
76. Sanjian, *Armenian Communities in Syria*, 36; Bardakjian, 'Armenian Patriarchate of Constantinople', 94–5.
77. Masters, 'Millet Wars', 137–8.

2

Participation of Lay Elites in Community Administration

In 1839, the Ottoman Empire promulgated the Gülhane Rescript and officially declared the inauguration of the Tanzimat Reforms. Amid this atmosphere of change, the Armenians of Istanbul implemented their own reforms to their community administration during the 1840s. First, Armenian artisans led a movement in 1840 to take over the financial affairs of the community. The movement resulted in the establishment of a short-lived committee of oversight, followed by a similar attempt in the next year. Second, disagreement among Armenian lay elites led to the establishment in 1847 of two councils in the Armenian Patriarchate of Istanbul to discuss religious and non-religious affairs of the community.[1] These developments offer a window into the question of lay participation in the non-Muslim community's administration.

Ottoman scholars have widely recognised that – in contradiction to the traditional account of the *millet* system – it was not only prelates who were granted official responsibility for communal affairs by the Ottoman government, but also lay notables were deeply involved in community administration both in Istanbul and at the local level. Thus, it is insufficient to consider the clergy alone as the main actor when discussing the administration of non-Muslim communities and their relationship with the imperial government. The most conspicuous examples were the lay notables of the Orthodox and Armenian communities who rose to prominence in Istanbul in the eighteenth century. Lay Orthodox elites, called *phanariot*s, acquired wealth and celebrity through their positions in imperial governance as interpreters and as governors of Walachia and Moldavia. Armenian elites, called *amira*, gained their wealth through their roles as financiers to the sultans and high-ranking officials. Both *phanariot*s and *amira*s employed the wealth that they earned through their service to the state in supporting their own communal institutions and cultures, establishing their fame within their religious communities and having an increased say in community administration.[2]

The novelty of the developments among Armenians in the 1840s was the creation of an institutional basis for lay participation in community administration. This chapter argues that Armenians' willingness to obtain state recognition was the defining characteristic of their reforms. Lay artisans and elites gained official government recognition of their positions in their community and shouldered responsibility for its administration. By doing so, they dragged the state into communal politics to gain the upper hand over other communal actors. They were able to do this because Ottoman statesmen, facing pressure from the European Great Powers, were becoming increasingly concerned about the affairs of non-Muslim communities in this period and were searching for new partners in their relationship with non-Muslims.

The reforms that occurred in the Istanbul Armenian community were the product of multiple factors. The timing suggests that the atmosphere of change encouraged Armenian artisans to take daring action. The decline in the relative power of the Armenian lay elites motivated other members of the community to discuss new ways to administer communal affairs.[3] This chapter emphasises that a further circumstance promoting this series of events was the changing profile of the Armenian community which followed the spread of school-based education beginning in the 1820s.[4] This chapter therefore first traces the development of school-based education in the 1820s and 1830s, and then turns its attention to the reforms of Armenians' community administration in the 1840s. It demonstrates that the pressure from the Great Powers and the reforms of community administration created a desire to distinguish the religious from the non-religious when discussing community administration.

The Early Nineteenth Century

The reign of Sultan Mahmut II (r. 1808–39) is recognised as the inaugural period of drastic reorganisation in the Ottoman Empire. By successfully eliminating the obstacles to reforms (that is, the Janissary corps and provincial notables), the sultan pursued the centralisation of power and the restructuring of the military and state administration. His efforts laid the foundation for the subsequent Tanzimat Reforms (1839–76), which consecutively reorganised the taxation system, the military, the judiciary and central and local administrations during the mid-nineteenth century.

The reforms initiated by Mahmut and continuing into the Tanzimat period aimed to increase state control over society. In the 1820s, an internal passport system was introduced to restrict and control the movement of people within the empire. Additionally, a census was implemented for Muslim and non-Muslim men. To administer these systems at the grassroots level, lay headmen, called *muhtar*, were appointed in Muslim neighbourhoods, Christian parishes and Jewish congregations of Istanbul. Eventually, the appointment of *muhtar*s was extended to the provinces. The religious authority of each non-Muslim community was entrusted by the Ottoman government with the administration of the *muhtar* system in Istanbul.[5]

The reign of Mahmut was also a period in which the treatment of non-Muslims in general – and their religious affairs in particular – assumed greater political meaning in the empire's foreign relations. In 1821, Greek revolts broke out in Morea, later prompting the intervention of the Great Powers on behalf of the Greeks, which ultimately led to their independence from the Ottoman Empire. This political independence accompanied the religious separation of the Church of Greece from the Istanbul Patriarchate. As for the Armenians, the Catholicosate of Echmiadzin, their highest religious authority, was incorporated into the Russian Empire in 1828, along with the Erivan Khanate in the Caucasus. This acquisition enabled the Russians to leverage the catholicosate to gain the support of Ottoman Armenians, causing concern among other Great Powers.[6] British and Austrian ambassadors cautioned the Ottoman Foreign Ministry, drawing an analogy between the Armenians' religious subordination to the catholicosate and the Catholics' subordination to the Roman Pope.[7] In 1828, France intervened in the Ottoman Empire when the latter expelled Armenians who had converted to Catholicism from Istanbul.[8] Meanwhile, Britain acted on behalf of Protestant missionaries from the United States, who started evangelising in Ottoman lands in the early nineteenth century and intensified their work in Istanbul and Anatolia around 1830.[9]

The state's increased control over society and the politicisation of the treatment of non-Muslims prompted Mahmut II's regime to strengthen ties with the non-Muslim religious authorities based in Istanbul. For the Ottoman statesmen of this period, these authorities were, if brought under state control, useful tools that facilitated population control and allowed them to address non-Muslim religious affairs as domestic problems.[10] Consequently, the government chose to appoint new religious heads for Armenian Catholics and Jews in a manner similar to the Istanbul Patriarchates of the Orthodox and Armenian Churches and assigned them administrative roles. In 1830, the government recognised the separation of Armenian Catholics from the jurisdiction of the Armenian Patriarchate, appointing an Armenian Catholic bishop as the head of all Catholic subjects – with the exception of Latin subjects – within the empire.[11]

In 1834, the government allowed the holder of this position to bear the title of patriarch, announcing its decision in its newly founded official gazette.[12] The state, responding to a request from Jewish subjects, granted an official appointment to a Chief Rabbi of Istanbul the following year.[13]

In the same period, the supervisory role of the patriarchate expanded among Armenians in Istanbul with the spread of school education and the establishment of other communal institutions. Some wealthy Armenians who had accumulated great fortunes as *sarraf*s and technocrats dedicated their wealth to improving the social, religious and cultural welfare of their coreligionists.[14] They contributed financially to the reconstruction of churches, publication of books and construction of schools. Mgrdich Amira Mirijanian, who had established schools in Istanbul in the late eighteenth century, was the forerunner in this trend.[15] During the 1820s and 1830s, he was followed by other wealthy laymen whose financial contributions enabled more Armenian schools to open, first in Istanbul and later in the provinces.[16] Harutyun Amira Bezjian, who paid the reconstruction fee for one of the schools that Mirijanian had built after it burned down in 1828, was the most prominent Armenian benefactor in this period.[17] As Orthodox Christian schools spread and as state concern for educating Muslims in general grew, the early nineteenth century exhibited increased attention overall to education in the different religious groups of the Ottoman Empire.[18]

Contrary to the assumptions of previous studies, the spread of schooling among Armenians was not a simple story of secularisation or the emancipation of education from the clergy's control.[19] Some sources suggest that the support of the high clergy played a major role in the educational trend. In 1824, Garabed, the Armenian patriarch, issued a letter of instruction to the clergymen under his jurisdiction. While five of the six orders in the letter refer to the restoration of discipline among the clergy, the final one encourages heads of dioceses to establish local schools.[20] The preamble to the letter states that these instructions were formulated by several bishops and *vartabed*s gathered at the patriarchate.[21] The fact that the surviving copy of this document was addressed to clergy in the remote provinces of Hasankale (currently Pasinler in Erzurum) suggests that the letter was actually sent to all provinces under the patriarchate's jurisdiction. Moreover, the patriarchate revised and extended these instructions twice further and issued them again in 1826 and 1830 as printed pamphlets. The 1830 regulations included two articles that mandated the establishment of schools and guidelines for the behaviour of teachers. These instructions and regulations suggest that high-level Armenian clergymen hoped to provide education to all the Armenian children in the empire and use it as a means of making these children loyal to the Armenian Church, thus guarding against the challenge from Catholic (and later Protestant) missionaries.[22]

The growth of Armenian schools in the provinces is confirmed by reports drafted by the patriarchate in 1834 and 1847. The surviving data produced by the 1834 investigation is limited to simply the number of schools in each diocese: there were 114 Armenian schools across the empire, from Van (in the eastern provinces) to Filibe (currently Plovdiv in Bulgaria). The İzmit diocese was conspicuous for its large number of schools (thirty-eight), in which graduates of the Armaş monastery school served as teachers before they were ordained as priests.[23] Some of the results of the 1847 Armenian investigation were published in *Hayasdan*, the patriarchate's official newspaper. Although the available data is limited to eight dioceses (Walachia, the Balkans, İzmir, Kütahya, Ankara, Eğin, Trabzon and Diyarbakır), the report allows the inference that, as a result of the patriarchate's project of spreading school education and the financial contributions of lay elites, most of the cities and towns in the Balkans and Western and Central Anatolia that had an Armenian population also had at least one elementary school by 1847, although their prevalence was lower in the eastern provinces.[24] For example, the number of schools in the İzmir diocese increased from three in 1834 to seventeen in 1847. Of its seventeen districts, fifteen had one school each, while Manisa had two. However, Bayındır did not even have one because 'its priest was incompetent and inhabitants were poor'.[25] The schools in the Ankara diocese also increased from eight to thirteen; of these, full-time teachers were employed in eight, priests served concurrently as teachers in five and priests held reading and writing courses in two districts without schools.[26] Although schools were previously open in some towns in the Diyarbakır diocese (in the eastern provinces), many of these were out of operation at the time of the investigation. Only two Armenian schools could now be found there.[27] It was only after the 1860s that Armenian schools increased in the eastern provinces.

In Istanbul, where the Armenians had twenty schools in 1847, the rivalry with Catholics and Protestants encouraged the Armenians to establish other communal institutions.[28] Both Catholics and Protestants offered education and medical treatment as part of their missionary activities. Although the Armenians had been running two hospitals in Istanbul since the eighteenth century, both had deteriorated by the early nineteenth century. The Armenians obtained imperial permission to establish a new hospital in 1832, one year after Armenian Catholics had obtained imperial permission to build their own hospital in Istanbul. Owing to the financial contributions of Bezjian and other *amiras*, an Armenian hospital – intended to serve not only as a place of medical treatment but also as an orphanage and poorhouse – was opened in Yedikule in 1834.[29] A monastery owned by the Jerusalem monastic order in Üsküdar was renovated and put into service as a higher educational institution called Jemaran in 1838.[30] In addition, the patriarchate launched an official newspaper to rival those of the Catholics and Protestants, who had begun to publish their own periodicals around 1840.[31] In 1846, Madteos, the Armenian patriarch of Istanbul, petitioned the government and obtained permission to publish its own newspaper, *Hayasdan* (Armenia, in Armenian).[32] *Hayasdan* was a weekly newspaper that printed official statements from the patriarchate as well as news of foreign and state affairs. In 1852, it was succeeded by *Masis*, which had a semi-official status with respect to the patriarchate. Several other newspapers in Armenian and Armeno-Turkish, such as *Meghu*, *Noyyan Aghawni* and *Münadi-yi Erciyas*, were also founded in the 1850s and 1860s.

Armenian elites did not see any inconsistency between their development of communal education and their allegiance to the state. An act of Patriarch Madteos provides a good example of this. He did not leave the state officials – who channelled limited resources to the development of higher educational institutions and left non-Muslim schools to their own devices – uninformed about the advancement of schooling among Armenians. In 1847, he sent a petition to the government to request that members of the Council of Public Education, which had been newly established in 1846, be sent to an examination conducted at an Armenian school in the Samatya district of Istanbul to motivate the Armenian children.[33] The Armenian Patriarchate reported on the examination in *Hayasdan*. The newspaper emphasised that the 'Armenian allegiant nation' was following the good example of the sultan by spreading school education. According to the report, four state officials, including Fuat Efendi, a member of the council and eventually a grand vizier, and Mütercim Mehmet Pasha, another future grand vizier, attended the examination. Fuat, who was a future leading proponent of Ottomanism – the project to integrate religiously diverse subjects as citizens under the principle of equality – reported positively on the development of school education among Armenians, which in his view did not conflict with their allegiance to the Ottoman Empire or its policy of integration. He told the students that the sublime will of the merciful monarch was that all his dear subjects would recognise each other as 'children of the one and same fatherland' (*mi ew noyn hayreneatsʻ zawag*) and love and respect each other through education, so that this love and harmony would further develop the empire.[34] Later that century, many graduates of the Armenian schools would enter the state's higher schools and bureaucracy, further demonstrating that the Armenian schools functioned as part of, rather than in opposition to, this integration policy.[35]

Community Administration Contested

Previously, the main community institutions that the Ottoman Armenians were required to collectively administer had been their churches. The growth in communal institutions in the 1820s and 1830s, especially schools, brought with them the responsibility of further management, and the patriarchate was expected to exercise a supervisory role over these institutions. Meanwhile, the increase of communal institutions augmented the community's financial burdens, which could no longer be shouldered by a few wealthy *amira sarraf*s and technocrats alone. Artisanal groups became obligated to contribute to their upkeep as well. Moreover, the temporal abolishment of the tax farming system in 1839 and the rise of Greek bankers in the 1840s led to a decline in the number and wealth of Armenian *sarraf*s. These developments led to the growing involvement of artisans in community administration and the creation of committees in the early 1840s.

At the time, high-ranking Ottoman officials were facing pressure from the Great Powers, who had increased their level of involvement in the religious affairs of Ottoman Christians. Foreign intervention reached unprecedented heights, forcing the Ottoman government to transfer its responsibility for non-Muslim affairs from the financial department to the Ministry of Foreign Affairs in 1838.[36] Responding to this pressure, Mustafa Reşit Pasha, the most prominent leader in the early Tanzimat Reforms, 'began contemplating measures as early as the summer of 1840 to reduce the secular powers of the clergy' and to appoint 'lay chiefs for the administration of the temporal affairs'. His and other statesmen's concern prompted Orthodox Christians in Istanbul to establish a committee of lay notables in 1843, which the patriarch soon abolished.[37]

Even before the Orthodox Christians, Istanbul Armenians had taken the first step towards reforming their community administration in 1840 by creating a financial management body called the Committee of Twenty-Four. A major disagreement was sparked when the patriarch collected money from the Istanbul Armenians for Jemaran's operating costs but did not give the entire amount to the school. The resulting financial difficulties drove the school into temporary closure, and the patriarch's attitude did not satisfy the artisans who had helped pay for the school's costs.

They took the initiative to form the Committee of Twenty-Four without the recognition of *amira*s or the patriarch, deciding that each of the twenty-four Armenian artisan guilds would send one representative to sit on the committee.[38]

The artisans then dared to directly petition the government themselves and dragged the state into their community politics. They found recourse in its support to challenge the powerful *amira*s and the patriarch. In their petition, they requested the recognition of the committee, attaching the committee's proposed regulations.[39] The regulations stated that the Committee of Twenty-Four was created to shoulder not only Jemaran's finances but 'all affairs related to the Armenian community's finances'. Moreover, these regulations forbade the involvement of *sarraf*s and patriarchs in the community's finances and in the appointment and dismissal of committee members. However, they did not challenge the role of the patriarch himself, stipulating that he would continue to manage religious and other affairs, only excepting community finances.[40] They justified their challenge, asserting that they had been chosen by the community and represented its voice. This bottom-up move invited opposition from both the *amira sarraf*s and the patriarch, who did not acquiesce to this loss of authority. In response, the artisans held a protest in front of the patriarchate, which was broken up by governmental intervention.[41]

The documents written after this intervention demonstrate the attitudes of state officials towards the administration of non-Muslim communities. They believed that the administration of the community was the responsibility of the patriarch. This was a natural conclusion from the fact that the patriarch was appointed as the official representative of the community through a charter of investiture. Officials also recognised that 'some lay notables whom the sublime state knows' (*devlet-i aliyenin bildiği bazı muteberan-ı millet*) were also responsible for the administration of their community, even in the absence of any official standing. In contrast, state officials held a negative view of the participation of ordinary lay members of the community. Thus, they were dismissive of movements from below and affirmed elite rule. Additionally, they recognised that Armenians' communal concerns included both religious matters and 'other communal affairs', and that the former were attributed to the responsibility of the patriarch, while the latter were the responsibility of both the patriarch and elite laypeople.[42] Finally, officials believed that there was a similarity in the methods of community administration of Orthodox Christians, Armenians and Catholics (but not Jews). Thus, when they investigated the Armenian protest, they invited Orthodox Christian and Catholic elites to give their opinions on the financial committee that the Armenians had established.

Unsurprisingly, these leaders found the involvement of ordinary laymen to be inappropriate.[43]

Nevertheless, the challenge posed by the artisans compelled the high clergy and lay elites to understand the necessity of appeasing them. The newly confirmed Patriarch Asduadzadur petitioned the government for permission to form a new committee for financial administration. This committee would have twenty-seven members, chosen from among the artisanal guilds, and it would be assigned the financial affairs of 'churches, hospitals and other similar [institutions] of the community'. In December 1841, the Ottoman government gave its tacit permission. Yet it was also short-lived. When the catholicos of Echmiadzin died in 1842, and the catholicosate sent a letter of invitation for the election of the new catholicos to the Patriarchate of Istanbul, the committee's inability to deal with this religious-cum-political issue became a problem.[44]

For Istanbul Armenians, their relationship with the Echmiadzin Catholicosate took on a new political meaning when it was incorporated into the Russian Empire in 1828. Ottoman Armenians unilaterally severed relations with the catholicosate to avoid the growing distrust of state officials.[45] In 1842, the patriarch needed to act cautiously to avoid inviting suspicion from the government. He presented the letter of invitation to the Ottoman Foreign Ministry. A report to the sultan stated that it would be inappropriate to forbid the acceptance of the invitation because the state should not intervene in issues related to the 'religion and principles of the community' (*ayin ü usul-i millet*). The report went on to mention that the *sarraf*s and elites would have handled the issue if a similar invitation had been delivered to the patriarchate before the formation of the committee. At the time, however, the community administration was in the hands of the twenty-seven guild representatives, and state officials saw this body as incapable of dealing with the issue. They therefore decided to dissolve the committee of twenty-seven and let a group of notables take its place.[46] State officials once again preferred to have the lay elites handle non-Muslim communal affairs.

The Separation of Religious and Non-religious Affairs

In 1844, Armenian lay elites chose Madteos, known for his popularity among artisans, as the new patriarch of Istanbul to win artisan support.[47] His patriarchate heralded a split in the prominent Armenian laypeople of Istanbul.

Two religious policies that Madteos promulgated alarmed both lay Armenian elites and Muslim statesmen, and they impressed on the latter how deeply the religious affairs of Armenians had become intertwined with international politics, as had also happened for the Orthodox Christians. The first of these policies was Madteos's support for the restoration of the Istanbul Patriarchate's relationship with the Echmiadzin Catholicosate. In the first mass that he held as patriarch, Madteos named Nerses as Echmiadzin catholicos without giving notice that he would do so. This act recognised the supremacy of Echmiadzin, and it was the first time that this had occurred in Istanbul since the incorporation of Echmiadzin into the Russian Empire. In response, the lay and ecclesiastical elites called a meeting at the patriarchate. During this discussion, it was decided to recognise Nerses as the supreme catholicos, restoring the Istanbul Patriarchate's relations with the Echmiadzin Catholicosate after an interval of eighteen years.[48] According to a Russian diplomatic report, this decision upset both clergy and *sarrafs*, who would have preferred caution in the relationship with the catholicosate.[49]

Although Madteos was not pro-Russian, his pro-Echmiadzin attitude did attract Russian interest. In 1846, the tsar consulted with Nerses about the possibility of awarding Madteos a decoration. Nerses proposed that it would be more appropriate if the catholicos, rather than the tsar, were to grant the decoration, and the tsar acceded to this proposal. Madteos was cautious enough to submit the decoration to the Ottoman Foreign Ministry and ask for permission to accept it. Although the political intentions of the Russian government were apparent, the Ottoman government considered that it had no choice but to give Madteos the permission he asked for.[50]

Madteos's other controversial stance was his firm treatment of Armenians who had converted to the Protestant faith. In 1846, Madteos anathematised the entire group and forbade other Armenians from having social or economic relations with them.[51] This decision displeased Britain, self-designated protector of Protestant missionaries in the Ottoman Empire and its most important political ally in the mid-nineteenth century. It must therefore have disturbed both Muslim state officials and the lay Armenian elites – particularly *sarrafs*, state officials and entrepreneurs – who had close ties with Muslim officials. A British diplomatic intervention on behalf of the Protestant Armenians led to the Ottoman government's recognition of the independence of the Protestant community in 1850.[52]

Two documents show how Madteos's declaration of anathema alarmed Ottoman officials. One was a formal response to Madteos's April 1846 petition for permission to publish the newspaper *Hayasdan*.[53] Madteos had promised to impose limits on the newspaper, restricting it from ever referring to 'politics' (*politika*). State officials granted this permission, but under the condition that no reference ever be made to rumours about the

Protestants. The other document is a draft of an order from the grand vizier, dated May 1846.[54] This order attests to the serious effects of the anathema, mentioning that Protestant Armenians had lost their guarantors for their businesses and were suffering considerable hardship. Interestingly, the draft also comments on Madteos's decision, its legality and its potentially disastrous impacts:

> Nothing can be said against the ecclesiastical punishments [*tedibat-ı ruhaniye*] that the patriarch inflicted on them [Armenians converted to Protestantism] according to their [Armenians'] religion [*ayinlerince*]. However, the punishments do not remain within the scope of religion [*mezhep dairesinde kalmayıp*] but have harmed their secular affairs [*umur-ı dünyeviye*], earnings and sustenance. Thus, considering that [the punishments] will cause various political [*politikaca*] dangers ~~on the part of the government~~ [~~*devletçe*~~] and various improprieties in the future…[55]

Importantly, the draft mentions the principle of non-intervention in non-Muslims' religious affairs, which, as will be discussed in later chapters, would gain more political significance in subsequent decades. As noted in Chapter 1, the rights of the patriarchs in the charters of investiture were expanded in the direction of restricting state officials and judges from interfering in Armenians' religious affairs in the eighteenth century. The drafter of this document might have hesitated due to this idea, but he justified the necessity of the intervention on the grounds that the religious punishment of the patriarch had secular effects.

As the seventeenth-century charters and the 1840s committees suggest, it was not unprecedented for Muslim officials to differentiate Armenians' religious affairs from other issues in discussions of the patriarchs' responsibilities. The novelty in this draft is the term used to describe other issues, that is, *dünyevi* (worldly, secular). With this word, the drafter refers to the division between religious and secular affairs and attributes the former to the jurisdiction of the patriarch, expressing a negative attitude towards the influence of the patriarch in the latter. Moreover, the drafter directs the reader's attention to the possibility of such an involvement acquiring political meaning.

The words used to refer to religion require some further explanation. The drafter uses the terms '*ayin*' and '*mezhep*' in relation to the principle of non-intervention in religious affairs. *Ayin* means religious rites in addition to manners and customs, including non-religious ones. Meanwhile, as Elif Bayraktar Tellan has argued, it was also frequently used in charters of investiture granted to the patriarchs in the early modern period and meant religion in general.[56] In earlier periods, *mezhep* also meant a religious denomination, but it came to be used to mean religion in general in the nineteenth century.[57] In a dictionary published in Venice in 1836 by Catholic Armenians who had emigrated from the Ottoman Empire, *mezhep* and *ayin* were the second and third synonyms listed for *grōn* (religion) after *din*.[58]

The desire of state officials to distinguish religious and non-religious affairs was observed in the discussion of the reforms in the community administration of Orthodox Christians as well. In 1847, a drafter of a document employed this distinction as a criterion to determine whether the government should recognise the regulations that the Orthodox Patriarchate had prepared for community administration. State officials considered it problematic that the patriarchate had shown these regulations to the Russian embassy first. Meanwhile, they claimed that the regulations were unacceptable because, although Orthodox Christians asserted that all the regulations were concerned with 'religious affairs' (*umur-ı diniye ve mezhebiye*), 'most of the regulations fell outside of religion' (*nizamatın ekseri mezhebin haricinde olmasıyla*), and therefore, they were not appropriate for implementation outside of government control. State officials believed that their intervention in Orthodox religious affairs could be a pretext for the Russians to complain about Ottoman treatment of Christian subjects. Thus, the document notes that the Russians would not be able to object so long as 'anything to violate their religion would not be done' (*mezheplerine dokunur bir şey yapılmadıkça*).[59]

In the same period, Istanbul Armenians also found it necessary to distinguish religious from non-religious matters when discussing their own community administration. Madteos's strong inclination to pursue his own religious policies motivated him to take measures to restrict the intervention of lay elites. According to the Armenian chronicles, he employed the rhetoric of separating political (*k'aghak'agan*) affairs, which included the administration of schools, hospitals and community finance, from the religious (*grōnagan*) or spiritual (*hokewor*) aspects of community administration.[60] He prevented the intervention of lay elites in the latter by releasing his hold on the former.

Some prominent laypeople demanded that Madteos resign from the patriarchate, which led to conflict between the pro- and anti-Madteos factions within that class. Hagop Grjigian, an Armenian state official, acted as mediator and called a meeting that was attended by lay elites and Madteos himself.[61] This meeting resulted in the 1847 formation of lay and ecclesiastical councils within the patriarchate under government approval. In this arrangement, lay elites would shoulder the management of the non-religious aspects of the community, and the clergymen would oversee the religious aspects. Meanwhile, the position of *logotet* – the lay leader of the Armenian community and the head of the lay council – was created. Grjigian was the first appointed to this role.[62] In 1848, the Ottoman authorities decided to dismiss Madteos in response to the demands of the Armenian lay elites. According to the government's investigation, Madteos had intended to invite clergymen from Russian territory and 'let them intervene in the ecclesiastical affairs of the community' (*umur-ı ruhaniye-i millete karıştırtmak*), which Ottoman officials found harmful (*muzır*) to the state.[63]

Grjigian's strong ties with Mustafa Reşit Pasha had been the driving force behind the councils' creation. Grjigian had begun his career as the interpreter for Reşit Pasha's French ambassadorship and had gained his trust. According to the former's obituary, when he consulted with Reşit Pasha on reforms for the Armenian community's administration and the creation of councils, he obtained Reşit's promise to appoint him as *logotet*.[64] Reşit Pasha must have regarded Madteos's policies as problematic and found it profitable to appoint a lay leader to the Armenian community in addition to the patriarch. Reşit Pasha learned from experience how difficult non-Muslim religious affairs could be. After he was appointed foreign minister in 1840, he faced British demands that the Ottoman government dismiss the Orthodox Christian patriarch.[65] The creation of the councils in the Armenian Patriarchate must have been a convenient opportunity for him, especially since his political power relied on his ability to manage foreign relations. By appointing trustworthy lay elites to positions of power in the Armenian community, Reşit Pasha intended to establish indirect control over the community's affairs and diminish the risk that it could harm Ottoman relationships with the European Great Powers. Mgrdich Jezayirlian, an Armenian *sarraf* and entrepreneur who had Reşit Pasha's trust, also joined the lay council.[66] Reşit's reliance on lay elites was also observable in his relationship with Orthodox Christians; he had close connection with Stefanos Vogorides, a state official with a diplomatic background.[67]

Grjigian's special position is attested by the fact that the Ottoman government granted him a charter of investiture as *logotet*.[68] While the term for other members of the lay council was two years, Grjigian remained in his position until 1855, when he was appointed as the councillor to the French ambassadorship of Mehmet Cemil, the son of Reşit. After Grjigian's departure for Paris, Sahag Abro, another Armenian official in the Foreign Ministry, assumed the position of acting *logotet* for a year, and in 1856, Krikor Margosian, who was also in the Foreign Ministry, became *logotet*.[69] As we will discuss later, Reşit Pasha's relation with

Grjigian was not exceptional. Several high-ranking Muslim officials of the Tanzimat period maintained close ties with leading figures in the Armenian community.

Behind state officials' willingness to recognise the Armenians' councils was a deeper concern regarding the state of the Orthodox Christian community. As they considered recognising the Armenians' councils, they realised that these would set a favourable precedent for Orthodox Christians.[70] Under pressure from Britain, Ottoman officials urged the Orthodox Christian hierarchy to reform their community's administration. However, they had difficulty persuading them to accept the institutionalisation of lay participation.[71] In the 1840s, high-ranking officials searched for a new way of managing the relationship between the state and Christian community, in which lay elites would play a greater and more formal role, and the high clergy would no longer be the sole official representatives of their communities.

Lay and Ecclesiastical Councils

The Armenian Patriarchate stipulated regulations for lay and ecclesiastical councils, to which the Ottoman government granted recognition. The regulations stated that

> Permission was granted to form two councils under the superintendence of the Armenian patriarch in order to manage the affairs of the allegiant Armenian community of the everlasting Sublime State according to just order and law. One of these councils was composed of nineteen members chosen by guilds. With the additional appointment of a logotet, twenty members would shoulder the management of all communal affairs. The other was composed of fourteen members chosen by the aforementioned council to shoulder the management of affairs related to religion.[72]

The selection method for members suggests that the bottom-up movement in the early 1840s impacted the lay council. Meanwhile, the idea of separating communal affairs into religious and non-religious ones survived.

The Armenians again requested state recognition for their new councils that were created to resolve political opposition in their community. Moreover, they requested government permission before they chose new members for these councils and reported the new members to the government after they were chosen.[73] Meanwhile, Armenian leadership kept the general public informed about the councils; the official and semi-official newspapers reported information on assemblies convened to elect council members every two years. As stipulated in the regulations, all the guild representatives gathered at the assembly in 1849 and elected lay council members.[74] In later years, the newspapers reported that *amiras*, notable artisans, other elites and sometimes clergy participated in the assembly and elected members of both the lay and ecclesiastical councils.[75]

The reform of community administration conducted by the Ottoman Armenians was not limited to Istanbul. An Armenian newspaper reported in 1841 that the Armenians in İzmir had elected four representatives, four advisors, two church managers, a hospital manager and a school manager.[76] The creation of a lay council in Istanbul led to demands for a similar council in İzmit in 1848. Patriarch Madteos granted his permission and ordered that its members be elected from İzmit and its environs.[77] In Muncusun, in the Kayseri diocese, Armenians established a council for the administration of the affairs of churches and schools in 1853.[78] According to Yaşar Tolga Cora, Armenians in Erzurum had a 'Civic Assembly' in the late 1850s.[79] It is worth noting that newspaper articles on these reforms commonly mentioned the administration of churches, schools and hospitals. As in Istanbul, the establishment of schools and hospitals in the early and mid-nineteenth century required a new style of community administration among provincial Armenians.

The establishment of the lay council and the expansion of the Tanzimat Reforms increased communication between the Istanbul Patriarchate and the Armenians of the eastern provinces. After the inauguration of the Reforms in 1839, the central government implemented administrative reforms first in the nearer provinces before gradually extending them to other areas. By 1845, they reached the eastern provinces. The semi-autonomous rulers of this region resisted the implementation of the Reforms, which seemed to imperil their privileges. The most significant resistance was shown in the 1847 revolt led by Bedirhan Bey, the most powerful local ruler in the eastern provinces. In the suppression of this revolt, the central government took the step of incorporating the provinces into its direct rule. The central government's elimination of the privileges of local rulers led to a reconfiguration of power relations in the eastern provinces.[80]

These political changes aroused concern among Istanbul Armenians for the fate of their coreligionists in the eastern provinces. The lay council sought to improve conditions for Armenians in the eastern provinces, an act that partially filled in for the absence of the state. The council dispatched an Armenian teacher named Fizika Boghos to Muş and generated new regulations for the Surp Garabed monastery in that province to reform its administration. These regulations included articles on the monks, donations, schools and a council formed in the monastery.[81] Later newspaper reports suggested that the main aim of the patriarchate would be to promote school education in the eastern provinces.[82] Using the Surp Garabed monastery as a model, the patriarchate encouraged other monasteries in the eastern provinces to follow its example and open schools. *Hayasdan* celebrated the fact that Fizika Boghos's activities had encouraged Armenians in Muş to donate to the monastery school.[83] *Masis* also reported in 1853 that graduates from the monastery school in Muş would be appointed as teachers at the school in the Surp Hohannu monastery and in another school in Muş.[84]

Armenian elites in Istanbul again requested state recognition for this project. They submitted the regulations they had drafted for the administration of the Muş monastery, in which they expressed their expectation that the protection of the state would be continuous, adding that the favours that the sultan granted to Armenians by removing the 'Kurdish bandits' would be remembered every year on market days. The government permitted the implementation of the regulations, seeing them as regarding merely the 'internal administration of the churches'.[85] Fizika Boghos's project was among the initial steps in the gradual growth of concern for the eastern provinces among Istanbul Armenians.

Conclusion

In the late eighteenth century, Ottoman Armenians began establishing schools, first in Istanbul and later in the provinces. This development expanded the supervisory role of the Istanbul Patriarchate for the administration of communal institutions and led to greater attention directed by lay members of the community to its administration. Meanwhile, the European Great Powers expressed increased concern for the religious affairs of Ottoman Christians in the 1830s and 1840s. This led Ottoman state officials to seek new ways to put the affairs of Christian communities under stricter control. One method was to rely on Christian lay notables to a greater degree. These factors encouraged the creation of an institutional basis for the participation of laymen in the administration of the Armenian community, which in turn led actors to discuss the division between religious and non-religious affairs within the community, specifically using the terms 'religious' and 'secular'/'political'.

The attitude that Istanbul Armenians took towards the Ottoman state is also noteworthy. They did not restrict imperial authorities from involvement in their communal affairs; rather, they frequently communicated with them about their administrative reforms. Istanbul Armenians petitioned the government for recognition of the establishment of their financial committees, ecclesiastical and lay councils and regulations for a local monastery. Patriarch Madteos even requested visits by state officials to an examination conducted in a communal school. The strategy of Istanbul Armenians was to build an amicable relationship with the state. During their reforms, they sought state support, indicating their belief that obtaining it would improve their position with respect to other local and communal actors and facilitate the achievement of their goals.

Notes

1. Artinian, *Armenian Constitutional System*, 53–8, 72–4.
2. Christine Philliou, 'Communities on the Verge: Unraveling the Phanariot Ascendancy in Ottoman Governance', *Comparative Studies in Society and History* 51, no. 1 (2009): 151–81; Barsoumian, 'Armenian *Amira* Class'; Araks Şahiner, 'The Sarrafs of İstanbul: Financiers of the Empire' (Master's thesis, Boğaziçi University, 1995).
3. Artinian, *Armenian Constitutional System*, chap. 4.
4. In the study of education among Ottoman Armenians, the period before the mid-nineteenth century has largely been neglected due to the limited amount of information available. On their education after the mid-nineteenth century, see Young, 'Knowledge, Nation'; G. A. Nazikyan, *Arevmtahay Mankavarzhakan Mitk'n u Dprots'ě: 19-rd Dari Skzbits' Minch'ev 19-rd Dari 50–60akan T'vakannerě* (Erevan: Luys Hratarakch'ut'yun, 1969); Selçuk Akşin Somel, 'Osmanlı Ermenilerinde Kültür Modernleşmesi, Cemaat Okulları ve Abdülhamid Rejimi', *Tarih ve Toplum Yeni Yaklaşımlar* 5 (2007): 71–92.
5. For the *muhtar* system among non-Muslims in Istanbul, see Ueno, 'Laicized Urban Administration'.
6. Paul W. Werth aptly argues that the Russian government faced a dilemma in its relation with the catholicosate. While the government needed to 'uphold and enhance the prestige of the Catholicos' to bring foreign Armenians to their side, this made it rather difficult to subordinate the catholicos to the decisions of the government. See 'Imperial Russia and the Armenian Catholicos at Home and Abroad', in *Reconstruction and Interaction of Slavic Eurasia and Its Neighboring Worlds*, ed. Osamu Ieda and Tomohiko Uyama (Sapporo: Slavic Research Center, Hokkaido University, 2006), 203–35; Eileen M. Kane, 'Pilgrims, Holy Places, and the Multi-Confessional Empire: Russian Policy toward the Ottoman Empire under Tsar Nicholas I, 1825–1855' (PhD diss., Princeton University, 2005), chap. 5.
7. BOA, İ.HR 604 (1 September 1841).
8. Kemal Beydilli, *Recognition of the Armenian Catholic Community and the Church in the Reign of Mahmud II. (1830)* (Cambridge, MA: The Department of Near Eastern Languages and Civilizations, Harvard University, 1995), 21–6.
9. Uygur Kocabaşoğlu, *Anadolu'daki Amerika: Kendi Belgeleriyle 19. Yüzyılda Osmanlı İmparatorluğu'ndaki Amerikan Misyoner Okulları* (Istanbul: Arba Yayınları, 1989; repr. Istanbul: İmge Kitabevi, 2000), 23–50.

10. Ueno, 'Laicized Urban Administration'.
11. Beydilli, *Armenian Catholic Community*, 32–3, 222–31, 257–61.
12. *Takvim-i Vekayi'*, no. 82 (6 May 1834); Beydilli, *Armenian Catholic Community*, 273–4. In January 1835, the government clarified that the Istanbul patriarchs of the Orthodox Christians, Armenians and Catholics had the same standing by granting decorations to all of them at once and reporting it in the official gazette. *Takvim-i Vekayi'*, no. 94 (15 January 1835).
13. *Takvim-i Vekayi'*, no. 96 (22 February 1835). Karmi, *Jewish Community of Istanbul*, 34–8; Avigdor Levy, 'Millet Politics: The Appointment of a Chief Rabbi in 1835', in *The Jews of the Ottoman Empire*, 425–6.
14. Barsoumian, 'Armenian *Amira* Class', chap. 4.
15. Ibid., 143–4.
16. This can be confirmed by the comprehensive list of events related to Ottoman Armenians in Pars Tuğlacı, *Tarih Boyunca Batı Ermenileri*, vol. 1 (Istanbul: Pars Yayın, 2004), 496–677.
17. Barsoumian, 'Armenian *Amira* Class', 144–5.
18. Gerasimos Augustinos, *The Greeks of Asia Minor: Confession, Community, and Ethnicity in the Nineteenth Century* (Kent, OH: The Kent State University Press, 1992), chap. 6; Somel, *Modernization of Public Education*, 25–7.
19. Nazikyan, *Arevmtahay Mankavarzhakan Mitk'n*, 25–6; Barsoumian, 'Armenian *Amira* Class', 143.
20. Matenadaran, KD, 48/254 (22 July 1824).
21. *Vartabed*s are educated celibate monks in the Armenian Church. Although *vartabed*s are ranked beneath bishops, many of them were in charge of episcopal dioceses in the nineteenth-century Ottoman Empire. This suggests that the Armenian Church in the Ottoman Empire suffered a shortage of bishops, probably because the church tradition required Armenian clergymen under the jurisdiction of the Istanbul Patriarchate to visit the Catholicosate of Echmiadzin to be ordained.
22. *Sahman Azkayin Zhoghovoyn* (Istanbul: n.p., 1826); *Sahman Azkayin Zhoghovoy* (Istanbul: n.p., 1830).
23. Arshag A. Albōyajean, *Badmut'iwn Hay Gesarioy: Deghakragan, Badmagan, ew Azkakragan Usumnasirut'iwn* (Cairo: Hradaragut'iwn Gesarioy ew Shrchagayits' Hayrenagts'agan Miut'ean Kahirēi Varch'ut'ean, 1937), vol. 1, 1096; Hovhannēs Dēr Bedrosean, *Grt'agan Sharzhumĕ T'rk'ahayots' Mēch 1600–1900* (Cairo: Hay Azkayin Himnatram, 1983), 172; *Hayasdan*, no. 100 (3 June 1848); 2nd. series, no. 15 (27 May 1850).
24. *Hayasdan*, nos. 27 (9 January 1847), 36 (13 March 1847), 41 (17 April 1847), 43 (1 May 1847), 46 (22 May 1847), 48 (5 June 1847), 53 (10 July 1847), 61 (3 September 1847).
25. *Hayasdan*, no. 48.
26. *Hayasdan*, no. 46.
27. *Hayasdan*, no. 53.
28. *Hayasdan*, no. 31 (6 February 1847).

29. Piwzant K'ēch'ean, *Badmut'iwn S. P'rgch'i Hiwantanots'in Hayots' i G. Bolis* (Istanbul: Db. K. Baghdadlean, 1887, 2–19; *Azkayin Sahmanatrut'iwn Hayots'* (Istanbul: Dbaran H. Miwhēndisean, 1863), art. 51. The hospital also functioned as a place of incarceration. Suciyan, *Outcasting Armenians*, 136–7.
30. K'ēch'ean, *Badmut'iwn S. P'rgch'i Hiwantanots'in*, 73–4.
31. Starting in the 1840s, Protestant missionaries began to actively utilise printed materials in Armenian and Armeno-Turkish, including a newspaper launched in 1839 in İzmir. See H. G. O. Dwight, *Christianity in Turkey: A Narrative of the Protestant Reformation in the Armenian Church* (London: James Nisbet, 1854), 356–60.
32. BOA, İ.MSM 936 (26 April 1846).
33. BOA, HR.MKT 17/26 (31 January 1847).
34. *Hayasdan*, no. 31 (6 February 1847).
35. Masayuki Ueno, 'Arumeniajin Osuman Kanryo no Kyoikuteki Haikei', in *Kindai Isuramu no Kyoiku Shakaishi: Osuman Teikoku karano Tembo*, ed. Jun Akiba and Nobuya Hashimoto (Kyoto: Syowado, 2014), 138–64.
36. Ali Akyıldız, *Tanzimat Dönemi Osmanlı Merkez Teşkilâtında Reform (1836–1856)* (Istanbul: Eren, 1993), 85.
37. Fairey, *The Great Powers*, 93, 101, 102.
38. BOA, İ.HR 633 [1841].
39. Ibid.
40. BOA, İ.HR 684 [1841].
41. BOA, İ.HR 633 (7 September 1841).
42. BOA, İ.HR 604 (1 September 1841); İ.HR 684.
43. BOA, İ.HR 633.
44. BOA, İ.HR 712 (14 December 1841).
45. George A. Bournoutian ed., *Russia and the Armenians of Transcaucasia, 1797–1889: A Documentary Record* (Costa Mesa: Mazda Publishers, 1998), 344: Baron Rosen to Counselor Butaev (10 July 1834).
46. BOA, İ.MSM 935 (23 December 1842).
47. Maghak'ia Ōrmanean, *Azkabadum: Hay Ughghap'aṛ Egeghets'ioy Ants'k'erē Sgizpēn Minch'ew Mer Ōrerē Haragits' Azkayin Barakanerov Badmuadz* (Istanbul: Hradaragut'iwn V. ew H. Nersesean, 1927; repr. Beirut: Db. Sewan, 1961), vol. 3, 3797–8.
48. Ibid., vol. 3, 3799; *Arshaloys Araradean*, no. 209 (5 October 1844).
49. Bournoutian, *Russia and the Armenians*, 390: Envoy Titov to Count Vorontsov-Dashkov (29 September 1844).
50. Ōrmanean, *Azkabadum*, vol. 3, 3800; BOA, İ.MSM 733 (2 June 1846).
51. Dwight, *Christianity in Turkey*, 215–38, 326–32.
52. BOA, A.DVNSMHM.d 258, p. 5, no. 8 (16–25 Nov. 1850); Mustafa Numan Malkoç, *İstanbul'daki Protestan Kiliseler* (Istanbul: Kaya Basım Yayın, 1999), 23.
53. BOA, İ.MSM 936 (26 April 1846).

54. BOA, HR.İD 1600/18 (5 May 1846).
55. Ibid. The strikethrough is present in the original.
56. Bayraktar Tellan, 'Patriarch and the Sultan', 28.
57. In the early modern period, Islam and other religions were distinguished by adding 'true' (*hak*) or 'false' (*batıl*) to *din* respectively. In the nineteenth century, however, the usage of *din* for religions other than Islam seems to have decreased, and the usage of *mezhep* became conspicuous. *Mezhep* was sometimes used to mean 'sect' or 'denomination', but at other times it was used to mean 'religion', especially religions other than Islam. For example, in a series of documents on the treatment of an Armenian who accepted Islam and then reconverted to Christianity, the drafter first used *din* and replaced it with *mezhep*. BOA, A.MKT.MHM 649/10 (21 June 1896; 4 May 1896). In 1869, Garabed Panosian used *mezhep* in his Armeno-Turkish newspaper to mean 'religion' in general and *dinsizlik* (that is, the absence of *din*) to mean irreligiousness in a single paragraph. See *Manzumēi Ēfk'ear*, no. 847 (16 January 1869). A Christian also used *mezhep* to mean 'religion' when describing Islam in a document in Ottoman Turkish. See BOA. DH.İD 116/44 (15 August 1912).

    According to a note attached to the French and Greek translations of the Reform Edict of 1856, *mezhep* was the word preferred for religions other than Islam (for which *din* was used). See Aristarchi, *Législation ottomane: Recueil des lois, règlements, ordonnances, traités, capitulations, et autres documents officiels de l'empire ottoman* (Istanbul: Bureau du journal Thraky, 1874), vol. 2, 18; Johann Strauss, 'Ottomanisme et "ottomanité": Le témoignage linguistique', in *Aspects of the Political Language in Turkey (19th–20th Centuries)*, ed. Hans-Lukas Kieser (Istanbul: Isis Press, 2002), 28. According to Johann Strauss, this claim was based on the writings of Alphonse Belin, a French diplomat and Orientalist. See 'A Constitution for a Multilingual Empire: Translations of *Kanun-i Esasi* and Other Official Texts into Minority Languages', in *The First Ottoman Experiment in Democracy*, ed. Christoph Herzog and Malek Sharif (Würzburg: Ergon in Kommission, 2010), 30.
58. H. G. Awetik'ean et al., *Nor Bargirk' Haykazean Lezui* (Venice: Tparan Srboyn Ghazaru, 1836; repr. Erevani Hamalsarani Hratarakch'ut'yun, 1979), vol. 1, 1138. Although this dictionary explains the meaning of Armenian words in Armenian, the Turkish equivalents are frequently inserted using Armenian script.
59. BOA, İ.MSM 922 (13 June 1847).
60. Awetis Pērpērean, *Patmut'iwn Hayots': Skseal i 1772 Amē P'rkch'in Minch'ew Hamn 1860* (Istanbul: Tpagrut'iwn Pōghosi K'irishchean, 1871), 318; Ōrmanean, *Azkabadum*, vol. 3, 3811–12. 'Political' here had a different meaning from the idea of politics in Madteos's petition for the permission to publish *Hayasdan*, in which politics fell outside of his jurisdiction.
61. On the life and career of Hagop Grjigian, see Masayuki Ueno, 'Empire as a Career: Hagop Grjigian or an Armenian in the Ottoman Bureaucracy', *The Memoirs of the Toyo Bunko* 76 (2018): 57–80.

62. BOA, İ.MSM 937 (25 April 1847); Ōrmanean, *Azkabadum*, vol. 3, 3812.
63. BOA, İ.MSM 941 (28 September 1848).
64. *Masis*, no. 713 (11 November 1865).
65. Fairey, *The Great Powers*, 82–6.
66. Jamgocyan, 'Finances de l'Empire ottoman', 507–15; Kevork Pamukciyan, *Biyografileriyle Ermeniler* (Istanbul: Aras Yayıncılık, 2003), 225–6.
67. For the life and career of Vogorides, see Christine M. Philliou, *Biography of an Empire: Governing Ottomans in an Age of Revolution* (Berkeley: University of California Press, 2011).
68. *Hayasdan*, no. 56 (31 July 1847); BOA, A.DVNS. GMC. d 9, p. 52; A.DVN. MHM 4/48 (5–14 July 1847).
69. *Masis*, nos. 180 (19 July 1855), 713; BOA, İ.HR 7150 (28 November 1856); Albōyajean, 'Azkayin Sahmanatrut'iwnĕ', 316–19.
70. BOA, İ.MSM 937 (25 April 1847).
71. Fairey, *The Great Powers*, chap. 4.
72. BOA, İ.MSM 937 [1847].
73. BOA, İ.HR 2613 (30 June 1849); 2689 (1 September 1849); 3918 (30 August 1851); 4043 (23 December 1851); 4796 (12 May 1853).
74. *Hayasdan*, no. 159 (21 July 1849).
75. *Hayasdan*, 2nd series, no. 90 (22 November 1851); *Masis*, nos. 69 (1 June 1853), 180.
76. *Arshaloys Araradean*, no. 27 (9 April 1841).
77. *Hayasdan*, no. 85 (19 February 1848).
78. *Masis*, no. 60 (30 March 1853).
79. Cora, 'Transforming Erzurum/Karin', 345.
80. Musa Çadırcı, *Tanzimat Döneminde Anadolu Kentleri'nin Sosyal ve Ekonomik Yapısı* (Ankara: Türk Tarih Kurumu Basımevi, 1997), 192–6; Martin van Bruinessen, *Agha, Shaikh and State: The Social and Political Structures of Kurdistan* (London: Zed Books, 1992), 175–95; Sarkis Atamian, *The Armenian Community: The Historical Development of a Social and Ideological Conflict* (New York: Philosophical Library, 1955), 47–59; Louise Nalbandian, *The Armenian Revolutionary Movement: The Development of Armenian Political Parties through the Nineteenth Century* (Berkeley: University of California Press, 1963), 78–9; Özok-Gündoğan, *The Kurdish Nobility*, chap. 5.
81. *Hayasdan*, 2nd series, no. 76 (11 August 1851).
82. *Hayasdan*, no. 153 (9 June 1849).
83. *Hayasdan*, 2nd series, no. 48 (8 January 1851).
84. *Masis*, no. 50 (19 January 1853).
85. BOA, İ.HR 2784.

3

The Promises of the Tanzimat Reforms

In the early 1850s, the Ottoman Empire faced the unwanted diplomatic intervention of the Russian Empire, leading to the Crimean War: a war over the very survival of the Ottomans. In the same years, the Ottoman Empire issued two edicts that had significant implications for the standing of non-Muslims in its legal regime: the Privileges Edict of 1853 and the Reform Edict of 1856. The former was issued on the eve of the conflict, amid diplomatic negotiations with Russia, and guaranteed the religious privileges of non-Muslim groups. The latter, issued near the end of the war, expressed to Britain and France the will to reform the empire and a promise to correct the inequality between Muslims and non-Muslims. This chapter deals with these edicts and the responses they elicited from non-Muslims, especially Armenians.

As discussed at the beginning of this book, while scholars have largely ignored the Privileges Edict, they have paid due attention to the promise of equality in the Reform Edict as a milestone in the empire's long history and as the starting point for Ottomanism, the project of integrating diverse subjects, regardless of their religion, as citizens. In their discussions, the Reform Edict was the product of top-down reforms that reflected the political intentions of Muslim statesmen but had little impact on non-Muslims.[1] In contrast, this chapter focuses on Armenians' responses to the two edicts and discusses the resulting shift in the empire's institutional dealings with non-Muslims. By doing so, it demonstrates the importance of this shift in light of recent studies on the treatment of non-Muslim religious authorities since the early modern period.

Whatever the intentions of the Muslim officials were, the institutional change in the 1850s stimulated the activism of Armenian lay elites. They did not sit back and wait to be granted their rights; rather, they sought to win them for themselves. The guaranteeing of religious privileges in 1853 and its repetition in the Reform Edict facilitated the development of a way of thinking that there was a sphere of religion distinct from the sphere over which the state had jurisdiction and that it should be left in the hands of non-Muslim communal leaders. Seeing an opportunity in these edicts, the Istanbul Armenian lay elites led comprehensive administrative reforms in the framing of a 'National Constitution' and sought to expand the scope of activities in which they could make decisions at their own discretion.

The Privileges Edict of 1853

In 1852, a dispute erupted between Russia and France over the Christian holy places in Palestine, especially the Church of the Holy Sepulchre in Jerusalem, which was then under Ottoman rule. The former based their claim on an expansive interpretation of the 1774 Treaty of Küçük Kaynarca, while the latter relied on the capitulations of 1740.[2] During this dispute, the Russians demanded that the Ottoman government conclude an agreement with them guaranteeing the privileges of their Orthodox Christian subjects. Ottoman statesmen refused, claiming that the Ottoman Empire had already guaranteed religious privileges to its non-Muslim subjects of its own accord. Instead of concluding the agreement, they decided to issue an edict of their own making that would publicly guarantee religious privileges for non-Muslims.

Ottoman officials made three strategic choices when drafting and issuing this edict. First, they refused to come to any terms with Russia regarding their own subjects to prevent any further expansion of Russian influence over Ottoman Orthodox Christians or set a precedent for future foreign intervention.[3] Second, while Russia limited its demands for privileges for Orthodox Christians due to its concern for the Orthodox Church's superiority in the Holy Land, Ottoman state officials avoided prioritising Orthodox Christians, instead delivering these edicts to five non-Muslim religious communities – Orthodox Christians, Armenians, Catholics, Jews and Protestants – thus limiting the number of officially recognised groups and placing these five on an equal footing.[4] Third, while Russian demands merely referred to privileges in general, Ottoman officials added the adjectives 'religious' (*mezhebiye*) and 'ecclesiastical' (*ruhaniye*) during their negotiations with the Russian envoy.[5] While the application of the term 'privileges' to the rights and exemptions accorded to non-Muslim religious authorities in the Ottoman mainland was a relatively new phenomenon, the promulgation of the 1853 Privileges Edict brought it to much wider currency.[6] The novelty here was the combination of the idea of privileges with the adjective 'religious'.[7] This combination is frequently found in Ottoman documents written after May 1853, when officials decided of their own accord to promulgate an edict guaranteeing privileges to non-Muslims.[8] A letter sent on 10 May by Ottoman Foreign Minister Sadık Rifat Pasha to Alexander Sergeyevich Menshikov, the Russian envoy dispatched to Istanbul, is a typical example.[9]

The emphatic repetition of the phrase 'religious (or ecclesiastical) privileges' indicates that the addition of the term was highly intentional, likely meant to limit the scope of non-Muslims' future claims of privilege to religious issues alone. This idea is supported by the fact that when some members of the Ottoman cabinet proposed that the words 'school' and 'hospital' be inserted into the edict as items that would be within the scope of non-Muslim privileges, the cabinet decided to avoid public mention of these institutions. Nonetheless, the cabinet record also indicates that the members believed that the inclusion would have been appropriate.[10] This shows the difficulty faced by the government in defining the rights granted to non-Muslim communities due to the increase in the breadth of communal institutions. At the same time, statesmen decided not to remove non-Muslims' schools and hospitals from the jurisdiction of their religious authorities. In fact, they continued to leave the management of elementary education in the hands of non-Muslims.[11]

The contents of the edict can be confirmed from its drafts and copies in the Ottoman archives and from the Armenian translation published in *Masis*.[12] Interestingly, state officials repeatedly used the word 'caliphate' in its text. This was likely a strategic allusion to the religious influence of the Ottoman sovereign over Muslims outside the Ottoman domains, particularly those under Russian rule, in response to symmetrical claims made by Russia. This suggests that the guarantee of religious privileges for non-Muslims (which was meant to prevent foreign influence) and the Ottoman politicisation of Islam were parallel developments.

The 1853 edict thus focused on the religious aspect of the rights of non-Muslims, stating that it was the sultan's will for his subjects to continue enjoying complete protection and consummate ease in their religious practices and in spiritual questions. The edict also stated that the sultan desired that the churches, monasteries and ecclesiastical privileges he and his ancestors had maintained would always be protected from violation. The privileges included were not specified but were loosely described as 'such privileges and permissions that are inserted in and written on the charters of investiture'. Although early modern Ottoman policy towards non-Muslim clergymen and churches had been contingent,[13] the drafter of the edict claimed an unchanging continuity in Ottoman treatment of non-Muslims, professing that nothing new was being added and that religious privileges would continue to be protected in the same way as they always had. This emphasis on continuity can also be seen in state officials' use of the foundation myth, in which Mehmet II was called the first to grant religious privileges.[14]

Non-Muslim Responses

Although religious privileges were asserted to be timeless, non-Muslims nevertheless treated the issuance of the Privileges Edict as a highly remarkable event. According to *Masis*, Istanbul Armenians convened an assembly to read the edict and then decided that it would be recited in the churches of Istanbul and that copies should be sent to the provinces.[15] The Ottoman archives contain numerous letters of appreciation not only from religious authorities in Istanbul but also from local non-Muslim communities.[16] These letters also allowed non-Muslim Ottoman subjects to declare their allegiance to the Ottoman Empire on the eve of the Crimean War. One of the first such letters came from the Istanbul Armenians.[17] Highlighting the faithfulness of the Armenian patriarch, the government reproduced this letter of appreciation in the Ottoman Turkish newspaper *Ceride-i Havadis*.[18] The Armenians' swift response was convenient for the government, which intended to display to its potential allies – Britain and France – its harmonious relations with its non-Muslim subjects.[19] Similarly, when the Russian advance on the Danubian Principalities led to war, the Armenian patriarch and *logotet* Grjigian sent the government another letter, signed by forty-five clergy and fifty-one laymen, stating the willingness of Armenians to serve in the army. State officials decided to also publish this letter in their official gazette as well as in *Ceride-i Havadis* to 'evoke good feelings among Muslims about the aforementioned [Armenian] community' and considered it 'politically' beneficial to publish it in both French and Greek.[20] Julia Phillips Cohen argues that acting as 'model imperial citizens' was a strategy that Ottoman Jews adopted in the nineteenth century to navigate this period of drastic change.[21] Apparently, Armenian elites in Istanbul chose the same approach.

The reactions of some smaller non-Muslim groups were also noteworthy. Greek Catholics in Syria, Orthodox Christians in Serbia and Jews migrating from Kerch in the Crimea sought to have the 1853 edict addressed to them as well. This would support state recognition for their groups, which would in turn give them an advantage in their ongoing rivalries with larger non-Muslim groups. From the perspective of state officials, these three groups enjoyed religious privileges as members of larger non-Muslim groups – that is, Catholics, Orthodox Christians and Jews, respectively.

For example, the Greek Catholics, considered part of the Catholic community, were sent a copy of the edict that had been addressed to Nigoghos, the Catholic patriarch in Istanbul and an Armenian. Maksimos Mazlum, the Greek Catholic patriarch, in fact claimed the status of an independent patriarch and, as such, requested that the edict be addressed to him as well.[22]

This case demonstrates the discrepancy of interpretations between the officials of the central government and local actors. When the Ottoman government decided to distinguish Armenian Catholics from the wider Armenian community in 1830, the government put all Catholic subjects, including Greek Catholics, under the jurisdiction of the religious authority of the Armenian Catholics.[23] This decision did not satisfy the leading clergy of the Greek Catholics in Syria, who needed government backing to support competition with Orthodox Christians in their locality. In 1848, Mazlum lobbied for – and somehow obtained – a charter of investiture from the central government, and he was appointed patriarch of the Greek Catholics.[24] On this basis, he insisted that he and his community be treated as having equivalent status with Orthodox Christians, Armenians and other sects. State officials, however, seemed not to be fully aware of – or simply to have ignored – this fact. When other non-Muslim groups – and particularly Orthodox Christians – obtained the edict, Mazlum considered it necessary to petition the government because he saw it as an indication of the state's recognition of the status of other non-Muslim communities. On receiving his petition, state officials found a record of his appointment and decided to accept his demands.[25]

One noteworthy document suggests Mazlum's objections were neither frivolous nor unusual. In discussing the response to his petition, state officials compared the status of the Greek Catholic patriarch to that of the high clergy of the Orthodox Church (not including the Istanbul patriarch); these included the patriarchs of Jerusalem, Alexandria and Antioch and the archbishop of Cyprus. According to their understanding, the high clergymen of both churches had independent status, but the latter were part of the single Orthodox Christian community represented by the patriarch of Istanbul, while the former maintained no relationship with any other patriarch. This led them to conclude that granting separate edicts to the high clergy of the Orthodox Church was against the conditions of the privileges granted to the Orthodox patriarch of Istanbul, whereas granting an edict to the Greek Catholic patriarch was admissible.[26] In other words, state officials believed that edicts should be granted only to the singular head of each religious community.

The state's response to the Orthodox Christians in Serbia shows more clearly that granting the 1853 edict meant a general state recognition of non-Muslim groups in the multiconfessional Ottoman Empire. The Serbian representative in Istanbul told the French ambassador that the group intended to form a national general council (*milletçe bir meclis-i umumi*) to obtain religious privileges. He claimed that they could not otherwise enjoy the privileges granted to the Orthodox Christian community. After hearing this information from the ambassador, the Ottoman government launched an investigation and found that the claim was not entirely unfounded, although the Serbians had not yet reached their own decision. Ottoman state officials discussed the issue and decided to suppress the movement, as they thought that the separation of Serbians from the Orthodox Christian community, while potentially justifiable, might also cause trouble by inflaming the 'Slavic cause'. The justification they offered was that religious privileges 'were not something relating to nationality' (*kavmiyet ve milliyete ait şey olmayarak*) but rather to religion; therefore, Serbians enjoyed those privileges as part of the wider Orthodox Christian community.[27] Ottoman non-Muslims were thus expected to claim their collective rights solely as religious groups.

Jews migrating from Kerch petitioned the Ottoman government and asked to be accepted as Ottoman subjects in 1856. They further requested that the government grant them the same privileges as other Ottoman non-Muslim communities because they were Karaite Jews and therefore religiously distinct from the Jewish community represented by Istanbul's Chief Rabbinate. The Ottoman government accepted their claim and decided to grant Kerch Jews an edict that placed them under the authority of their own rabbi for religious affairs (*umur-ı mezhebiye*) and under that of the chief of public security in other matters.[28] The decision to appoint a separate rabbi for the Kerch Jews invited a complaint from the existing Chief Rabbinate of Istanbul, who contested the Karaite origins of the Jews from Kerch. He claimed that Kerch area held no Karaite Jews and asserted that Crimean Jews should be put under his jurisdiction; if they were not, the government was violating the conditions of the charter given to him. The government's response, if any, has not been found.[29]

The Reform Edict of 1856

In February 1856, the Ottoman Empire issued its Reform Edict to satisfy Britain and France, with whom the settlement of the Crimean War was being negotiated. The primary concern of the edict was the integration of non-Muslims into full Ottoman citizenship. To this end, the edict repeated its guarantees of religious privileges while also promising non-Muslims equality with Muslims as citizens of the Ottoman state.[30]

Although some researchers maintain that the Gülhane Rescript of 1839 had already declared the equality of Muslims and non-Muslims, there is no mention of this equality in the Rescript itself. Ottoman state officials were rather reluctant to change the deep-rooted traditions that had been upheld over a thousand years.[31] The idea of altering the political and legal structures of inequality for Muslims and non-Muslims in 1856 was therefore a radical venture. Unlike the Gülhane Rescript, the Reform Edict repeatedly employed the terms 'equality' (*müsavat*) and 'equal' (*müsavi*). Mustafa Reşit Pasha regarded this political choice – made by junior state officials who had advanced their careers under his patronage – to be too radical. Interestingly, when he criticised the promise of equality in his memorandum, he used the phrase 'political rights' (*hukuk-ı politikiye*) interchangeably with 'equality' and paired this idea with religious privileges.[32]

Nevertheless, the progress towards social equality in the Ottoman Empire had begun much earlier. Donald Quataert has highlighted the impact of Mahmut II's 1829 abolition of 'the old social markers based on wearing apparel'. The sultan, beginning with state officials, imposed 'visual uniformity among all male state servants and subjects', except for Muslim ulamas, Christian clergy and Jewish rabbis, replacing the tradition in which types and colours of headgear and clothing indicated differences in social class and religious affiliation.[33] The costumes of religious functionaries would symbolise the exceptional treatment given to religious affairs in the later history of the Ottoman Empire. A quarter of a century later, a ban on discriminatory language followed in the Reform Edict, and this further blurred social distinctions. Specifically, the Reform Edict forbade the use of discriminatory terms against any groups based on 'religion, language and ethnicity'.[34] This mainly referred to the traditional Ottoman terminology used to describe non-Muslims. The words for 'infidel' (*kafir*, *kefere* or *gavur*) were abandoned. The term *reaya*, which had formerly been used regardless of religion but in the eighteenth and early nineteenth centuries had come to specifically indicate non-Muslim subjects, was also completely abandoned.[35] Instead, the Reform Edict frequently used the relatively new term *tebaa*, whose use became prevalent in the 1830s, to refer to all subjects, regardless of religion.[36] Najwa Al-Qattan argues that this reform had a real impact. After the promulgation of the Reform Edict, the scribes in Damascus sharia courts abandoned the terminology formerly used to differentiate Muslims and non-Muslims. For example, *walad*, which was used for non-Muslims before 1856, was replaced by *ibn*, which had been used for Muslims. The scribes also abandoned the intentional alteration of non-Muslims' names for which Muslims' analogues also existed, such as Yusuf, Musa and Sulayman. Although they continued to employ different terms to refer to deceased Muslims and non-Muslims, the discriminatory term *al-halik*, which was used only for deceased non-Muslims, was replaced by the neutral term *al-mutawaffa*.[37]

Progress towards equality of duty had begun in 1855. Ottoman state officials chose to institutionally equalise the tax burden by abolishing the poll tax, which had been imposed only on non-Muslims.[38] At the same time, the government declared that non-Muslim males would be subject to military conscription like Muslim males.[39] The phrase invoked by state officials to justify this novelty was the defence of 'the general fatherland'. According to Tobias Heinzelmann, the concept of service to 'the state and the fatherland' (*devlet ü vatan*) replaced the ideology formerly used to justify conscription, that is, the concept of service to 'the religion and the state' (*din ü devlet*). The latter had been suitable only as long as the Ottoman conscription was limited to Muslims because in this phrase 'religion' referred to Islam alone.[40] However, despite the adoption of universal conscription in principle, in practice state officials chose to impose a new tax on non-Muslims in lieu of military service. This was done mainly out of consideration for the negative responses that they feared this new policy might invite from Muslims and non-Muslims, as well as making up for the financial loss caused by the abolition of the poll tax. This decision was repeated in the Reform Edict.

While equality of duty remained theoretical in the Reform Edict, the equality of opportunity was substantial. The edict declared that non-Muslims would be admitted to the Supreme Council, the consultative body of the central government. It further stated that the government would accept non-Muslims into state bureaucracy, which had, until that time, only accepted a few non-Muslims who were in possession of special skills. Moreover, the edict announced that all Ottoman subjects would be accepted into the state's military and civil schools, whose main aims were to train future members of the state apparatus.[41] Mehmet Emin Ali Pasha, the leading figure in the preparation of the Reform Edict and the most prominent statesman of the 1860s, wrote in 1868 that, as educated non-Muslims were inclined to seek upward mobility, the Ottoman government needed to accept them into the state bureaucracy, or they would become dissatisfied with their unequal treatment and choose other countries to serve. He further claimed that it was necessary for the Ottoman government to employ learned and able non-Muslims to deal with European countries.[42]

These changes presented more new opportunities for Ottoman Armenians, especially among the elites in Istanbul, as they had fallen behind the Orthodox Christians in finance and commerce and thus needed an alternate path for upward mobility. Of the non-Muslims in the Ottoman Empire, the Armenians were the most eager to enter state bureaucracy.[43] As is discussed below, the large numbers of Armenian state officials that emerged after the decline of the Armenian *amira sarraf*s in the 1840s and 1850s became leading figures in the communal politics of the 1860s and 1870s.

The Reform Edict also triggered institutional changes in the government's relationship with non-Muslim religious authorities. As in the Russian and French cases, the institutionalisation of the rights of non-dominant religious groups led to bureaucratic changes in the Ottoman government.[44] Around 1861, the Bureau of Religious Affairs (*mezahib odası/ mezahib müdürlüğü*) was created within the Ministry of Foreign Affairs to deal with the religious affairs of non-Muslims.[45] The main task of this small bureau was correspondence with non-Muslim religious authorities, and its chief was engaged in settling outstanding issues related to the non-Muslim population, such as disagreements between Orthodox Christians and Catholics in Jerusalem or a diplomatic problem involving properties situated in Walachia and Moldavia that had been donated to Orthodox Christian monasteries in Jerusalem and Mount Athos.[46] These chiefs were chosen from among Muslim state officials.[47] In 1877, the government decided to attach the Bureau to the Ministry of Justice to avoid giving the impression that the government 'regarded non-Muslim Ottoman subjects as foreigners' (*tebaa-i Gayrimüslime-i Osmaniyeyi ecnebi addetmek*).[48]

As discussed in Chapter 1, the tax farming system defined early modern relationships between the Ottoman government and Christian religious authorities. Until the Reform Edict, the tributes expected from Christian communities were indicated in the preambles of the charters of investiture given to their religious authorities.[49] After the Reform Edict abolished tax farming, tributes were no longer mentioned.[50] A document dated from 1859 states that, although the method of abolishment had not yet been determined, the government had already decided to stop collecting tributes from non-Muslim religious authorities and had not collected them since the Hijri year of 1272 (1855/6).[51]

After tax farming no longer defined relations between the Ottoman state and non-Muslim religious authorities, religious privileges filled this role. Non-Muslim religious authorities – who had institutionally been treated as tax farmers in the Ottoman administrative system for several centuries – became the holders of these privileges. In the later years of the empire, privilege (*imtiyaz*) became the blanket term used to express the rights and exemptions that pertained to non-Muslims. For example, the tax exemption for non-Muslim clergymen was termed a privilege, as was the Jewish right to impose a tax on kosher meat.[52] This term was further employed in the discussion of the independence of Bulgarians from the Greek-dominated Orthodox Christian Patriarchate.[53] The Armenian patriarch also claimed that the Syriac Christians' attempt to merge with the Church of England was a violation of his rights and privileges.[54]

The Reform Edict invited non-Muslims to examine their vested privileges and exemptions and propose any reforms to the government that had become necessary over the passage of time.[55] The first non-Muslim group to respond to this request was the Armenians. Leading figures from their community began to prepare regulations on community administration before the promulgation of the Reform Edict, probably after obtaining information on the negotiations between the Ottoman Empire and the European Great Powers. In 1855, they held an assembly and created a 'Constitutional Committee' composed of seven clergymen and ten laymen.[56] This committee completed a draft of the regulations, which was presented to and accepted by the Armenian Assembly in March 1857.[57] The document included 100 articles, sorted into twelve chapters, and it dealt with the organisation of community administrations: the patriarchate, the standing General Assembly, the lay and ecclesiastical councils and several committees. The Armenian Patriarchate presented this document to the government in June as the result of the Armenians' consideration of their vested privileges and exemptions.[58]

State officials refused to approve their regulations on the grounds that the community administration of the Orthodox Christians needed to be reformed first. In addition, they claimed that some aspects of the Armenians' proposals were not acceptable, without specifying which ones.[59] Although the Reform Edict only required non-Muslims to propose necessary reforms, the Armenians' initiative appears to have set a precedent; in October, state officials instructed Orthodox Christians to prepare a document for their own community administration. State officials also issued guidelines for the planning of communal reforms, which pertained mainly to Orthodox Christians but also held for non-Muslims in general. These guidelines stipulated that non-Muslim communities were to convene an assembly to discuss communal reforms, including the method of electing patriarchs and metropolitans, ecclesiastical and lay councils, salaries for clergymen and communal taxes.[60]

Interestingly, the guidelines also indicated a distinction between three spheres: the affairs of general administration (*idare-i umumiye*), which fell under the jurisdiction of the state; ecclesiastical affairs (*umur-ı ruhaniye*), which related to the religious authorities of each community; and secular affairs of the community (*milletin umur-ı mahsusa-i cismaniyesi*), for which the guidelines recommended the creation of a council composed of both laymen and clergymen. The guidelines further mentioned that the newly created council could not have authority that overlapped with that of the other two spheres, and a special reference was made to the ecclesiastical sphere, stating that 'purely ecclesiastical affairs' – including the church, religion and laws and affairs related to community rituals – would not be interfered with.[61]

Here, state officials had two divisions in mind: one related to the lay and ecclesiastical spheres within each non-Muslim community and the other related to the relationship between the spheres of the state and those of each non-Muslim community. As discussed in Chapter 2, the former division was at issue in conversations between Ottoman state officials and foreign diplomats regarding reforms of community administration in the 1840s. In the 1850s, as state officials admitted the entry of non-Muslims into the state apparatus as individuals to achieve the political integration of multireligious subjects, they became more cautious and pessimistic about the possible overstepping of non-Muslim communities as groups into the jurisdiction of the state.

Armenians in the State Services

The Reform Edict and the state's subsequent instructions urged the leading figures of non-Muslim communities to gather around their religious authorities in Istanbul and examine their vested privileges and exemptions to propose any necessary reforms to the government, which led to the formulation of regulations for their community administration. The Armenians revised their first draft and began to administer their community affairs according to the regulations without state approval in 1860. After the Ottoman government approved the regulations proposed by the Orthodox Christians in 1860–2 and the Armenians made some required revisions under the supervision of state officials, the government approved their regulations in 1863.[62] After the Jewish community's regulations were approved in 1865, the regulations of these three non-Muslim communities were inserted into the empire's code of laws (*Düstur*).[63]

As Vartan Artinian has noted, the four principal architects of the Armenians' regulations – Serovpe Vichenian, Nigoghayos Balian, Nahabed Rusinian and Krikor Odian – were all lay intellectuals who had studied in Paris.[64] More importantly, along with other leading figures in the Armenian community in this and later periods, many chose careers in Ottoman bureaucracy or other state services. They represented a new type of Armenian communal elite, taking the place of the *amira* class, which had been mainly composed of *sarraf*s and had almost disappeared by the mid-nineteenth century.

The four intellectuals mentioned above were also inaugural members of the Armenian community's education committee when it was established in 1853 under the initiative of Hagop Grjigian. Artinian argues that Grjigian requested that the members of the education committee draft the regulations for community administration.[65] Vichenian, who was chosen as chairman, studied medicine in Paris during Grjigian's service at the Ottoman embassy there, and he was also highly regarded by Ambassador Reşit Pasha.[66] This suggests that in Paris, Vichenian had built connections not only with this promising Ottoman official but also with the future leading figure in the Armenian community. This connection perhaps led to his gaining the position as chairman. After his return to Istanbul, he was appointed first as a doctor at the hospital of the War Ministry and later as a professor at the military medical academy. In the early 1850s, he accompanied Mehmet Fuat Pasha's special mission to Cairo to negotiate with the autonomous governor of Egypt.[67] During these years, Vichenian likely cultivated close relations with Fuat Pasha. This promising Muslim statesman advanced in his career under the patronage of Reşit Pasha and would become one of the most prominent statesmen in the 1850s and the 1860s, along with Ali Pasha. Upon Vichenian's recommendation, Rusinian also became Fuat Pasha's family physician.[68] Vichenian went on to become an influential figure in Armenian communal politics in the 1860s.

Thus, in their relationship, Fuat Pasha and Vichenian followed the example of Reşit Pasha and Grjigian. Fuat Pasha inherited the method of using lay non-Muslim elites as informal intermediaries, while Vichenian inherited the method of gaining influence in the Armenian community through connections with high-ranking Muslim officials. This was not a coincidence. As discussed in Chapter 2, Muslim officials wanted prominent Christian laymen they could trust as the leaders of their communities, in the hopes that they would play an intermediary role. From the viewpoint of Muslim officials, the availability of an informal means of dealing with non-Muslims' problems must have been valuable in this period, as the Ottoman treatment of non-Muslims could invite the interference of European Great Powers and provoke international crises, and guarantees of non-Muslims' religious privileges were making it difficult to formally intervene in their communal affairs. After Fuat Pasha and Vichenian came Midhat Pasha and Krikor Odian, another remarkable pair of leaders in the 1860s and 1870s. Odian entered state service in the late 1850s and was eventually promoted to undersecretary of the Ministry of Commerce in 1871 and then of the Ministry of Public Works in 1875.[69] The *amira sarrafs* of the early nineteenth century had been similarly close to government and palace circles; likewise, they had also played an informal intermediary role between Muslim statesmen and the Armenian community. Thus, there was a continuity between the old and new elites of the Armenian community. All that changed was the fact that an institutional basis had now been established for their position.

The principal architects of the Armenian regulations embedded clauses in the document that made it easier for them to obtain influence in the community. Seven of the Istanbul-based members of the General Assembly – which became the main organ of the Armenians' community administration after the regulations were in place – were required to have a rank in the Ottoman Empire.[70] The regulations therefore encouraged voters to choose the members of the assembly from among those already in the state services. Meanwhile, suffrage was limited to Ottoman subjects over twenty-five years old who paid at least seventy-five *kuruş* in communal tax or who had personal merit. Those with personal merit were defined as those in the state services, doctors, authors of useful books, teachers and those making contributions to the Armenian community.[71] These conditions gave special positions to those in the state services. I have identified forty-nine of the eighty assembly members elected in 1863.[72] Of these, ten were Ottoman state officials, six were in state service due to their special skills and one provided bread for the imperial army. Among those with special skills were members of two renowned families: the Dadians, managers of the imperial gunpowder factory, and the Balians, imperial architects. The first assembly members elected Serovpe Vichenian as chairman and Krikor Odian as secretary-general.[73] As time went on, members of the assembly continued to prefer state officials as their chairs.[74] The 1863 regulations served as a tool to strengthen and justify the rule of the elite.

Among the high-ranking Muslim officials, ties with Armenian elites were also useful for revising the Armenians' regulations. In 1862, the patriarchate appointed a committee composed of four Armenian clergymen and eight laymen to examine the 1860 draft. Thereafter, the government required the Armenians to create a new committee under its superintendence. Each committee included several Armenians in the state services: Serovpe Vichenian, Hovhannes Dadian and Krikor Aghaton in the first and Krikor Odian and Sdepan Aslanian in the second.[75] As discussed below, the differences between the versions of the regulations indicate that Muslim officials' intervention led to some important changes.

The Armenian National Constitution

The regulations adopted by the Armenians were prepared in three languages: Armenian, Ottoman Turkish and Armeno-Turkish.[76] The Armenian elites in Istanbul attached great importance to this achievement, titling the Armenian version of their regulations the Armenian National Constitution. Their choice of the word 'constitution' (*sahmanatrut'iwn*), which was not used by the Orthodox Christians and was not reflected in the title of the state-approved Ottoman Turkish version (titled Regulations on the Armenian Patriarchate (*Ermeni Patrikliği Nizamatı*)), suggests the influence of European constitutionalism on the Armenian elites who had studied in Paris in the mid-nineteenth century.[77] From its inauguration in 1855, the committee that drafted the regulations was called the Constitutional Committee, and it pursued communal reforms that it likened to the constitutional movements in Europe.[78] Considering that the committee did not use the word 'constitution' in its first draft of 1857 but began to use it in the 1860 draft, we can assume that the change in wording was intentional.[79]

Previous researchers have discussed whether this nomenclature was appropriate.[80] To resolve this question, we should consider the impact that the choice had in the 1860s rather than seeing it from today's understanding of 'constitution'. An Armeno-Turkish pamphlet published by Garabed Panosian in September 1861 shows how radical and serious the choice was. According to the pamphlet, the word 'constitution' invited accusations from 'a group of seditious men' (*bir takım fesadaver ve fitnetengiz ademler*), who reported to the government that the Armenians had chosen the word constitution because 'their intention was to create a sovereign state' (*bunların fikri padişahlık çıkarmak dır*). In response to this 'lie', Panosian upheld the choice, insisting that the Armenians' creation of regulations for community administration and assembly were within the scope of the privileges that the government guaranteed.[81]

Panosian's pamphlet helps us develop an understanding of the idea behind this radical choice. He insisted that the regulations on community administration were necessary for the Armenians to be recognised as a *millet*, writing that a *millet* without regulations would be 'regarded as a barbaric group that was devoid of proprieties and discipline and abandoned in injustice of ignorance'. He continued that, although Armenians deserved to have the title of *millet* due to 'our religion and old honour', they had once been barbarians, due to their lack of regulations.[82] His argument was driven by the transformation of the word *millet*, which in the nineteenth century gradually came to bear the new sense of 'nation' in the modern understanding, in addition to its old sense of 'a group of people who share religious and/or ethnic identity'. Panosian understood that being recognised as a *millet* in the new sense was crucial. Importantly, this understanding coexisted with his clear denial of any intention by the Armenians to pursue independence.

According to previous research, the state ideology of the Tanzimat period, commonly known as Ottomanism, aimed at integrating all subjects into a single Ottoman nation regardless of religion or ethnicity. This concept was often accompanied by the assumption that non-Muslims had never accepted Ottomanism because it was not compatible with their national feeling.[83] In Panosian's view, however, being a nation in the modern sense did not require political independence and did not conflict with the empire's Ottomanism policy. Why, in this case, was being recognised as a modern nation important for a minor group intending to stay within a multireligious and multiethnic empire? By whom did Armenians need to be recognised as a modern nation? Answering these questions will help us understand the Armenians' idea of nation in the context of the Tanzimat Reforms.

For Armenian elites in Istanbul, the diplomatic discussions beginning with the disputes over the Holy Land must have led to their understanding of the strategic importance of international recognition for maintaining and improving their status in the Ottoman Empire. Thus, Armenians became increasingly convinced that they needed recognition as a nation in the eyes of the European Great Powers to improve their status in the Ottoman context. The more frequent use of the word *millet* in the nineteenth century should be understood from this perspective rather than that of the Ottoman *millet* system. To be recognised as a nation, Armenians needed a constitution, and they needed to administer their community affairs in accordance with it. This partly explains why Armenian elites in Istanbul became so eagerly involved in running the communal assembly, councils and committees in the following decades.

Elke Hartmann argues that Armenians' understanding of their 'constitution' in the 1860s produced a positive attitude among them towards the empire's constitutional regime when it was introduced in the following decade, earning them pride at being 'the first constitutional people [*sahmanatragan zhoghovurt*]' in the Ottoman Empire. Krikor Odian may have bridged the Armenians' experience with the creation of the Ottoman Constitution through his close relationship with Midhat Pasha.[84] Some Armenians radically referred to themselves as a 'constitutional nation' (*sahmanatragan azk*). For example, while *Masis* lamented the state of Ottoman Armenians in 1868, it emphasised that European newspapers had once praised them for becoming a 'constitutional nation', and their development of the Armenian National Constitution.[85] In 1875, a lay member of the Armenian Assembly referred to the Armenians as a 'constitutional nation' when discussing whether the patriarchate could impose non-spiritual punishments.[86] Armenians thus strategically adapted ideas of nationalism and constitutionalism to the multireligious and multiethnic conditions of the empire. The term *millet* in Turkish was suitable for their purposes because this word meant both 'nation' and 'community'. With this in mind, I will refer to the Armenians' regulations as their National Constitution but will continue to use 'community' when referring to them collectively because of their position within the empire.[87]

The divergence between the Ottoman Turkish version of the Armenian National Constitution and the other versions was not limited to the title. The Armenian and Armeno-Turkish versions contained six articles at the beginning called the Basic Principles that were omitted from the official Ottoman Turkish version.[88] The drafters apparently made a distinction between the Constitution's official appearance in Ottoman Turkish and the actual functions expected of it. The Basic Principles stipulated the interactions between the Armenian community and its individual members, regarding it as a mutual relationship of duties and rights. These principles placed responsibility for the protection of the faith and tradition of the Armenian Church, the education of children, the maintenance of communal institutions, the protection of the poor, mediation among community members and so on firmly on the community's shoulders. Individuals had responsibility to provide financially for the community, accept communal positions and observe communal decisions. The Basic Principles further declared that the community would be represented by a body called the Community Administration (*Azkayin Varch'ut'iwn*), which would take a representative form and to which the Ottoman government would entrust communal administration by granting privileges and approving the Constitution. The drafters of the National Constitution interpreted the empire's granting of privileges to their patriarch in accordance with their own purposes and grounded their communal autonomy on those privileges.

The fact that the Ottoman Turkish version did not include the Basic Principles suggests that the state officials may have been reluctant to approve them. This point is related to a theoretical but substantive change that Armenian leading figures intended to achieve. Previously, the administrative centre of the Armenian community had been the patriarchate, and several councils and committees had existed under this institution. The second draft of the Constitution in 1860 stipulated that the entire administrative body of the Armenian community would be called the Community Administration and that the patriarch of Istanbul was to be situated within this body. This idea was incorporated into the Basic Principles in the 1863 version, although the main body of the Constitution did not actually include the expression 'Community Administration'.[89] Nonetheless, the idea was reflected elsewhere in its content. As we will discuss in the next chapter, this theoretical change came to have significance for later developments.

The main organ of the Community Administration was the newly institutionalised standing General Assembly, which embodied the principle of representation; it was composed of 20 clerical and 120 lay members, including 40 members elected by provincial Armenians. The power to elect the patriarch of Istanbul was granted to the assembly, which was also convened to discuss significant communal issues, participate in the election of the catholicos and elect the patriarch of Jerusalem, along with choosing the members of lay and ecclesiastical councils.[90] Thus, although the regulations were called the Regulations on the Armenian Patriarchate in the Ottoman Turkish version, and the patriarch of Istanbul remained the formal representative of the Armenian community before the Ottoman authorities, the National Constitution transformed the Armenians' administrative centre from the Church to a body dominated by lay members of the community.[91]

Armenian Journalism and Community Administration

The drafting of the Constitution stimulated a wider discussion on communal issues in the 1850s, raising expectations among Istanbul Armenians of greater participation in communal politics.[92] This led to a growth in Armenian publications and periodicals that critically discussed their community's situation, as well as the rise of journalists as important actors in communal politics. Lay elites' attempts to bring these periodicals under control would also become a telling overstep into the jurisdiction of the state.

In the Ottoman Empire, periodicals in diverse languages – including Ottoman Turkish, Greek, Armenian and Ladino – appeared in the 1830s and 1840s and proliferated in the 1860s. While in early decades these periodicals were devoted to simply delivering news under the strict censorship of the state, articles in Ottoman Turkish that criticised state politics emerged in the late 1860s, leading to the constitutional movement by the Young Ottomans, a group of Muslim constitutionalist intellectuals.[93]

A decade earlier, the Armenians' constitutional movement at the community level had accompanied the emergence of critical discussion about their communal politics. In the 1840s and early 1850s, Armenian journalists had devoted most of the pages of their periodicals to news on foreign, state and communal topics, while avoiding argument, criticism or the expression of political positions regarding either the Ottoman state or the Armenian community. The Ottoman government had been suspicious of the contents of non-Muslim periodicals since their first appearance. In 1844, the government closed a Greek newspaper published in İzmir, which it claimed published 'things against the administrative principles and political benefits of the Sublime State'.[94] When the Armenian Patriarchate petitioned the government for permission to publish *Hayasdan* in 1846, it was granted only on the condition that the newspaper would not discuss state politics. Moreover, the government decided to impose censorship as well, appointing Hagop Grjigian as the censor of Armenian periodicals.[95]

While state politics were out of bounds for Armenian journalists, Harutyun Svajian opened a discussion of the politics of the Armenian community. Like the principal architects of the Armenian Constitution, Svajian had studied in Paris in the mid-nineteenth century. After returning to Istanbul, he launched a career in journalism, inaugurating the satirical periodical *Meghu* (*Bee*) in 1856.[96] Garabed Panosian, who was not recognised in Armenian historiography, was another conspicuous participant in this trend. He was a Turkophone Armenian from Kayseri in Central Anatolia who moved to Istanbul to study. In 1859, he founded the Armeno-Turkish periodical *Münadi-yi Erciyas* (*Herald of Argeus*), probably with financial support from his fellow Turkophone countrymen in Istanbul.[97] In 1866, Panosian founded a new Armeno-Turkish newspaper called *Manzume-i Efkar*, which achieved great popularity among Istanbul Armenians in the 1860s and 1870s.[98] While many other journalists were eventually elected members of the General Assembly due to their fame, Svajian and Panosian often refused this role, preferring to make their voices heard through their publications. Meanwhile, other journalists generally supported the leading figures of the Community Administration. Among these were Garabed Utujian, the editor of *Masis*, and Sdepan Papazian, the editor of *Jamanag* (*Time*).

Until the mid-nineteenth century, most printed materials in Armenian script were religious works published under the superintendence of the patriarchate or by Catholics and Protestants. Among those published in Istanbul, most Armenian books and pamphlets noted the permission of the patriarchate on their title pages.[99] The 1857 draft of the communal regulations proposed that the ecclesiastical council was to take on the role of authorising the publication of religious books and documents, although there was no mention of non-religious materials.[100]

Nevertheless, the criticism of Armenian leadership that was sometimes published alarmed leading figures of the Armenian community and inspired them to bring these publications under their control. In January 1861, for example, the lay council discussed an issue that arose due to an article in *Meghu*, which accused Vartabed Boghos of Van of committing diverse evil deeds, such as flogging a pregnant woman for no reason, causing a miscarriage, and wrongfully sentencing several Armenians to being beaten with chains.[101] According to *Meghu*, the ecclesiastical council of the patriarchate did not punish him because he was under the protection of a powerful patron in Istanbul. *Meghu* therefore claimed that it would do what the council had not, declaring that 'we do not want such an unlawful and scandalous man in our church' and that this *vartabed* should henceforth have no power to conduct the sacred profession. Moreover, the periodical announced that it would collect signatures supporting its call for Boghos to be stripped of his rank.[102] The lay council considered this problematic and forced the editor to publish an admission that his article had violated the jurisdiction of the Church.[103]

In June, the leading figures of the Armenian community began a discussion of the necessity of regulating Armenian publications in the General Assembly.[104] At the beginning of this discussion, two complaints against articles published in *Meghu* and *Münadi-yi Erciyas* were delivered to the assembly. The first was brought by twenty-three *vartabed*s of the Jerusalem monastery, claiming that the two periodicals carried unpleasant writings. The second was presented by fifty-nine members of the assembly itself, who claimed that the same periodicals did not correctly characterise assembly discussions and proposed that hereafter no newspaper should be allowed to print anything that would slander the assembly, the community, the lay or ecclesiastical councils or any individual person.

Responding to this, Serovpe Vichenian made a proposal as a member of the assembly rather than as its chair. His prefatory remarks affirmed the importance of the freedom of thought. He reminded the assembly that the Ottoman government allowed newspapers to exercise this freedom by giving them publication licences; thus, it was not possible to deprive only Armenian newspapers of this freedom. Nevertheless, Vichenian insisted that some restriction was necessary because certain Armenian newspapers went well beyond the limits of toleration. He proposed that every accusation must be accompanied by evidence; otherwise, it was mere slander. Freedom, he claimed, had its limits. Vichenian proposed that the assembly should appoint a committee to prepare regulations that would place appropriate limits on the freedom of Armenian newspapers. Most of the assembly supported the idea and elected a committee to prepare the regulations. The future patriarch Nerses Varjabedian and the priest of Samatya were elected as its ecclesiastical members, and Vichenian, Sdepan Aslanian, Krikor Odian, Krikor Aghaton and Arakel Dadian were the lay members. Notably, all the lay members were employed in the state services, and no journalists were included.[105]

State and Community

Vichenian's proposal invited several responses, one of which asked how editors who had published offensive writings before the establishment of the regulations should be punished. Vichenian responded that state law guaranteed honour to everyone, and those slandered by the newspapers could appeal to the Sublime Porte.[106] This response summed up the difficulty surrounding the issue: who would be responsible for penalising Armenian periodicals?

Armenian newspapers could be problematic for high-ranking Muslim officials. When the committee was preparing its regulations on Armenian publications, certain articles published in *Münadi-yi Erciyas* concerning the Armenians of Zeytun attracted their attention. Isolated by a mountainous barrier in south-central Anatolia, Zeytun's Armenians formed a semi-autonomous community.[107] In 1862, a regional conflict led to an attack by Armenians from Zeytun on the Muslim village of Ketman. In response, Aziz Pasha, the governor of Maraş, sent force to the Armenian village of Alabaş.[108] In his article on the incident, Panosian wrote about rumoured acts of violence conducted by Aziz Pasha's troops, including the killing of 200 people, plundering, the burning of a church and an attack on a nearby Armenian monastery. The report further stated that Aziz Pasha then moved to a plain only two hours away from Zeytun and urged the Armenians there to surrender.[109] In another article, Panosian decried Aziz Pasha's brutal acts, although he also wrote that the Zeytun Armenians deserved to be punished according to the law for attacking a Muslim village.[110] A state document accused Panosian of spreading falsehoods against the just policy of the Ottoman state and proposed punishing him as stipulated by the penal code. The government closed the *Münadi-yi Erciyas* printing office, imposed a fine of twenty *mecidiye* gold coins on Panosian and confiscated the last three issues of the newspaper.[111]

The state's approval of the Armenian Constitution in 1863, meanwhile, generated momentum among the leading figures in Armenian communal politics. This group was thus given a sufficient basis to claim that they had secured government backing for greater involvement in transforming the Armenian community. One of the first questions tackled was the regulations on Armenian periodicals.

In November 1863, when the draft of the regulations was to be presented to the General Assembly, the lay council summoned representatives from six Armenian periodicals in Istanbul to instruct them about the rules that they were required to follow until the enactment of the new regulations. According to contemporary reports, the council forbade the periodicals from publishing anything that could be an insult to the Armenian 'religion, constitution or Community Administration' or to make accusations against any individual, regardless of whether the accusations were grounded. The council further instructed editors to go to court to make any complaints. While the representatives of *Meghu* and *Zepiwr* (*Zephyr*) refused to accept these instructions, those of *Giligia* (*Cilicia*), *Varaka-yı Havadis* (*Newspaper*), *Masis* and *Jamanag* authored a pledge in which they promised to 'respect the religion, the constitution, the Community Administration and the honour of every individual' and presented it to the lay council.[112]

Two weeks later, *Jamanag* published a draft of the regulations on Armenian periodicals.[113] Its preamble drew on Vichenian's earlier argument in the assembly. In it, the members of the committee discussed the importance of the freedom of thought, which would facilitate the appearance of public criticism of false ideas. However, the committee still called for limits to this freedom, saying that some topics should be exempted from criticism. Furthermore, they specified three things that should always be respected: religious belief, authority and members of the Community Administration. This group of topics corresponded to their previous warnings to editors.

The regulations themselves contained fourteen articles referring to the prohibition of insults and criticism, setting out punishments in case of infringement.[114] The first article discussed the freedom of publication within the scope of the Ottoman government's permission. Meanwhile, it stated that religious affairs were under the jurisdiction of the Church, suggesting that these were outside of the scope of journalistic criticism. The prohibition of insults against religion, the Constitution and the Community Administration was also inserted into regulations. Protection from insult and criticism was thus granted to all those serving in the Community Administration. A committee nominated by the General Assembly would decide the punishment in case of infraction, which could be a fine from 100 to 500 *kuruş*, suspension from publication for two weeks to three months or even absolute prohibition from publication.

The publication of the draft invited a prompt response from several Armenian journalists, although others maintained a deliberate silence. *Jamanag* presented a positive attitude towards the regulations. Its editor, Sdepan Papazian, was a well-known teacher, working at several communal schools in Istanbul. He was also an active participant in communal politics as a member of the General Assembly and sat on several committees. Publishing the whole text of the draft, Papazian announced his support for the regulations. He believed that it would be good for all Armenians to adopt a position of support for the Community Administration; he therefore considered the prohibition against insulting them to be appropriate. Moreover, he claimed that the regulations were necessary because many editors of Armenian periodicals were still inexperienced.[115]

By contrast, Harutyun Svajian, the editor of *Meghu*, criticised the regulations. He insisted on the importance of the freedom of the press, through which people could keep a close eye on whether the Community Administration was functioning properly.[116] A similar negative response came from Panosian, the former editor of *Münadi-yi Erciyas*. Because the Ottoman authorities had closed his newspaper, Panosian published a book in Armeno-Turkish entitled *Free Thought*, in which he argued that newspapers were of crucial importance for Armenians, who had embraced constitutionalism. For a constitutional administration to function, it was vital to keep a close eye on the members of the assembly and councils. Thus 'the soundness of constitutional administration [*Sahmanatragan idarenin sıhheti*] can be attained only by the freedom of the press [*kalem serbestiyeti*]'.[117]

Panosian admitted that limits were necessary for the freedom of the press, but he argued that the Ottoman government, not the patriarchate, should determine these limits. On these grounds, Panosian criticised the regulations that the patriarchate was imposing on Armenian periodicals. It should be noted that he specifically referred to the patriarchate as the Armenians' administrative centre rather than the Community Administration. Panosian insisted that the patriarchate had no authority to formulate communal regulations where state laws existed. Though the editors of the papers were Armenian, they published newspapers within the realm of 'protected [Ottoman] domains' (*memalik-i mahruse*) and obtained permission for publication not from the patriarchate but from the Sublime Porte or the Ministry of Public Education. Thus, state law should apply to Armenian newspapers in the same way it applied to the newspapers of other communities, and the Ottoman government already had clauses in its penal code on infringements and punishments in relation to publishers.

Panosian extended this line of thought to the matter of jurisdiction, indicating the difficulties inherent to a pluralistic society. He wrote, 'The patriarchate does not have any responsibility for [affairs] other than the community, that is, churches and schools, and does not have any political obligation at all' (*politikaca zerrece bir vacibatı yok dur*). Therefore, the patriarchate had no authority to enact regulations for a group of people who were subjects of the Ottoman Empire. Even if a group of Armenians were drunk in a bar or caused disorder in a theatre, these issues were out of the patriarchate's responsibility.[118] Here, Panosian used the term 'political' to refer exclusively to the state's jurisdiction. In addition, he argued that enacting regulations on publications could alienate the Armenian public from the Armenian Church and possibly encourage them to approach the Catholic or Protestant churches, adding that if the patriarchate succeeded in silencing the followers of the Armenian Church by enacting the regulations, they would send their complaints to newspapers published by the adherents of other confessions.[119]

Conclusion

The most recent study investigating the Armenian National Constitution argued that it was the result of 'the strong will of the Ottoman administration to gain power over the provinces'[120]; nevertheless, it is difficult to discern such an intention from the contents of the regulations of other communities, which rarely referred to centre–province relations, and the 1857 guidelines. As this chapter demonstrates, and considering its differences from the other communities' regulations, the highly progressive and centralising character of the Armenian National Constitution stemmed from the persistent efforts of the Armenian elites in Istanbul. They perceived the promise of reforms as an opportunity and actively sought to expand the scope of their communal autonomy rather than conforming to the expectations of Muslim officials. In response to their bold actions, Ottoman ruling circles, pursuing reforms to increase state control over society, considered these efforts as an encroachment on the jurisdiction of the state.

In December 1863, *Masis* reported that a draft of the regulations on Armenian periodicals had been presented to the General Assembly, but less than half of its members participated in the session, which was the threshold for a quorum.[121] The assembly's minutes, which were printed and sold to the public, did not include a record of this session, and contemporary sources made no mention of these regulations thereafter. The abrupt disappearance of any information on the regulations suggests that leading Armenian figures abandoned the enactment, not because of any disagreement within the assembly or community but due to external intervention.

During the early 1860s, some private periodicals began circulating in Ottoman Turkish, and high-ranking state officials recognised the necessity of putting the press under state control. In 1862, the government formed its Bureau of Publications and appointed an Armenian Catholic as its chief.[122] In 1864, it enacted its Law on Publications, which regulated periodicals.[123] Thus, while the Armenian committee was preparing its proposed regulations for Armenian periodicals at the end of 1863, the government was also preparing its own system to regulate periodicals published in the empire, regardless of language. They were likely reluctant to tolerate a parallel development in the Armenian community, instead intending to put all periodicals under the control of their unitary legal system. The 1857 guidelines on non-Muslim community reforms contained the specific instruction that community councils created for secular affairs should not infringe on the sphere of state administration.[124] High-ranking state officials may therefore have informally halted the development of the regulations in the Armenian community, which had been led by Armenian elites in state employment.

The Law on Publications stipulated the prohibitions imposed on periodicals and the punishments for infringement. Among the prohibitions were inappropriate or slanderous writings against various figures and topics, including public order, religions, the Ottoman government, sultans, ministers, state officials, the heads of state and diplomats from other countries. Article Thirty-One stipulated who could file a suit in case of infringement. It first stated that no trial would be held unless the offended party filed a suit. Subsequently, the article mentioned three exceptional possible cases. The first was slander against the sovereign, the imperial family, the government or the ministers of the Ottoman state, and the second was writings against public virtue. In these cases, the Law on Publications conferred on the Ottoman government itself the right to file suit. The third was regarding slander against 'religions and denominations' (*edyan ve mezahib*). In this case, the law conferred the right to file suit on 'the agents of the religion and denomination targeted by such slander'.[125] Thus, state officials avoided directly involving themselves in the religious affairs of non-Muslims, leaving this to the respective clergy by carving out an exceptional area for them in the unitary legal system.

In the eyes of state officials, then, religion was an exceptional area that required specific discussion in the legislation of the empire. Another example of this type of thinking was the Law on Public Education, which was drafted in the late 1860s. While this law was intended to put all educational institutions under government control, it guaranteed non-Muslim community leaders the right to operate and administer their own schools. The references to religious education in the Law on Public Education stipulated exceptional treatment for non-Muslims, mentioning that religious education fell under the jurisdiction of non-Muslim religious authorities.[126] Thus, religious affairs were exempted from the political integration of the Ottoman nation and kept apart from political interference. It must be noted that this special treatment was applied to non-Muslims in general. For Muslims, meanwhile, the upper echelons of the empire did not consider it necessary to separate out religious affairs or apply a special rule to them. The distinctions between and the intertwining of the spheres of religion and politics will be a main topic in the following chapters. The next chapter focuses on the international connection of the Armenian Church and details how Armenian religious affairs took on political meaning for Ottoman ruling circles due to the existence of the Echmiadzin Catholicosate under Russian rule.

Notes

1. Davison, *Reform in the Ottoman Empire*, 407–8; Ruben Safrastjan, 'Ottomanism in Turkey in the Epoch of Reforms in XIX C.: Ideology and Policy. I', *Etudes balkaniques* 24 (1988): 72–86; Ruben Safrastjan, 'Ottomanism in Turkey in the Epoch of Reforms in XIX C.: Ideology and Policy. II', *Etudes balkaniques* 25 (1989): 34–44; Somel, 'Osmanlıcılık Düşüncesi', 88–116.
2. Fairey, *The Great Powers*, 122–43.
3. BOA, İ.HR 21198 (11 May 1853).
4. BOA, İ.HR 21210 (6 June 1853).
5. *Correspondence Respecting the Rights and Privileges of the Latin and Greek Churches in Turkey: Presented to Both Houses of Parliament by Command of Her Majesty* (London: Harrison and Son, 1854), 134–8, 143–50, 164–70. The Russian ambassador even employed the phrase 'secular privileges' to describe Orthodox Christians in relation to the Palestinian holy places. Ibid., 147.
6. Fujinami, 'Ecumenical Patriarchate', 244–5.
7. The document dated to 1847 refers to both the privileges of non-Muslims and the existence of their distinct religious sphere. Nevertheless, the drafter did not add 'religious' to 'privileges' in this document. BOA, İ.MSM 922 (13 June 1847).
8. For example, BOA, İ.HR 21203 (19 May 1853), 21234 (6 July 1853). To the best of my knowledge, the first appearance of this combination was in a report submitted to the Sultan in April 1853. BOA, İ.HR 21191 (10 April 1853).
9. *Correspondence Respecting the Rights*, 197; BOA, İ.HR 21198 (11 May 1853).
10. BOA, İ.HR 21207 (30 May 1853).
11. Somel, 'Osmanlı Ermenilerinde Kültür Modernleşmesi', 85; Somel, *Modernization of Public Education*. As will be discussed in Chapter 6, the Ottoman government was inclined to establish firmer control over non-Muslim schools in the late nineteenth century. After the Young Turk Revolution, the Ministry of Public Education sought the 'unification of education' and the subjection of non-Muslim educational institutions to stricter supervision. Nobuyoshi Fujinami, 'Privileged but Equal: The Privilege Question in the Context of Ottoman Constitutionalism', in *Balkan Nationalism(s) and the Ottoman Empire*, vol. 3, ed. Dimitris Stamatopoulos (Istanbul: Isis Press, 2015), 33–59.

12. BOA, İ.HR 21207 (30 May–7 June 1853), A.DVN 89/55 (30 May–7 June 1853), C.ADL 3124 (1–10 March 1854); *Masis*, no. 71 (15 June 1853).
13. Greene, *History of the Greeks*, 68–9.
14. *Takvim-i Vekayi'*, no. 491 (13 August 1853). For more on the 'foundation myth', see Braude, 'Foundation Myths'.
15. *Masis*, no. 71.
16. For example, BOA, İ.HR 4835 (16 June 1853), 4843 (23 June 1853), 4848 (27 June 1853).
17. BOA, İ.HR 4841 (16 June 1853).
18. BOA, İ.HR 4841 (21 June 1853); *Ceride-i Havadis*, no. 631 (15 July 1853).
19. BOA, İ.HR 21217 (no date; the document is attached to one dated 9 June 1853).
20. BOA, İ.HR 5001 (7 October 1853); *Takvim-i Vekayi'*, no. 494 (27 October 1853).
21. Cohen, *Becoming Ottomans*.
22. BOA, İ.HR 5191 (28 November 1853).
23. Beydilli, *Armenian Catholic Community*, 33.
24. BOA, İ.MSM 974 (18 December 1847). The government's granting of the charter was regarded as recognition of the Greek Catholic (or Melkite) *millet*. Bruce Masters, 'The Establishment of the Melkite Catholic *Millet* in 1848 and the Politics of Identity in Tanzimat Syria', in *Syria and Bilad al-Sham under Ottoman Rule: Essays in Honour of Abdul-Karim Rafeq*, ed. Peter Sluglett and Stefan Weber (Leiden: Brill, 2010), 455–73; Hidemitsu Kuroki, 'Neither "Western" nor "Orthodox": Establishing Greek Catholic Identity in the Ottoman Empire and Beyond', in *Religious Interactions in Europe and the Mediterranean World: Coexistence and Dialogue from the Twelfth to the Twentieth Centuries*, ed. Katsumi Fukasawa, Benjamin J. Kaplan and Pierre-Yves Beaurepaire (London: Routledge, 2017), 287–98.
25. BOA, İ.HR 5191 (6 February 1854).
26. Ibid.
27. BOA, İ.HR 21234 (6 July 1853), A.AMD 46/47 (6 July 1853), A.MKT.UM 139/26 (15 July 1853).
28. BOA, İ.HR 6857 (20 May 1856; 7 July 1856), HR.MKT157/20 (29 July 1856). This method resembled what was proposed for Armenian Catholics in the 1830 negotiations between the representatives of the Ottoman Empire and France. Beydilli, *Armenian Catholic Community*, 226–31.
29. BOA, A.DVN 119/13 (16 December 1856).
30. *Takvim-i Vekayi'*, no. 539 (3 March 1856). On the implication that the equality between Muslims and non-Muslims had for non-Ottoman Muslims in Ottoman lands, see Bruce Masters, 'The Treaties of Erzurum (1823 and 1848) and the Changing Status of Iranians in the Ottoman Empire', *Iranian Studies* 24, no. 1–4 (1991): 9; Michael Christopher Low, 'Unfurling the Flag of Extraterritoriality: Autonomy, Foreign Muslims, and the Capitulations in

the Ottoman Hijaz', *Journal of the Ottoman and Turkish Studies Association* 3, no. 2 (2016): 308.

31. Masami Arai, '"Osuman Shimin" no Jiyu to Byodo: Midohato Kempo kara 1924 Nen Kempo he', in *Kokumin Kokka to Shimin: Hosetsu to Haijo no Shoso*, ed. Hirotaka Tateishi and Taku Shinohara (Tokyo: Yamakawa Shuppansha, 2009), 147–52.
32. Cevdet Paşa, *Tezâkir 1–12*, ed. Cavid Baysun, 2nd ed. (Ankara: Türk Tarih Kurumu Basımevi, 1986), 77.
33. Donald Quataert, *The Ottoman Empire 1700–1922*, 2nd ed. (Cambridge: Cambridge University Press, 2005), 148–51.
34. *Takvim-i Vekayi'*, no. 539.
35. Suraiya Faroqhi, 'Ottoman Guilds in the Late Eighteenth Century: The Bursa Case', in *Making a Living in the Ottoman Lands 1480 to 1820* (Istanbul: Isis Press, 1995), 95–6; Baki Tezcan, 'Ethnicity, Race, Religion and Social Class: Ottoman Markers of Difference', in *The Ottoman World*, ed. Christine Woodhead (London: Routledge, 2011), 165–7; Aleksandar Fotić, 'Tracing the Origin of a New Meaning of the Term *Re'āyā* in the Eighteenth-century Ottoman Balkans', *Balcanica* 48 (2017): 55–66.
36. For the term 'tebaa', see Özgür Türesay, 'Un nouveau type de sujets ottomans: l'apparition des *tebaa* au début du XIXe siècle', in *Ethno-geópolitique des empires: de l'antiquité au monde contemporain*, ed. Yann Lignereux, Alain Messaoudi, Annick Peters-Custot and Jérôme Wilgaux (Rennes: Presses universitaires de Rennes, 2021), 181–202; Özgür Türesay, '*Nizam*dan *Tanzimat*a, *Reaya*dan *Tebaa*ya Gidilirken: 1830'ların Başında Takvîm-i Vekayi'nin Siyasi Dili ve Söylemi', *Tarih ve Toplum Yeni Yaklaşımlar* 20 (2022): 98–142.
37. Najwa al-Qattan, 'Discriminating Texts: Orthographic Marking and Social Differentiation in the Court Record of Ottoman Damascus', in *Arabic Sociolinguistics: Issues & Perspectives*, ed. Yasir Suleiman (Richmond: Curzon Press, 1994), 57–77.
38. In practice, the collection of taxes depended on local officials and social conditions, and tax reforms and the state's financial difficulties worsened the situation of the local population. Nadir Özbek, 'The Politics of Taxation and "Armenian Question" during the Late Ottoman Empire, 1876–1908', *Comparative Studies in Society and History* 54, no. 4 (2012): 770–97.
39. Ufuk Gülsoy, *Osmanlı'nın Gayrimüslim Askerleri* (Istanbul: Timaş Yayınları, 2010), chap. 2; Tobias Heinzelmann, *Cihaddan Vatan Savunmasına: Osmanlı İmparatorluğu'nda Genel Askerlik Yükümlülüğü 1826–1856*, tr. Türkis Noyan (Istanbul: Kitap Yayınevi, 2009), 244–50.
40. Heinzelmann, *Cihaddan Vatan Savunmasına*, 144–5, 247–8. Virginia H. Aksan has argued that *din ü devlet* gained importance as the ideology of the Ottoman Empire in the late eighteenth century. 'Ottoman Political Writing, 1768–1808', *International Journal of Middle East Studies* 25, no. 1 (1993): 53–69. For example, in the Charter of Alliance of 1808, the government

advocated for the necessary revitalisation of *din ü devlet*. Yaycioglu, *Partners of the Empire*, 206.

41. *Takvim-i Vekayi'*, no. 539.
42. Engin Deniz Akarlı ed., *Belgelerle Tanzimat: Osmanlı Sadrıazamlarından Ali ve Fuad Paşaların Siyasi Vasiyyetnameleri* (Istanbul: Boğaziçi Üniversitesi Yayınları, 1978), 14–15.
43. Sarıyıldız, *Sicill-i Ahvâl Komisyonu'nun Kuruluşu*, 151–63.
44. Werth, *Tsar's Foreign Faiths*, 52–3.
45. BOA, A.DVN 164/72 (27 May 1861); A.MKT.MHM 220/65 (27 May 1861); *Salname*, H1278 (1861/2), 52; Carter V. Findley, *Bureaucratic Reform in the Ottoman Empire: The Sublime Porte, 1789–1922* (Princeton: Princeton University Press, 1980), 185–6. Among the documents held in the Ottoman Archives, the term 'religious affairs' (*mezahib hususatı*) begins to appear in December 1859 in the archival classification, including in the communications between ministries and other government agencies in Istanbul. BOA, A.MKT.NZD 298/77 (16 December 1859), 302/55 (23 January 1860). In 1861, this expression was replaced by the reference to the Bureau of Religious Affairs in the same classification. BOA, A.MKT. NZD 363/99 (20 August 1861), 409/59 (4 April 1862). It is likely that the documents held by this bureau were transferred to the Ministry of Justice when the bureau was attached to it. The documents held by the ministry were lost when a fire broke out in the building housing them.
46. BOA, İ.HR 15508 (4 May 1873); 21447 (4 May 1864); İ.MMS 1964 (1 May 1873).
47. Because its tasks often concerned relations with European countries, the chiefs – and probably the staff members – were required to be proficient in French. We can confirm this from the curricula vitae of two state officials who shouldered these duties. BOA, DH.SAİD.d 2/982 (Sadullah Paşa); 4/268 (Mustafa Ziver Bey).
48. İ.DH 61932 (25 November 1877); Demirel, *Adliye Nezareti*, 64–70.
49. For example, see the appointment charters of the Orthodox Christian patriarchs dated 1840 and 1855. BOA, A.DVNS.GMC.d 3, pp. 41–5, 113–16.
50. For example, see BOA, A.DVNS.GMC.d 3, pp. 119–22.
51. BOA, A.MKT.NZD 298/21 (11 December 1859).
52. BOA, İ.HR 11907 (13 April 1864), İ.DH 77132 (31 April 1886).
53. BOA, A.MKT.UM 472/28 (13 June 1861).
54. BOA, HR.İD 1597/53 (8 October 1874).
55. *Takvim-i Vekayi'*, no. 539.
56. *Meghu*, no. 8, 173–5 (12 January 1857).
57. Artinian, *Armenian Constitutional System*, 81–2.
58. BOA, İ.MVL 16736 (3 April 1857). Unlike the later versions, this first draft of the National Constitution was not published. Although researchers were aware that it was prepared in 1857, the whereabouts of this document were unknown. During my research in the Ottoman Archives, I found the

draft in manuscript form, which was written in both Armenian and Ottoman Turkish. For the preliminary analysis and the transcription of the Ottoman Turkish version, see Ueno, 'First Draft'.

59. BOA, İ.MVL 16736 (17 October 1857); İ.HR 7850 (16 October 1857).
60. BOA, İ.HR 7850 (16 October 1857).
61. Ibid.
62. Artinian, *Armenian Constitutional System*, 82–91.
63. *Düstur*, 1st series, vol. 2 (Istanbul: Matbaa-i Amire, 1872/3), 902–75.
64. Artinian, *Armenian Constitutional System*, 84–6.
65. Ibid., 77–8.
66. Vahram H. T'orkomean, *Pzhishg Dōk't'. Servich'ēn Ēfēndi* (Vienna: Mkhit'arean Dbaran, 1893), 11–12.
67. BOA, DH.SAİD.d 1/60 (Servichen Efendi).
68. Artinian, *Armenian Constitutional System*, 85.
69. Arthur Beylérian, 'Krikor Odian (1834–1887): Un haut fonctionnaire ottoman, homme des missions secrètes', *Revue du monde arménien moderne et contemporain* 1 (1994): 52–3.
70. *Azkayin Sahmanatrut'iwn* (1863), art. 68.
71. Ibid., arts. 65, 66.
72. The names of the first representatives of the General Assembly can be found in the report of the first election in 1863. *Deghegakir Kordzatir Hantsnazhoghovoy Azkayin Sahmanatrut'ean Nergayats'eal Handean Ěnthanur Zhoghovoy Azkayin Eresp'okhanutean i 20 Sebdemper Amsoy 1863* (Istanbul: Dbakrut'iwn Hovhannu Miwhēndisean, 1863). In many cases, researchers have had no other choice but to utilise the list of communal taxpayers of 1870–1 to identify the representatives of 1863. *Deghegakir Hamaraduut'ean Dndesagan Khorhrtoy aṛ Azkayin K'aghak'agan Zhoghovn Getronagan Varch'ut'ean* (Istanbul: Dbakrut'iwn Ō. Khōjasarean, 1872). Although the occupational information recorded in this list might be different from that of 1863, we can assume that the differences are not great enough to affect the general tendency.
73. *Adenakrut'iwnk' Azkayin Ěnthanur Zhoghovoy* (2 October 1863), 90.
74. Vartan Artinian, *Osmanlı Devleti'nde Ermeni Anayasası'nın Doğuşu 1839–1863*, tr. Zülal Kılıç (Istanbul: Aras Yayıncılık, 2004), 163.
75. *Azkayin Sahmanatrut'iwn* (1863), 7.
76. The Armenian Patriarchate published the Armenian and Armeno-Turkish versions in a single volume. *Azkayin Sahmanatrut'iwn* (1863). The Ottoman Turkish version was inserted in the Code of Laws. *Düstur*, 1st series, vol. 2, 938–61.
77. Nevertheless, it is noteworthy that the Ottoman Turkish version of the text frequently uses the expression *Nizamname-i Esasi*. Rarely used in the regulations of other communities, this expression can be seen as a precursor to the later name of the Ottoman constitution, *Kanun-ı Esasi*, and as a reflection of the constitutional character of the Armenian name. Talin Suciyan

downplays this and frequently uses the word *Nizamname* in her book, interpreting it as an expression that simply means regulation and reflects the government's perspective, with the understanding that the Armenians' regulations were called *Nizamname-i Ermeniyan* in Turkish. *Outcasting Armenians*, 8, 237. However, *Nizamname-i Ermeniyan* (or *Nizamname-i Millet-i Ermeniyan*) is the expression used in the Armeno-Turkish version, not the one used in the state-approved Ottoman Turkish version.

78. *Meghu*, no. 8, 173–5.
79. BOA, İ.MVL 16736 (3 April 1857); *Azkayin Sahmanatrut'iwn Hayots'* (Istanbul: Azkayin Dbaran Surp P'rgch'i, 1860).
80. Kharatyan, 'Arevmtahayeri Azgayin "Sahmanadrut'yunĕ"'; Koçunyan, 'Nizâmnâme-i Millet-i Ermeniyân'.
81. Garabed H. P'anosean, *Miwst'ēdiyi Sahmanatrut'iwn* ([Istanbul]: Miwhēndisean T'abkhanēsi, 1861), 2.
82. Ibid., 1.
83. Safrastjan, 'Ottomanism in Turkey'; Somel, 'Osmanlıcılık Düşüncesi'; Davison, *Reform in the Ottoman Empire*, 407–8.
84. Elke Hartmann, 'The "Loyal Nation" and Its Deputies: The Armenians in the First Ottoman Parliament', in *The First Ottoman Experiment in Democracy*, ed. Christoph Herzog and Malek Sharif (Würzburg: Ergon Verlag, 2010), 193–5, 209–10; *Masis*, no. 1930 (30 January 1877).
85. *Masis*, no. 843 (18 April 1868).
86. *Adenakrut'iwnk'* (2 April 1875): 238.
87. I have therefore translated *millet*/*milli* (and *azk*/*azkayin* in Armenian) sometimes as 'nation'/'national' and sometimes as 'community'/'communal'.
88. *Azkayin Sahmanatrut'iwn* (1863), 11–12.
89. A single exception can be found at the beginning of the body of the Armenian version, while the Ottoman Turkish version does not contain it.
90. *Azkayin Sahmanatrut'iwn* (1863), arts. 57, 60, 61.
91. This transformation affected the venue of the General Assembly, which was not specified in the Constitution. In 1863, the assembly convened at the Armenian Patriarchate in the Kumkapı district of Istanbul. After 1864, however, it was generally convened in the conference room of the Holy Illuminator Church in Galata. *Masis*, nos. 609 (24 October 1863), 613 (21 November 1863), 639 (21 May 1864), 645 (2 July 1864), 679 (25 February 1865), 1014 (19 October 1870), 1427 (6 September 1873). This church was also used as the venue for communal councils and committees. *Masis*, no. 852 (20 June 1868). Although Armenian elites did not prefer to belong to the parish of Galata, it was more easily accessible for members of the assembly – who came from all around Istanbul – than Kumkapı had been when the city was geographically expanding to the north and the newly developing parts of that area (namely, Beyoğlu, Beşiktaş and Ortaköy) were attracting the wealthier residents of Istanbul. Data from the early 1870s shows that the aforementioned regions were the top three parishes

in which the Armenian Assembly members preferred to reside, while the Istanbul parishes on the Marmara coast (Kumkapı, Samatya and Yenikapı), which had dense Armenian populations, were less attractive to the wealthy and powerful. *Deghegakir Hamaraduut'ean Dndesagan Khorhrtoy*; *Masis*, nos. 950 (9 March 1870), 1000 (31 August 1870). In 1862, Paspatis, an Orthodox Christian doctor, referred to the decline of the Marmara coast region, writing that Muslim and Christian residents were moving out of the Marmara coast region to the 'commercially active quarters'. Aleksandros Paspatis, *Balıklı Rum Hastanesi Kayıtlarına Göre İstanbul'un Ortodoks Esnafı, 1833–1860*, tr. Marianna Yerasimos (Istanbul: Kitap Yayınevi, 2014), 115.

92. For the connection between the emergence of the venues of political discussion and the public sphere, see Der Matossian, *Shattered Dreams*, chap. 5.
93. For the Young Ottomans, see Şerif Mardin, *The Genesis of Young Ottoman Thought: A Study in the Modernization of Turkish Political Ideas* (Princeton: Princeton University Press, 1962).
94. BOA, HR.MKT 2/33 (1 March 1844).
95. BOA, İ.MSM 936 (26 April 1846; 28 April 1846). Grjigian was told to censor not only Armenian but also French newspapers. It was simultaneously decided to assign the censorship of Greek newspapers to an official (probably of Greek origin) in the Translation Bureau who handled the translation of Greek documents. There was no mention of the appointment of a censor for Ottoman Turkish newspapers, which at this point were limited to the official and semi-official gazettes. The archives of the Topkapı Palace hold reports that attest the actual application of censorship, in which I found two reports on articles of *Hayasdan*. BOA. TS.MA.E 558/69 (no date); 560/27 (no date).
96. *Haykakan Sovetakan Hanragitaran* (Erevan: Haykakan SSH Gitut'yunneri Akademia, 1985), vol. 11, 88–9.
97. Erciyas was the name of the mountain near the city of Kayseri. Armenians in Kayseri generally only spoke Turkish. For Garabed Panosian, see Ueno, 'One Script, Two Languages'.
98. Oksen Khojasarian built his career writing for *Manzume-i Efkar* and achieved fame through journalism. When Khojasarian started his own newspaper in 1869, he mentioned that he had written for *Manzume-i Efkar* until then. *Ōrakir Dziln Awarayrioy*, no. 1 (18 September 1869). In his articles published in *Manzume-i Efkar*, Khojasarian signed himself 'Ō'.
99. Albert Khaṛatyan, *Arevmtahay Parberakan Mamulě ev Grak'nnut'yuně Ōsmanyan T'urk'iayum* (Erevan: Haykakan SSH GA Hratarakch'ut'yun, 1989), 20.
100. BOA, İ.MVL 16736 (3 April 1857), art. 21.
101. *Adenakrut'iwnk'* (16 April 1861), 42, 46.
102. *Meghu*, no. 118 (22 December 1860). On the local network and power of Vartabed Boghos, see Antaramian, *Brokers of Faith*, 108–17.

103. *Adenakrut'iwnk'* (16 April 1861), 42; *Masis*, no. 466 (23 January 1861).
104. *Adenakrut'iwnk'* (6 June 1861), 63–6.
105. Ibid., 63–6.
106. Ibid., 64–5.
107. Most of south-central Anatolia was in the hands of several local rulers, including the Kozanoğlu family, a notable provincial Muslim family that controlled the Kozan region. Andrew G. Gould, 'Lords or Bandits? The Derebeys of Cilicia', *International Journal of Middle East Studies* 7, no. 4 (1976): 494.
108. Nalbandian, *The Armenian Revolutionary Movement*, 70–4; Stephan H. Astourian, 'On the Genealogy of the Armenian–Turkish Conflict, Sultan Abdülhamid and the Armenian Massacres', in *Collective and State Violence in Turkey: The Construction of a National Identity from Empire to Nation-State*, ed. Stephan H. Astourian and Raymond H. Kévorkian (New York: Berghahn, 2021), 17–20.
109. *Miwnadiyi Ērjiyas*, no. 213 (26 August 1862).
110. *Miwnadiyi Ērjiyas*, no. 214 (28 August 1862).
111. BOA, İ.MVL 21426 (11 September 1862). Some scholars prefer to regard the incident in Zeytun as a rebellion against the Ottoman Empire and the sign of the Armenian national liberation movement. From this viewpoint, Panosian was wrongfully depicted as a journalist who supported the rebellion and, more generally, the liberation movement. Khaṛatyan, *Arevmtahay Parberakan Mamulě*, 39–40, 94–106; G. Step'anyan, 'Hayataṛ T'urk'eren Hay Mamulě', in *Hay Parberakan Mamuli Patmut'yunits'*, ed. A.B. Karinyan (Erevan: Haykakan SSR GA Hratarakch'ut'yun, 1963), 239–74. Because the Ottoman government confiscated the last three editions (213, 214 and 215) of *Münadi-yi Erciyas*, we can find them in the Ottoman Archives. BOA, İ.MVL 21426.
112. *Masis*, no. 614 (28 November 1863); *Jamanag*, no. 23 (21 November 1863).
113. *Jamanag*, no. 23.
114. Ibid.
115. Ibid.
116. Khaṛatyan, *Arevmtahay Parberakan Mamulě*, 56–7.
117. Garabed H. P'anosean, *Ēfk'earě Mukhayyērē* (Istanbul: Hovhannēs Miwhēndisean T'abkhanēsi, 1863), 66–9.
118. Ibid., 81–94, 106.
119. Ibid., 118–19.
120. Suciyan, *Outcasting Armenians*, 30.
121. *Masis*, no. 618 (26 December 1863).
122. Server İskit, *Türkiyede Matbuat Rejimleri* (Istanbul: Ülkü Matbaası, 1939), 13–14.
123. *Düstur*, 1st series, vol. 2, 220–6.
124. BOA, İ.HR 7850 (18 October 1857).
125. *Düstur*, 1st series, vol. 2, 225.

126. Ibid., 185, 188–90, 196–7. For the English translation of the Law of Public Education, see Emine Ö. Evered, *Empire and Education under the Ottomans: Politics, Reform, and Resistance from the Tanzimat to the Young Turks* (London: I. B. Tauris, 2012), 205–46.

The law on the exemption of customs duties for Christian clergymen was the fruit of similar exceptionalism. Although the law was mainly intended for foreign Christian clergymen (especially missionaries) living in the Ottoman realm, it was applied to Ottoman subjects as well. In the preamble, the drafter calls the exemption of customs duties the most important of the privileges that had been granted to non-Muslim clergymen. The exemption was therefore applied to the clergymen and institutions that they administered. The institutions mentioned in the law exhibit the scope of the exceptionalism, including not only churches and monasteries but also schools, hospitals, pharmacies, orphanages and soup kitchens. *Düstur*, 1st series, vol. 2, 310–17.

4

The Armenian Church and Transimperial Politics

In 1889/90, İbrahim Hakkı, who served the Ottoman Empire as a legal advisor and taught in the Imperial Law School, published a textbook for administrative law. In this textbook, he devoted a chapter to the religious administration of the Ottoman Empire and provided an explanation of the various non-Muslim groups and their religious authorities, with main reference to the regulations that Orthodox Christians, Armenians and Jews had created in the 1860s. He emphasised that the Ottoman Empire did not have official relations with religious authorities outside its territory, such as the Roman Pope or the catholicos of Echmiadzin. He insisted on the non-existence of the empire's official relations with the latter, repeating this assertion three times. On one of these occasions, he writes as follows:

> Similar to the Orthodox Christian community, the first religious privileges and favours were granted to the Armenian community by Sultan Mehmet Han the Conqueror, who rests in heaven, as well. Because the [Ottoman] state did not have an official relationship with the Catholicosate of Echmiadzin, which was in Russia and was the highest religious authority of the Armenian denomination, a patriarchate was established in Istanbul to administer the affairs of the community.[1]

From what has been discussed so far, it is clear that this explanation does not reflect the actual situation. The granting of religious privileges by Mehmet II was a later invention, and the appointment of the Istanbul patriarch was initially unrelated to the existence of the catholicosate in Russia. This explanation rather reflects what Muslim high-ranking officials in the nineteenth century desired: they hoped to deal domestically with the religious affairs of non-Muslims to avoid their politicisation through foreign intervention and wanted religious authorities in Istanbul to serve this purpose. In their understanding, the Armenian Patriarchate of Istanbul was established so that Ottoman Armenians would not need to have recourse to any religious authority outside the realm. Unlike the explanation of the *millet* system, Ottoman statesmen needed to consider the transborder religious connections of non-Muslim subjects when deciding on the treatment of its religiously diverse population.

Recent studies on the Ottoman legal regime have advanced our understanding about the growth of the Ottomans' concern about territorial integrity, boundaries and sovereignty during the nineteenth century.[2] This growth of concern inevitably foregrounded the transborder nature of religions. While the Ottomans used caliphal claim to cross their own borders, they were faced with the necessity of limiting the transborder connections that their non-Muslim subjects had with religious authorities outside the empire. This chapter uses the Ottoman Armenian connection to the Catholicosate of Echmiadzin as a case study for analysing these attempts at limitation.

The creation of the National Constitution in 1863 significantly affected relationships among the religious authorities of the Armenian Church. Although the Ottoman Empire accommodated four religious authorities of the Armenian Church (that is, the catholicoi of Sis and Aghtamar and the patriarchs of Istanbul and Jerusalem), the highest authority of the Church was located in the Russian Caucasus along with a considerable concentration of the Armenian population. As discussed in the previous chapter, the National Constitution was intended to substantially change the administrative centre of the Armenian community. Previously, this centre had been the Patriarchate of Istanbul, represented by the patriarch, a religious authority. In the Basic Principles section of the Constitution, however, the administrative body of the community was newly identified as the Community Administration, represented by the General Assembly. The National Constitution situated patriarchs within this body and conferred power on the assembly to elect these patriarchs and to participate in the elections of the catholicoi. The Constitution thus structurally subordinated the religious authorities to a newly established administrative body that was dominated by the lay elites of Istanbul.[3]

This transformation allowed lay elites to further involve themselves in ecclesiastical issues and imagine the formulation of a new type of relationship between the Community Administration and the religious authorities outside Istanbul, including the catholicosate under Russian rule. Thus, their action had a highly charged political meaning. In dealing with these religious-cum-political affairs, these actors framed their claims in a way that adopted the language of both politics and religion. This chapter, a discussion of the relationship of the Armenian elites with religious authorities and the attitudes of Muslim state officials towards these issues, will investigate the intertwined politics of the treatment of non-dominant religious groups in a multireligious empire.

Religious Authorities and their Jurisdiction

As discussed in Chapter 1, in the eighteenth century, the Ottoman Empire had allowed the Istanbul Patriarchate an extensive administrative jurisdiction, covering the entire empire, apart from the Arab provinces that had a small Armenian population. However, this did not match the jurisdiction that the patriarchate had in the church organisation. Ecclesiastically, the Catholicosates of Sis and Aghtamar and the Patriarchate of Jerusalem retained jurisdiction over south-central Anatolia, Aghtamar Island and the Arab provinces, respectively, while the Balkans and the rest of Anatolia fell under the jurisdiction of the Istanbul Patriarchate.[4]

The new administrative body that appeared in Istanbul after the National Constitution was not restricted by any ecclesiastical organisation. Indeed, the drafters of the Constitution intended to incorporate all Armenians living in the Ottoman Empire under the jurisdiction of the Community Administration. The 1857 draft of the Constitution stated that all Ottoman Armenians would be represented by the newly institutionalised General Assembly.[5] This intention was reflected in the provincial allotment of assembly seats, included in the 1860 draft, which assigned seats to the provinces under the jurisdiction of the Sis catholicos and the Jerusalem patriarch as well.[6] Although the Armenian elites in Istanbul had already begun the project of dominating the other three religious authorities in the Ottoman realm in the mid-nineteenth century, the Constitution greatly accelerated this process by providing them with justification.[7]

Thus, the change in geographical jurisdiction triggered by the National Constitution was oriented towards matching the jurisdiction of the Armenians' administrative centre to the political territory of the Ottoman Empire. This transition had another aspect, however. The Istanbul patriarch had jurisdiction not only over Armenians living in Ottoman territory but also over those who had emigrated out of the empire and those who were living in former Ottoman territories. The first draft of the Constitution written in 1857 was intended to apply not only to all Armenians living in Ottoman territory but also to those living outside of it who were still under the ecclesiastical jurisdiction of the Istanbul patriarch. The document stipulated that both groups of Armenians must obey it.[8] It also included articles on a protectoral committee that was to be formed to superintend existing or prospective Armenian schools throughout Europe.[9] All of this was removed from the final, state-approved version, in which the Community Administration was responsible only for the Armenians in existing Ottoman territory.[10] The jurisdiction of the Community Administration was thus limited to the existing political territory of the empire, separating it theoretically from that of the patriarch, who maintained his ecclesiastical jurisdiction over those who had emigrated or those living in former Ottoman territories.

This trend affected the stipulations in the Constitution on the Ottoman Armenians' relationship with the Catholicosate of Echmiadzin. In the 1857 draft, six articles mention the catholicos: four of these refer explicitly to the catholicos of Echmiadzin, while the others merely call him the catholicos.[11] Two of the six articles specify the relationship between the patriarch of Istanbul and the catholicos of Echmiadzin: Article Four states that the Istanbul patriarch is to be ranked next to the Echmiadzin catholicos, and Article Five stipulates that the Istanbul patriarch must be a bishop ordained by the Echmiadzin catholicos. Furthermore, Articles Nineteen and Twenty state that any highly significant religious issues that the ecclesiastical council in Istanbul cannot handle must be entrusted to the Echmiadzin catholicos and the Echmiadzin Synod. In the 1860 version of the Constitution, mentions of the catholicos were reduced to four: one merely mentioned the name catholicos, another mentioned the catholicos of Echmiadzin explicitly and the remaining two used the phrase 'the mother seat of Ararat', an indirect expression used to refer to the Catholicosate of Echmiadzin.[12] In the final, state-approved version, there were only two references to the catholicos.[13] Article Twenty-Nine concerned the means of approaching highly significant religious issues, but it avoided naming Echmiadzin, and Article Sixty-One stipulated that the General Assembly would be convened for the election of the catholicos, again avoiding a direct mention of Echmiadzin. We can conclude that Muslim state officials were reluctant to specifically determine the relationship between the Istanbul Patriarchate and a religious authority within Russian territory. The preference was for non-Muslims to deal domestically with their religious affairs.

In spite of these changes, the order of the grand vizier that approved the Armenian National Constitution only stated that some parts of the draft on 'purely secular affairs' (*sırf umur-ı dünyeviye*) had been modified during the revision process.[14] This expression must have been chosen with care by Muslim state officials to emphasise their lack of intervention into the religious affairs of non-Muslims as part of the existing separation of the concerns of non-Muslim communities into religious and secular ones. Although non-intervention into religious affairs was a guiding principle in the relationship between the Ottoman government and non-Muslim communities, Muslim state officials recognised the necessity of intervening in their relationship with religious authorities located in foreign countries, and for this purpose they probably relied on the intermediary work of Armenian state officials.

Religious Authorities within Ottoman Territory

The relationship between the Community Administration and the religious authorities whose seats were within Ottoman territory had even greater importance for the Armenian elites in Istanbul. They worked to obtain government recognition of the centrality of Istanbul within the Armenian community by including stipulations regarding the other authorities in the National Constitution.

According to Ahmet Cevdet Pasha, who participated in the revision of the Armenian National Constitution, the Armenian members of the revision committee wanted to include articles on the election of the Sis catholicos.[15] Since 1731, the Achbahian family had enjoyed hereditary rights to the Sis Catholicosate, with the approval of the Ottoman government. This family's close relationship with the Kozanoğlus, who controlled the region where the catholicosate was located, allowed the Achbahians to keep hold of their power.[16] Intending to subordinate the catholicosate to the Community Administration of Istanbul, the committee members demanded that the privileges granted to the Achbahian family be abolished and that the Constitution state outright that the Sis catholicos would be elected through a 'general election' (that is, by the General Assembly, convened in Istanbul). This proposal was set aside as impracticable because the Kozan region was not directly subject to the central government; the government had only taken over the area militarily in 1865.[17]

Another target for the drafters was the Patriarchate of Jerusalem, which had first been established by the Mamluks in the fourteenth century and was approved by the Ottomans after the city was conquered.[18] The presence of a patriarch in the Holy City conferred distinction and prestige on the Armenian Church relative to other Christian denominations, and this was all the more significant in the context of the ongoing competition between the Armenians and the missionary work of the Catholic and Protestant denominations. Subordinating this patriarchate to Istanbul would be a financial victory because it enjoyed extensive income from the pilgrimages undertaken to Jerusalem by Armenians from all over the world.[19]

Although the Patriarchates of Istanbul and Jerusalem were equal within the hierarchy of the Armenian Church, the transformation of the administrative centre liberated Armenian elites in Istanbul from this ecclesiastical tradition. In the early 1860s, Istanbul Armenians formed a committee to draft regulations for the Jerusalem Patriarchate. In February 1861, the draft was in the course of being presented to the assembly when news reached Istanbul of the death of Jerusalem's patriarch, and the Armenian elites in Istanbul hastened to enact regulations to ensure that the next patriarch would be elected following their agenda.[20] Serovpe Vichenian was a leading figure in this movement.

The regulations contained forty-two articles, including stipulations for the administration of Jerusalem's monastery and the election of the patriarch.[21] Some articles also dealt with the relationship between the Jerusalem Patriarchate and the Community Administration in Istanbul. For example, Article Twelve stated that the Jerusalem Patriarchate was required to obtain permission from the Community Administration before disposing of its own property. Article Thirty-Eight indicated that the Community Administration had the right to choose the Jerusalem patriarch from candidates proposed by the Jerusalem Patriarchate. After the draft was read, the members of the assembly also discussed whether it would be necessary to add stipulations on financial aid from the Jerusalem Patriarchate to Istanbul.

Because the draft was intended to subordinate the Jerusalem Patriarchate to the Community Administration, those in the assembly who represented Jerusalem were reluctant to approve it. For example, the representatives for Jerusalem's monks opposed the stipulations on financial aid, saying that the Armenian nation (*azk*) was present not only in the Ottoman Empire but also in Russia, Iran and India and that all Armenians had right of access to the Jerusalem monastery; therefore, the disposal of its property was not a matter for the Community Administration alone but the global Armenian community. Vichenian, as chair, responded that the assembly represented the majority of the Armenian nation (more than half of the world's Armenian population lived in the Ottoman Empire), and its decisions were therefore those of all Armenians. However, most assembly members did not approve of Vichenian's heavy-handed approach. The stipulations on financial aid from the Jerusalem monastery did not pass.[22]

Seeing the opposition from the Jerusalem contingent, Vichenian proposed to first elect the Jerusalem patriarch and only then enact new regulations. The assembly members voted and chose three candidates. However, some objected to these because none had a relationship with the Jerusalem monastery. Thus, the election of the patriarch and the enactment of regulations reached a deadlock.[23]

In the meantime, the Armenian members of the revision committee succeeded in inserting articles into the Constitution on the Jerusalem Patriarchate, the final version of which had seven articles on the topic.[24] Article Seventeen defined the status of the Jerusalem patriarch as the head of the St James Monastery, and Articles Eighteen and Nineteen stipulated that the monastery and the lay and ecclesiastical councils of Istanbul had the right to impeach him. In case of impeachment, the General Assembly of Istanbul would decide on the punishment. The other articles specified the method by which the Jerusalem patriarch should be elected: first, the Jerusalem monastery would choose seven candidates from among its bishops and *vartabed*s. Second, the lay and ecclesiastical councils in Istanbul would jointly choose three of the seven candidates. Finally, the General Assembly would elect the Jerusalem patriarch from among the latter three. The Constitution, with the approval of the government, thus subordinated the patriarchate to the Community Administration of Istanbul.

A Change of Climate

After the government's approval of the National Constitution, the General Assembly elected a Jerusalem patriarch, Esayi, in August 1864.[25] On 3 March 1865, the assembly returned to the discussion of regulations for the patriarchate, which had been suspended until the election. Patriarch Esayi also participated in this conversation, beginning with the second session on 9 March.

The government's approval of the Constitution – and therefore of the subordination of the Jerusalem Patriarchate to the Community Administration – must have changed the perspective of the assembly's members, who discussed the draft regulations article by article and voted on each. In 1861, they had hesitated to support Vichenian's heavy-handedness when he insisted on subordinating Jerusalem to Istanbul. In 1865, however, the assembly leaned towards supporting the clauses that upheld this subordination. It was decided that the newly elected candidate for the Patriarchate of Jerusalem would take his oath of assumption before the General Assembly rather than in Jerusalem itself. Moreover, they voted that the administrative council in Jerusalem would entrust the Community Administration with any matters that it could not resolve. Furthermore, the assembly decided that the curriculum of the ecclesiastical college in Jerusalem would be created by the local monastery but would require the approval of both the ecclesiastical council and the educational committee of Istanbul.[26]

The draft described the relationship between Istanbul and Jerusalem not as one between two equal patriarchates but as one between the newly formed Community Administration and a subordinated religious authority. Patriarch Esayi, understandably, resisted this. He engaged in a rather heated argument with Nerses Varjabedian, an ecclesiastical member of the assembly and an active participant in communal politics.[27] It is likely that Varjabedian had a favourable relationship with Vichenian, who would support him in his ill-fated 1869 bid for the Istanbul Patriarchate. Varjabedian eventually won the election in 1874 and remained patriarch for ten years.[28] His argument with Esayi demonstrates the need that the lay elites of the Armenian community had for ecclesiastical allies in their treatment of opposing clerical members.

A proposal made by a lay member on 24 March began the discussion.[29] In the Armenian Church, the catholicoi have the exclusive authority to ordain bishops. Because the Patriarchates of Istanbul and Jerusalem were both under the religious jurisdiction of the Echmiadzin catholicos, candidates for bishoprics within these two patriarchates were ordained in Echmiadzin. The lay member proposed that when a clergyman obtained permission from the Jerusalem Patriarchate to be ordained as a bishop, he should have to obtain approval from the Community Administration as well. Esayi resisted, citing Jerusalem's independence and saying that it could not submit to the jurisdiction of another, as it was a patriarchate and thus an apostolic seat. Varjabedian responded that the Ankara diocese was also an apostolic seat, but it was nevertheless under Istanbul's jurisdiction. He added that while the Jerusalem Patriarchate was established by 'the order of the Egyptian Sultan' in 1311, the Istanbul Patriarchate had been established by 'the order of Sultan Mehmet the Conqueror', implying that Istanbul was superior to Jerusalem on these grounds. Esayi, however, pursued the question more directly, asking whether Varjabedian meant to imply that the Istanbul Patriarchate was more honourable, as it had been established by Mehmet II. Varjabedian avoided giving a direct response, instead saying that 'The Armenian Church of Turkey accepted the patriarch of Istanbul as its head'.[30] Then, he added that there were more than sixty dioceses under the jurisdiction of the Istanbul Patriarchate, again appearing to suggest its superiority. In response, Esayi provocatively asked whether the Jerusalem Patriarchate was Apostolic or Islamic (*Mahmedagan*), suggesting that the ranks of the patriarchates should be determined according to ecclesiastical tradition rather than the political decisions of Muslim monarchs. His remark threw the assembly into an uproar.

Esayi called for laymen to exclude themselves from religious affairs, aiming to turn the discussion in his favour. He insisted that the ecclesiastical council resolve problems related to religious authority, suggesting that the General Assembly – which included some clergymen but was mainly composed of laymen – had no authority over religious issues. Agreeing that clergymen had exclusive authority over religious affairs, Varjabedian admitted that a final decision on religious questions should be reserved for the bishops. He added, however, that all the Armenians belonging to the Church of the Illuminator, especially the General Assembly, which represented the community of the Armenians, had the right to deliberate on, discuss and make proposals regarding religious affairs.[31] He thus justified the intervention of the General Assembly into religious affairs based on the principle of representation.

Although the General Assembly reached no decision on the ordainment of bishops, the chairman requested that Esayi swear to comply with the new regulations for the Jerusalem Patriarchate. Esayi here mounted his final resistance, claiming that he could swear to uphold the Armenian National Constitution but not these regulations. Although the Constitution, like the regulations, stipulated the subordination of the Jerusalem Patriarchate to the Community Administration, Esayi could not take a stance against a document that the Ottoman government had approved. Continuing to discuss the regulations, the Istanbul side chose to detain Esayi, who wished to return to Jerusalem before Easter to be able to fulfil his religious duties as patriarch. During the next session, on 31 March, the General Assembly attempted to force Esayi to swear by adding a policy directly unfavourable to him to the regulations.[32] This stated that when a clergyman obtained a certificate from the Jerusalem Patriarchate to be ordained as bishop, it must be sent to the Echmiadzin catholicos through the Istanbul patriarch. Esayi realised that his further resistance would only make matters worse and took the oath to introduce and uphold the regulations on Jerusalem.

Political Intervention

The momentum created by the state's approval of the Constitution led leading figures in the Armenian community to consider the time ripe to deal with two long-standing, significant issues: Istanbul's relationship with the catholicosates and the plight of the Armenians in the provinces. This movement, however, provoked a direct intervention by Mehmet Emin Ali Pasha, the most influential Ottoman statesman of the 1860s.

The Ottoman government kept a cautious eye on the relationship between their Armenian subjects and the Catholicosate of Echmiadzin after its incorporation into the Russian Empire. This religious authority could potentially be used by the Russians as a political tool to earn support from Armenians outside Russian territory. Russia's defeat in the Crimean War moved it towards an emphasis on soft power.[33] When the

Echmiadzin catholicos died in 1857, Aleksandr Baryatinsky, the governor of the Caucasus, strongly supported choosing a successor who would have influence over Ottoman Armenians.[34] Madteos, the former patriarch of Istanbul who had led the drive to restore the relationship between the Istanbul Patriarchate and the Echmiadzin Catholicosate, was then elected catholicos of Echmiadzin.[35] According to Gerasimos Augustinos, Russian agents persuaded Orthodox and Armenian Christians in the Ottoman Pontus to emigrate to Russian territory, promising a better life.[36] Margos Aghapekian wrote in 1865 that Baryatinsky sent Russian Armenians to influence the Ottoman Armenians living in the eastern provinces.[37] This claim is supported by Ottoman archival documents: reports in 1863 note that Armenians were emigrating (or trying to emigrate) from the eastern Ottoman provinces to the Russian Caucasus.[38] Because the Istanbul Patriarchate and the Community Administration took political responsibility for the deeds of Ottoman Armenians, Armenian elites in Istanbul in the 1860s could not simply avoid a relationship with the Echmiadzin catholicos and Russian Armenians. After the catholicosate alerted the lay and ecclesiastical councils of Istanbul to the death of Catholicos Madteos in 1865 and the election of a new catholicos, Istanbul Armenians were forced to address this delicate issue.[39]

The General Assembly served as the venue of discussion. The National Constitution stipulated that the General Assembly would be convened to participate in the election of a catholicos without mentioning the form that this participation would take.[40] On 5 January 1866, letters from the Echmiadzin Catholicosate to the lay and ecclesiastical councils of Istanbul were read aloud in the General Assembly. Sdepan Aslanian commented on the differences in the legal frameworks that existed for Russian and Ottoman Armenians. In 1836, the Russian Empire had enacted a statute governing the Armenian Church in a manner similar to other non-dominant religious groups. This statute stipulated that each diocese around the world would choose an ecclesiastical and a lay deputy, and the body composed of these deputies would propose two candidates for the catholicosate, leaving the final decision to the tsar.[41] Aslanian noted that the Echmiadzin Catholicosate intended to select a catholicos in accordance with this rule. Accordingly, the catholicosate asked Ottoman Armenians to participate in the election, not within the General Assembly but by sending an ecclesiastical and a lay deputy from each diocese. However, the Armenian National Constitution stipulated that the Ottoman Armenians had to participate through the General Assembly. Thus, Aslanian proposed that a committee be formed to investigate the present state of the catholicosate, its electoral legislation and traditions and the methods by which Ottoman Armenians could participate in it. The General Assembly approved this proposal, and a committee was formed.[42] While the committee was investigating the Echmiadzin Catholicosate, Ali Pasha, then the foreign minister, staged an intervention in non-Muslim communal affairs.

On 13 March 1866, Ali Pasha sent an order prohibiting non-Muslim religious authorities in Istanbul from submitting *takrir*s (official reports that non-Muslim religious authorities submitted to the Ottoman government) about non-religious situations, a move intended to consolidate state control over non-Muslims' communal affairs. A follow-up letter was sent to the Armenian Patriarchate on 1 April concerning the administration of the Armenian community alone.[43] This second order entirely suspended the Armenian Constitution and assigned the role of community leadership to a temporary council.[44] Developments in non-Muslim communities must have alarmed Ali Pasha enough to inspire this move, including the recent request by the Bulgarians for the creation of a Bulgarian Orthodox Church that was independent of the ecumenical patriarchate.[45] At the same time, as I have just noted, the Armenian elites in Istanbul were attempting to intervene in the election of a religious authority within the Russian Empire. Both or either of these developments might have given the Russian Empire a pretext to intervene in Ottoman internal affairs. Ali Pasha's orders were therefore to prevent significant international ramifications.

According to Maghakia Ormanian's *Azkabadum*, Ali Pasha also invited the leading figures of the Armenian community to his home for a discussion.[46] The ostensible topic was the stagnation of Armenian communal administration. By 1865, most members of the lay council had resigned for unspecified reasons, leading to months of dysfunction. Moreover, Istanbul patriarch Boghos had announced his intention to resign on 16 March, soon after Ali Pasha's prohibition of non-religious *takrir*s. In response to Ali Pasha's questioning about the state of the Armenian community, the Armenians replied that certain points in the National Constitution were causing dysfunction in the Community Administration, adding that the Constitution required revision. Although Ali Pasha refused to accept the patriarch's resignation, he permitted the Constitution to be revised, deciding to form two councils. The first was tasked with revising the Constitution, and the other – the 'mixed council' – was to be temporarily given the roles of both the lay and ecclesiastical councils until the end of the revision period.

Ali Pasha's choice suggests that he hoped to consolidate state control over the Armenian community by empowering the Armenians who were employed by the state. The council for revision had three ecclesiastical and eight lay members. Most of the lay members had close relationships with the government, including Serovpe Vichenian, Sdepan Aslanian and

Krikor Aghaton. The mixed council, meanwhile, had the same number of ecclesiastics and only six lay members. Among the latter were two state officials and three *sarrafs*. Krikor Margosian, a state official, was appointed chairman. Ali Pasha also allowed the Armenians to retain their General Assembly but required that it ask the permission of both the government and the council for revision each time it wanted to convene.[47]

Sending an Ottoman Candidate to Echmiadzin

Despite Ali Pasha's intervention, the leading figures of the Armenian community did not give up their involvement in the election of the Echmiadzin catholicos. Under the strict surveillance of the government, the General Assembly received a report on the catholicosate in June 1866.[48] The report had four sections. The first three related to the proposal of Sdepan Aslanian (that is, reporting on the present situation of the Echmiadzin Catholicosate, the procedures governing elections and prospective methods of participation open to Ottoman Armenians). From this report, it is clear that the committee that prepared the report wished to justify the participation of Ottoman Armenians in the election of the Echmiadzin catholicos to the Ottoman government. It did so by highlighting the potential undesirable effects of Russian control over the Armenian Church and emphatically defining the catholicos as a religious authority.

The first section criticised the present situation of the catholicosate. The committee argued that the catholicos of Echmiadzin had lost its jurisdiction over the entire Armenian Church and for thirty years had merely had 'the name of the Catholicosate of all Armenians' (*amenayn Hayots' Gat'oghigosut'ean anunĕ*). It attributed this to the statute that had been enacted by the Russian Empire in 1836, specifically discussing how this was opposed to the independence and tradition of the Armenian Church.[49] The second section analysed the elections of catholicoi that had taken place in the past. It discussed the statute for the election of catholicoi and pointed out problems with it. The committee then examined the two elections that had followed the Russian incorporation of the Echmiadzin Catholicosate and concluded that neither had been conducted in accordance with the statute, implying that the next election might not be, either.

The committee further examined the traditions and customs of the Armenian Church before Russian incorporation. It noted two principles that the Armenian Church had customarily employed in the election of catholicoi: the participation of the entire Armenian nation (including both clergymen and laymen) and the non-intervention of non-Armenians. While the committee discussed these principles, which were advantageous to Ottoman Armenians, it did not avoid mentioning that in practice they had not always been observed: some catholicoi had been designated by their predecessors, others had been elected by clergymen alone and still others had been chosen by non-Armenian monarchs. Because neither the present state of the catholicosate nor the regulations for the election of catholicoi were in accordance with any of their basic principles, the committee concluded that it was necessary to restore the old laws and traditions of the Armenian Church.[50] Therefore, the committee proposed a method for electing the Echmiadzin catholicos in the third section of their report. The committee asserted two premises: first, as the catholicos was a religious authority, he should be nationally (*azkovin*) elected, as 'the general Patriarch and the Spiritual Lord of all Armenians';[51] second, the election should be held in Echmiadzin because it was 'the centre of the spiritual unity of Armenians'.[52]

The committee went on to discuss how Ottoman Armenians should participate in the election. Although it criticised Russian rule and the legal restrictions that the Russian Empire had imposed on the Armenian Church, the committee proposed a method that satisfied both the Russian legal stipulations and the Ottoman Armenian Constitution: Ottoman Armenians would participate in the election as a single entity represented by the General Assembly, who would choose three candidates from a list drawn up by clergymen in Istanbul. To satisfy the stipulation of the statute that every Armenian diocese send an ecclesiastical and a lay deputy to vote, the committee proposed that the Ottoman Armenians combine all the votes of the sixty-five dioceses under Ottoman rule in favour of the results of the General Assembly. Thus, the General Assembly would choose a single pair of ecclesiastical and lay deputies and send them to Echmiadzin to cast sixty-five votes each for the candidates selected by the General Assembly. The deputies would also deliver an official document from the General Assembly to the catholicosate, presenting the names of the three candidates selected and the fact that the assembly was entrusting 130 votes to them.[53] The statute allowed the Armenians to choose two candidates for the catholicosate and left the final decision to the tsar, but the method that the committee proposed would allow the Ottoman Armenians to dominate the election of the candidates because there were more Armenian dioceses in the Ottoman Empire than in any other territory. The General Assembly approved the proposal as presented.

In August, the General Assembly selected their three candidates. Following the committee's method went smoothly. According to Paul Werth, the 'Russian emperor was reluctant not to confirm the candidate who received [the] most votes', not wanting to alienate the Ottoman

Armenians. Werth observes that 'one may say that the election of the catholicos happened as much in Constantinople as it did in Echmiadzin, with Armenians outside the Ottoman capital playing a limited role at most'.[54] Keork, a former patriarch of Istanbul who received the most votes from the General Assembly, was elected catholicos.[55] The Ottoman Armenians' successful intervention in the selection of the leadership for the Echmiadzin Catholicosate led the assembly members to begin discussion of the future of the other catholicosates.

Istanbul, Sis and Echmiadzin

After the Russian incorporation of the Echmiadzin Catholicosate, the Sis Catholicosate, which was in Ottoman territory, assumed an outsized political importance and complexity. It was a card up the sleeve of the Ottoman Armenians in their negotiations with the Russian Armenians and the Russian Empire more generally. The Ottoman Armenians were able to imply that they had an alternative catholicosate and could even sever their relationship with Echmiadzin whenever they considered untoward influence was being exerted from the Russian side. This attitude was effective as long as the Russian Empire wished to have the support of Ottoman Armenians through the Echmiadzin Catholicosate. High-ranking Muslim state officials of the Ottoman Empire would have preferred, meanwhile, to subordinate Ottoman Armenians to the Sis Catholicosate and break their dependency on a religious authority under Russian rule.

For the Istanbul Armenians, the jurisdiction of the Sis Catholicosate seemed a weak defence against Catholic missionaries. Within Ottoman territory, the missionaries were relatively more active in Greater Syria, which was adjacent to Sis Catholicosate jurisdiction. In the mid-eighteenth century, the archbishop of the Armenian Catholics in these regions visited Rome and was certified by the pope as patriarch without the approval of the Ottoman government.[56] In 1867 and 1871, several members of the General Assembly asserted the necessity of mounting a response to the ongoing missionary work in the area.[57] The Armenian elites in Istanbul considered it crucial to place the Sis Catholicosate under the direct control of the Community Administration in Istanbul.

In 1865, several further developments brought the issue of the Sis Catholicosate to the forefront of discussions among Armenian elites. The Ottoman central government removed the Kozanoğlus from power and placed south-central Anatolia, where the catholicosate was located, under direct state control.[58] The institution of the catholicoi was already drawing the attention of Armenian elites in Istanbul due to the discussion of the

Echmiadzin Catholicosate mentioned above. Moreover, the catholicos of Sis died during the same year. Taking this opportunity, Armenian elites in Istanbul intervened in the selection of the next catholicos, with the intention of ending the Achbahian family's monopoly over the catholicosate and subordinating it and its jurisdiction to Istanbul. To achieve this, they appointed the bishop of nearby Ayntab as Istanbul's deputy and, under his superintendence, ordered the Armenians in the Sis Catholicosate to elect a new catholicos. This divided them: the majority took the side of Istanbul, but a minority, including the Achbahians, secretly had Nigoghayos (whose mother was an Achbahian) installed to protect their hereditary rights.[59]

The response from Muslim state officials might have been favourable to the Achbahian faction. After the Kozan region was placed under their direct control, they encouraged Istanbul Armenians to make the Sis Catholicosate their supreme religious authority, rather than the Echmiadzin Catholicosate. To encourage this alteration, they augmented the authority of the Sis Catholicosate, donating 500,000 *kuruş* for its restoration and soliciting funds from Armenian elites as well. Nevertheless, the Armenian elites in Istanbul preferred to be subordinated to Echmiadzin, concluding that the pre-eminence of the Sis Catholicosate might lead to a challenge to Istanbul's superiority among Ottoman Armenians. Further, they did not approve of Nigoghayos as the catholicos, which created more antagonism between the Armenian elites in Istanbul and the Sis Catholicosate.[60]

When the clergy met to select candidates for the Echmiadzin Catholicosate in Istanbul, the conversation went further, concluding with the decision that the incumbent catholicoi of Aghtamar and Sis were illegitimate. The report of this meeting stated that the provincial council of Van accused Khachadur, catholicos of Aghtamar, of murdering his predecessor. Nigoghayos, meanwhile, had been ordained by a bishop who was alleged to have been Catholic. Hearing this report, the General Assembly voted to approve the decisions of the clerical meeting, declaring the two catholicosates were vacant.[61] The two suspect catholicoi were summoned to Istanbul.[62]

Nigoghayos went to Istanbul and filed a protest that was read before the General Assembly in February 1867. He claimed that the Armenians under the jurisdiction of the Sis Catholicosate did not approve of the deputy that the Istanbul Armenians had appointed, and they had asked Nigoghayos to assume the catholicosate. He did so in response to their appeal, claiming that he had popular support.[63] The General Assembly did not accept this explanation. In its March 1867 session, the General Assembly discussed what to do with the two catholicosates. Interestingly, Sdepan Aslanian proposed that the issue be referred to the Echmiadzin Catholicosate. This proposal was grounded in the aforementioned stipulation of the National

Constitution that highly significant religious issues that were beyond the scope of the ecclesiastical council in Istanbul should be entrusted to the catholicosate. However, the majority did not agree to this idea. The assembly thus decided to form a committee composed of four clergymen and four laymen to investigate how two catholicoi would be elected and to once and for all determine the relationship between the Community Administration in Istanbul and the three catholicosates. The committee, however, failed to achieve its goal because some members resigned for unknown reasons.[64]

Echmiadzin's Move

In 1868, the behaviour of a bishop invited an intervention from the Catholicosate of Echmiadzin. According to *Manzume-i Efkar*, when Nigoghayos visited the city of Tekirdağ on his return to Sis, the bishop of Tekirdağ treated him as a legitimate catholicos, opposing the decision of the General Assembly. This act must have been sufficient to sow doubt among the clergy at Echmiadzin, although the Istanbul patriarch soon summoned the bishop to Istanbul and petitioned the government to order the Aleppo province to prevent Sis Armenians from treating Nigoghayos as a legitimate catholicos.[65] Three weeks after this incident, Echmiadzin Catholicos Keork dispatched Bishop Sarkis Jalalian to Istanbul.

Jalalian arrived at Istanbul in September. He was a leading clerical figure for the Armenians in the Russian Empire: his name was at the top of the list of members of the monastery and education committees that Keork had created to improve the standing of Russian Armenians.[66] *Manzume-i Efkar* reported that he brought letters to the mixed council, the General Assembly, the grand vizier and the minister of foreign affairs from Keork, who had built relationships with the Muslim state officials of the Ottoman Empire during his tenure as Istanbul patriarch.[67] Unlike the nuncios periodically dispatched by the Echmiadzin Catholicosate to Armenian churches in the Ottoman Empire to deliver consecrated oil, Jalalian was not a temporary visitor. According to *Daily Masis*, Keork wrote that he had dispatched Jalalian to be Echmiadzin's representative stationed in Istanbul to deal with ecclesiastical affairs and the relationship between the Echmiadzin Catholicosate and the Armenians in the Ottoman Empire.[68]

Jalalian's visit attracted the attention of the Istanbul Armenians. According to a newspaper article published ten to fifteen days after his arrival, nearly all Armenians were talking about his arrival.[69] *Masis* reported the rumour that Jalalian had been dispatched to Istanbul to superintend a boarding school that the Echmiadzin Catholicosate was planning to build in Beyoğlu.[70] Jalalian was also allowed to deliver a sermon at the church in Kumkapı and visit the mixed council to present the letter from Keork.[71] *Manzume-i Efkar* suggested that the Istanbul Armenians received Jalalian favourably, writing that notable Armenian merchants in Istanbul paid official visits to him and that certain artisans were planning to do the same.[72] The Ottoman government displayed a cautious attitude in response to his application to visit the Sublime Porte to deliver the letters for the grand vizier and the foreign minister. In mid-October, Armenian newspapers reported that Jalalian's visit to the Sublime Porte, which had been planned for 13 October, was to be postponed until the grand vizier – now the aforementioned Ali Pasha – issued an invitation.[73] In late October, Armenian newspapers wrote that Jalalian had visited Grand Vizier Ali Pasha at home and delivered a letter to him. Jalalian spoke with Ali Pasha for twenty minutes, and the latter stated that he would respond to the letter later.[74] Jalalian also visited the home of acting Foreign Minister Safvet Pasha.[75]

Safvet Pasha replied to the catholicos' letter on behalf of the Sublime Porte and expressed disapproval of Jalalian's mission in Istanbul. *Manzume-i Efkar*, which was usually published in Armeno-Turkish, printed Safvet's reply in Armenian. Because the letter had clearly been written by someone with knowledge of the Armenian Church, one or several Armenians – probably colleagues of Safvet Pasha in the Ministry of Foreign Affairs – composed the letter in Armenian. At the very least, Safvet Pasha may have composed it with their help in Turkish or French and then had them translate it. The letter stressed that all religions, including the Illuminator's Armenian religion (*lusaworch'agan Hay grōn*), enjoyed freedom within the Ottoman Empire, adding that the catholicos himself must be well aware of this from his experience as patriarch of Istanbul. Assuming that the Russian Empire stood behind the catholicos, Safvet Pasha wrote that there was no need to remind him that no danger would threaten the rights of any Christian church in the Ottoman Empire. He said that this principle would always be 'the basis of internal politics of the state' (*Dērut'ean nerk'in k'aghak'aganut'ean himě*), thereby asserting a boundary against Russian interference in domestic Ottoman affairs.[76]

Safvet Pasha's reply once again demonstrates that high-ranking officials were inclined to deal domestically with the religious affairs of non-Muslims. Safvet Pasha justified his refusal to permit Jalalian's stay in Istanbul by calling it inappropriate and taking the point of view not of the Ottoman state but the Armenian community. First, he said that the duties of a representative of the Echmiadzin catholicos in Istanbul – which could only be to superintend the religious affairs of Ottoman Armenians – would overlap with those of the Istanbul patriarch. Second, he noted that it was unheard of to station a representative of the Echmiadzin catholicos in Istanbul. Previous catholicoi had dispatched nuncios to the Ottoman Empire, but they were merely sent to deliver consecrated oil and then quickly returned to Russia. Therefore, Safvet argued, even Jalalian's 'short presence [in the Ottoman Empire] was not free from inappropriateness' and would invite the complaints 'of the [Armenian] nation' (*azkin*). Tradition demanded that the Echmiadzin Catholicosate would send only consecrated oil, ecclesiastical decrees and the blessings of Grigor the Holy Illuminator. Thus, on behalf of the Sublime Porte, Safvet Pasha asserted that the Porte would not permit Jalalian's stay in Istanbul and that the local patriarch would continue to be the only representative of the Armenian Church in Istanbul.[77] His response suggests that high-ranking Ottoman officials believed the Russian Empire to be playing a game of political interference with a religious guise. The Crimean War had awakened the Ottomans to the dangers of such interference. The religious affairs of non-Muslims had a highly political meaning, and the distinction between the religious and the political was a focal point in the reception of Jalalian.

A few days after this reply, Catholicos Keork ordered Jalalian to make an official inquiry of the Istanbul patriarch. This inquiry, consisting of two questions, shows that the main reason for the mission was suspicion of Nigoghayos's movements. First, it was asked whether Nigoghayos, the dubious catholicos of Sis, had truly added a bejewelled cross to his hood. This was not customary, in either an ecclesiastical or a national sense, and it was a privilege granted to none but the catholicos of Echmiadzin by the Russian emperor. The text further asked that if Nigoghayos had worn the cross, then by whose order and according to which privileges was he allowed to do so. The second question also asked whether the bishop of Tekirdağ had truly treated Nigoghayos as a legitimate catholicos.[78] These questions seem to have gone unanswered.

After Jalalian's meeting with Ali Pasha, *Masis* noted that Istanbul Armenians did not need to inquire whether the government would accept Jalalian's stay in Istanbul, as his duties had no relationship with politics (*k'aghak'ganut'ean hed pnaw haraperut'iwn ch'uni*).[79] The newspaper emphasised that his duty was merely religious, as it consisted of superintending the reformation and development of the Armenian Church as the representative of the catholicos. *Masis* added that it had been a longstanding custom for catholicoi to dispatch nuncios to distant countries to console the flock. According to this article, the only difference between Jalalian and previous nuncios was the length of his stay, which, as discussed above, was the basis for Safvet Pasha's rejection of his presence.

Oksen Khojasarian, a journalist and an active participant in community politics, carefully used the language of religion and politics in his discussion of the Jalalian issue.[80] He argued that there could be no national affair concerning the Armenians in the Ottoman Empire that was not related to the Echmiadzin catholicos because all Armenian affairs – including those related to monasteries, churches, hospitals and schools – were 'sacred' (*nuiragan*) and religious and thus under the superintendence of the catholicos, the supreme authority. Khojasarian rhetorically asked who had overseen the national affairs of Ottoman Armenians until the present time. The answer, he said, was the local bishops, who had been ordained by catholicoi and who had handled such affairs in their jurisdictions. Nevertheless, the catholicoi did not grant any documentation to bishops in the Ottoman Empire: both the patriarch and the bishops had political charters of investiture (*k'aghak'agan bērat'*) from the Ottoman government. Thus, the patriarch and bishops were ecclesiastical officials when regarded individually but political officials in terms of their duty. This naturally led to the conclusion that the catholicosate in fact had no agents at all in the Ottoman Empire, and that this was causing confusion for the Armenian Church.

Demonstration

A week after Jalalian's inquiry, the bishops in Istanbul attempted to visit Patriarch Boghos but did not find him at the patriarchate. *Masis* reported that they had intended to criticise his response to recent religious problems, including the inquiries, the treatment of Nigoghayos and his response to the invitation of the pope to the ecumenical council that was planned for 1869 in the Vatican.[81] They held that Boghos was obligated to discuss these issues with the ecclesiastical members of the mixed council but had neglected to do so.[82]

After this publication, an anti-Boghos movement sprang up among Istanbul Armenians. According to a state document composed later, Jalalian's supporters expressed suspicion of Boghos.[83] This popular pressure caused Boghos to present his resignation to the government, which did not give a prompt response. The movement swelled on 10 January 1869, when some Armenians held anti-Boghos demonstrations at various churches in Istanbul by abstaining from the customary utterance of the incumbent patriarch's name during mass. This demonstration prompted a request to the Ottoman government – probably from the patriarchate – for intervention. Rumours spread that Jalalian was behind the demonstrations, and it was claimed that his supporters were planning to elect him patriarch of Istanbul after Boghos's resignation. The chief of public security summoned several Armenians who were thought to be behind the demonstration. Among these were the editors of three Armenian newspapers, *Manzume-i Efkar*, *Jamanag* and *Punch* (*Root*).[84]

Garabed Panosian, the editor of *Manzume-i Efkar*, detailed his meeting with the chief of public security. He waited a long time to see the Chief Hüsni Pasha, who demanded that Panosian be respectful of the patriarch, saying:

> the thing called religion (*mezheb denilen şey*) is the bit in the mouths of humans, and if there were no religion, the bonds and comfort of human society would be lost. Therefore, there is an obligation to respect religious authorities (*reis-i mezhebler*).[85]

Although Panosian denied any involvement in the demonstrations, Hüsni Pasha did not believe him and demanded that Panosian offer a guarantor and a promise that he cause no further confusion. After Panosian published his report of this meeting, the government suspended publication of *Manzume-i Efkar* for two months according to a 'sublime decision' (*karar-ı ali*) issued in March 1867, which enabled the government to arbitrarily suppress political criticism in the newspapers of the Young Ottomans.[86]

High-ranking state officials were working to control the Armenian community by appointing a new mixed council. According to a rumour reported by *Manzume-i Efkar*, Ali Pasha did not accept the patriarch's resignation because he feared that Jalalian would be elected as his successor. *Manzume-i Efkar* printed another rumour, according to which all members of the new council would be *Efendi*s from the Sublime Porte (that is, Armenian state officials).[87] The government's order for the appointment included a list of members, 'who had loyalty, sagacity and integrity from the viewpoint of both state and community'.[88] Not all were state officials, but most of the lay members were officials, financiers and doctors with good relationships with high-ranking Muslim officials, including Krikor Odian, Serovpe Vichenian and Harutyun Dadian.

However, the appointment of a new mixed council did not appease the anti-Boghos movement. Several petitions that called for Boghos's resignation and had gathered many signatures were delivered to the mixed council. In early February, the government finally officially allowed the resignation to pass. In a document on the matter prepared by the Ottoman bureaucracy, the Jalalian issue was described in detail.[89] This repeated Safvet Pasha's argument, emphasising that the Istanbul patriarch oversaw the religious affairs of the Armenian community, and asserting that it was unprecedented for the Echmiadzin catholicos – a Russian subject – to interfere in how Ottoman Armenians governed their affairs. The document further criticised the Echmiadzin catholicos for sending Jalalian to Istanbul, saying that it was clear that these foreign subjects would later become 'tools of penetration' and 'mischievous means' wielded by their home country under the pretext of religious affairs if they were permitted to interfere in Armenian Ottoman religious affairs now. An explanation of the anti-Boghos movement was then given, which concluded that, although it was inappropriate to approve Boghos's resignation in response to an unlawful demonstration, the government had had no choice but to do so to prevent the movement from escalating.

Conclusion and Aftermath

With the support of the state recognition provided in the National Constitution, Armenian elites in Istanbul ventured to subordinate religious authorities outside Istanbul to the Community Administration. Their attempt to subordinate the Sis Catholicosate entangled them in difficulties in which the Echmiadzin Catholicosate, Russia and the Ottoman government were involved, and impressed Ottoman officials with a sense of the political complexity attached to non-Muslims' religious affairs. The trouble caused by Jalalian further demonstrates the complexity inherent in the relationship with the Sis Catholicosate. To achieve their goal, Armenian elites in Istanbul needed to deal with their relationship to the Echmiadzin Catholicosate at the same time.

After the resignation of Patriarch Boghos, an election was held to choose his successor. A candidate was elected in August 1869 but died before he could be confirmed. In the following election, the relationship between the two catholicosates once again became an issue. In the General Assembly, Serovpe Vichenian asked why the general meeting of clergymen – the body that prepared the list of candidates for the patriarchal seat – did not include Nerses Varjabedian in the list. Varjabedian had been ordained as bishop by the Sis catholicos, and Vichenian believed this was why the clergymen's general meeting considered him ineligible. Vichenian, who may have wanted to make Varjabedian a patriarch, argued that Varjabedian had been sent on a mission as an envoy to the Echmiadzin Catholicosate and had been treated as a bishop there. This showed that Echmiadzin accepted Varjabedian's legitimacy, indicating that he was indeed eligible for the Istanbul Patriarchate.[90]

Bishop Khoren, another active participant in communal politics, reported this to the Echmiadzin catholicos by telegram, hoping to bar Varjabedian's candidacy.[91] In the next session of the General Assembly, Krikor Odian read it aloud. This request for intervention from Echmiadzin threw the assembly into an uproar, and Odian then asserted that only esteemed figures should be proposed for candidacy for the patriarchate, adding that Varjabedian could not be qualified due to his young age. Instead, he proposed Mgrdich Khrimian as the right person for the position, and the assembly agreed, electing him.[92] Three months later, the assembly announced the restoration of the National Constitution, to which Odian had been a contributor.[93] Under the restored Constitution, the assembly then elected Odian as its chair. His influence in communal politics had grown substantially after his return from tenure as an official in the Danube province under the governorship of Midhat Pasha.

This chapter detailed how the transborder religious connections of Armenians took on political meaning and prompted Ottoman actors to frame their claims in a way that adopted the language of both politics and religion. The next chapter turns our attention to domestic issues where Istanbul Armenians and the Ottoman statesmen adopted the same terminology to negotiate the scope of their communal jurisdiction.

Notes

1. İbrahim Hakkı, *Hukuk-ı İdare*, 1st edition, vol. 1 (Istanbul: Karabet Matbaası, 1889/90), 297.
2. Fujinami, 'Sovereignty and Suzerainty'; Fujinami, 'First Ottoman History'; Kostopoulou, 'Armed Negotiations'; Özsu, 'Ottoman Empire'; Genell, 'Autonomous Provinces'.
3. *Azkayin Sahmanatrut'iwn* (1863), 9–12. Paradoxically, the religious privileges conferred on the patriarch of Istanbul by the Ottoman government authorised the existence and functioning of this administrative body. Due to this complexity, Armenians in Istanbul were not entirely aware of the structural changes that their administration had experienced. Armenians sometimes referred to the Community Administration as their administrative centre; at other times, they regarded the patriarchate as the centre following the old tradition.
4. Interestingly, the yearbooks of the Ottoman Empire adopted this ecclesiastical jurisdiction when recording lists of the dioceses supervised by each religious authority. See, for example, *Salname*, H1264 (1847/8), 95–101. The jurisdiction of the Sis Catholicosate generally covered south-central Anatolia, including the cities of Maraş, Ayntab, Adana and Aleppo. The jurisdiction of the Jerusalem Patriarchate included the greater Syria, Egypt and Cyprus.
5. BOA, İ.MVL 16736 (3 April 1857), art. 1.

6. We can find the provincial allotment of assembly seats at the end of the second draft of the Constitution printed by the press of Holy Saviour. *Azkayin Sahmanatrut'iwn* (1860).
7. Sanjian, *Armenian Communities in Syria*, 236–7; Antaramian, *Brokers of Faith*, chap. 3. I will spend little time here on the Catholicosate of Aghtamar because the Armenian elites in Istanbul themselves cared little about it and its jurisdiction was limited to Aghtamar Island. On this catholicosate in the nineteenth century, see Richard Edward Antaramian, 'In Subversive Service of the Sublime State: Armenians and Ottoman State Power, 1844–1896' (PhD diss., University of Michigan, 2014), 87–99.
8. BOA, İ.MVL 16736 (3 April 1857), arts. 4, 99.
9. Ibid., arts. 28–30. *Masis* wrote that this committee was to superintend an Armenian school in Paris, jurisdiction over which was a source of contention between the Armenians of the Armenian Church and Armenian Catholics. The Armenian elites in Istanbul included articles on Armenian schools in Europe in the first draft of 1857, intending to gain the upper hand over Armenian Catholics. *Masis*, no. 271 (15 April 1857); James Etmekjian, *The French Influence on the Western Armenian Renaissance 1843–1915* (New York: Twayne Publishers, 1964), 95, 112. The Muradian School was originally established in Padua, Italy in 1834 and was moved to Paris in 1846. Although its relation with the Mkhitarian Order of Armenian Catholics was well known, some sources from Armenian state officials suggest that Armenians belonging to the Armenian Church also attended this school. BOA, DH.SAİD.d 36/209 (Yervant Melkon), 103/321 (Yervant Horasan). The Muradian School was especially useful for Armenians who wanted to study in Paris. For example, Yervant Horasan, the son of a jeweller, first attended an Armenian school in his birth city of Istanbul before moving to Paris and studying at the Muradian School. Thereafter, he attended the École Centrale Paris, which enabled him to enter the state bureaucracy as an engineer after returning to the Ottoman Empire.
10. Unlike the Russians, who tried to take advantage of the religious network of the Echmiadzin Catholicosate, Ottoman political circles apparently did not intend to use the network of the Armenian Patriarchate in Istanbul in the same way.
11. BOA, İ.MVL 16736 (3 April 1857), arts. 1, 4, 5, 19, 20, 67.
12. *Azkayin Sahmanatrut'iwn* (1860), arts. 8, 12, 22, 115.
13. *Azkayin Sahmanatrut'iwn* (1863), arts. 29, 61.
14. Ibid., 8.
15. Cevdet, *Tezâkir 21–39*, 237–8; Cevdet, *Tezâkir 40–Tetimme*, ed. Cavid Baysun, 2nd edition (Ankara: Türk Tarih Kurumu Basımevi, 1986), 204. Cevdet Pasha's writings include a certain amount of knowledge on the history of the Armenian Church. He joined the Ottoman campaign against the Kozanoğlus in the 1860s, familiarising him with that region and its peoples. In addition, his service as the Minister of Justice and Religious

Affairs in the 1880s gained him further knowledge on the religious affairs of non-Muslims.

16. As Richard Antaramian has discussed in the case of Vartabed Boghos in Van, the inter-confessional relationship enabled non-Muslim clergymen to strengthen intra-confessional power. *Brokers of Faith*, 108–20.
17. Gould, 'Lords or Bandits', 494–9.
18. Sanjian, *Armenian Communities in Syria*, 95–9; Ercan, *Kudüs Ermeni Patrikhanesi*, 15–32.
19. In 1860, the lay council of Armenians in Istanbul requested a loan of 600,000 kuruş from the Patriarchate of Jerusalem. *Adenakrut'iwnk'* (16 April 1861), 43.
20. Ibid., 43.
21. *Adenakrut'iwnk'* (1 March 1861), 30–3.
22. Ibid., 34, 35. Although Vichenian claimed that the decision of the Community Administration (*azkayin varchut'iwn*) reflected the global will of all Armenians, he admitted that it was basically a representative entity not of the worldwide Armenian nation (*azk*) but only of those in the Ottoman Empire.
23. *Adenakrut'iwnk'* (24 July 1861), 69–72; Artinian, *Armenian Constitutional System*, 87.
24. *Azkayin Sahmanatrut'iwn* (1863), arts. 17–23.
25. *Adenakrut'iwnk'* (26 August 1864), 139–41.
26. *Adenakrut'iwnk'* (3 March 1865), 153–4; (9 March 1865), 162–4.
27. *Adenakrut'iwnk'* (24 March 1865), 197–8.
28. *Adenakrut'iwnk'* (9 September 1869), 391–8; (16 September 1869), 399–405; Ōrmanean, *Azkabadum*, vol. 3, 4077–80.
29. *Adenakrut'iwnk'* (24 March 1865), 199–201.
30. Armenians in the nineteenth century used *Dajig* to mean an Ottoman Muslim, mainly those who spoke Turkish, and *Dajgasdan* to mean the Ottoman Empire. The use of these terms corresponded with the terms 'Turk' and 'Turkey' (and their equivalents in French, German, etc.) used by contemporary Europeans. For example, Oksen Khojasarian called the Ottoman Balkans 'the European part of *Dajgasdan*' and Anatolia 'the Asian part of *Dajgasdan*'. *Adenakrut'iwnk'* (22 September 1876), 185–6.
31. Grigor the Illuminator is the patron saint of the Armenian Church and is believed to have converted Armenia to Christianity in 301 and become the first catholicos. The adjective form of the term 'Illuminator' was used to denote members of the Armenian Church and to differentiate them from Catholic and Protestant Armenians.
32. *Adenakrut'iwnk'* (31 March 1865), 205–6.
33. Werth, 'Russia and the Armenian Catholicos', 213–14. The outbreak of the Crimean War in 1853 did not seriously affect the relationship between the Echmiadzin Catholicosate and the Istanbul Patriarchate, as had been the case when Russia advanced to the Erivan Khanate under the Qajars in 1826 and incorporated the catholicosate in 1828. Although the relationship

may have been temporarily interrupted, a letter that the patriarch of Istanbul sent to the Echmiadzin catholicos celebrating the end of the war suggests that there was an amicable relationship between the two authorities at that time. Matenadaran, KD, 181/197 (18 June 1856).

34. Bournoutian, *Russia and the Armenians*, 412–14: Prince Bariatinskii to Prince Orlov (26 June 1857).
35. Werth, 'Russia and the Armenian Catholicos', 214.
36. Augustinos, *Greeks of Asia Minor*, 30.
37. Margos Aghapēkean, *Deghegakir Amenayn Hayots' Gat'oghigosut'ean Ayzhmean Vijagin vray* (Istanbul: Dbakrut'iwn Aramean, 1865), 16.
38. BOA, HR.TO 240/23 (21 July 1863), 322/57 (5 June 1863).
39. *Adenakrut'iwnk'* (29 December 1865), 271.
40. *Azkayin Sahmanatrut'iwn* (1863), arts. 60, 61.
41. *Polozhēnia: Bardzragoyn Kargadrut'iwn Haghags Karavarut'ean Gortsots' Lusaworch'akan Hayots' Ekeghets'woy i Rusastan* (Echmiadzin: n.p., 1836), arts. 11–19.
42. *Adenakrut'iwnk'* (5 January 1866), 275–86.
43. *Manzumēi Ēfk'ear*, no. 18 (3 April 1866).
44. Ōrmanean, *Azkabadum*, vol. 3, 4129–31.
45. Vovchenko, *Containing Balkan Nationalism*; Dimitrios Stamatopoulos, 'The Bulgarian Schism Revisited', *Modern Greek Studies Yearbook* 24–5 (2008–9): 105–25; İpek Yosmaoğlu, *Blood Ties: Religion, Violence, and the Politics of Nationhood in Ottoman Macedonia, 1878–1908* (Ithaca: Cornell University Press, 2014), 53–60.
46. Ōrmanean, *Azkabadum*, vol. 3, 4129–31.
47. Ibid., 4129–31.
48. *Adenakrut'iwnk'* (8 June 1866), 290–313.
49. Ibid., 290–9.
50. Ibid., 299–312.
51. The word used here for 'Patriarch' is *hayrabed*, which literally means 'the head of father'. *Badriark'* was used for the patriarchs of Istanbul and Jerusalem, as well as for the catholicos of Echmiadzin.
52. Ibid., 312. The religious character of the catholicosate would be emphasised several decades later in 1892, when the Armenian patriarch claimed the right to participate in the election of the Echmiadzin catholicos in his petition to the Ottoman government. BOA, Y.PRK.AZN 6/12 (18 February 1892).
53. *Adenakrut'iwnk'* (8 June 1866), 312–13.
54. Werth, 'Russia and the Armenian Catholicos', 215–16.
55. *Adenakrut'iwnk'* (3 August 1866), 317–25, 327–8. In 1884, the Russian government took a countermeasure against the General Assembly, 'declaring that any delegate or written opinion from Constantinople would be construed as representing the will merely of the diocese of Constantinople, and not of all Ottoman Armenians'. Werth, 'Russia and the Armenian Catholicos', 215–16.

56. Frazee, *Catholics and Sultans*, 185–7.
57. *Adenakrut'iwnk'* (22 February 1867) 330–3; (24 November 1871), 524–5.
58. Cevdet, *Tezâkir 21–39*, 237–8; Cevdet, *Tezâkir 40–Tetimme*, 204; Gould, 'Lords or Bandits', 494–9.
59. Sanjian, *Armenian Communities in Syria*, 236.
60. Cevdet, *Tezâkir 21–39*, 238; Cevdet, *Tezâkir 40–Tetimme*, 205.
61. *Adenakrut'iwnk'* (3 August 1866), 325–6.
62. *Adenakrut'iwnk'* (8 March 1867), 340.
63. *Adenakrut'iwnk'* (22 February 1867), 334–7.
64. *Adenakrut'iwnk'* (1 November 1867), 352–3.
65. *Manzumēi Ēfk'ear*, no. 830 (29 December 1868).
66. *Masis*, no. 812 (14 September 1867).
67. *Manzumēi Ēfk'ear*, nos. 760 (7 October 1868), 761 (8 October 1868).
68. *Masis Ōrat'ert'*, no. 237 (8 October 1868). *Masis Newspaper* (*Masis Lrakir*), which I simply call *Masis*, was inaugurated in 1852 as a weekly publication. In addition to this weekly publication, the editor began publishing a smaller periodical, *Daily Masis* (*Masis Ōrat'ert'*), in 1865, which came out several times a week. In 1870, the editor increased the frequency of the publication of *Masis Newspaper* to two or three times a week.
69. *Manzumēi Ēfk'ear*, no. 763 (10 October 1868).
70. *Masis*, no. 867 (3 October 1868).
71. *Masis Ōrat'ert'*, nos. 237, 239 (13 October 1868).
72. *Manzumēi Ēfk'ear*, no. 793 (14 November 1868).
73. *Manzumēi Ēfk'ear*, no. 766 (14 October 1868); *Masis Ōrat'ert'*, no. 239.
74. *Manzumēi Ēfk'ear*, no. 777 (27 October 1868); *Masis*, no. 871 (31 October 1868).
75. *Masis Ōrat'ert'*, no. 250 (2 November 1868).
76. *Manzumēi Ēfk'ear*, no. 802 (25 November 1868).
77. Ibid.
78. *Masis Ōrat'ert'*, no. 265 (30 November 1868); *Manzumēi Ēfk'ear*, no. 808 (2 December 1868).
79. *Masis*, no. 871.
80. *Manzumēi Ēfk'ear*, no. 763.
81. This ecumenical council, which was held after an interval of three centuries, is known as the First Vatican Council and produced the dogmatic definition of papal infallibility.
82. *Masis Ōrat'ert'*, no. 269 (8 December 1868).
83. BOA, İ.HR 13927-1 (4 February 1869).
84. *Manzumēi Ēfk'ear*, no. 845 (14 January 1869); *Masis*, no. 882 (16 January 1869). I read this number of *Masis* at Matenadaran, Yerevan. Someone wrote 882 with a marker over the original printed issue number, which might have been a misprint, but the original number was impossible to read with the naked eye.
85. *Manzumēi Ēfk'ear*, no. 847.

86. *Manzumēi Ēfk'ear*, no. 870 (24 March 1869); Fatmagül Demirel, *II. Abdülhamid Döneminde Sansür* (Ankara: Bağlam, 2007), 34–6.
87. *Manzumēi Ēfk'ear*, no. 845. *Manzume-i Efkar* sometimes called Armenian state officials '*efendi* folk' (*efendi kısmı*), using the honorific title *efendi* to describe the entire group. *Manzumēi Ēfk'ear*, no. 819 (15 December 1868). This expression did not attain wide currency, unlike the case of *amira*. This is probably because a wider stratum of Armenians began to use the title *Efendi* shortly afterwards.
88. *Masis*, no. 882.
89. BOA, İ.HR 13927-1 (4 February 1869).
90. *Adenakrut'iwnk'* (9 September 1869), 391–8.
91. Ōrmanean, *Azkabadum*, vol. 3, 4167.
92. *Adenakrut'iwnk'* (16 September 1869), 399–405.
93. *Adenakrut'iwnk'* (21 December 1869), 417–18.

5

Negotiating the Scope of Communal Affairs

As I have demonstrated in previous chapters, the distinction between religious and political affairs assumed considerable importance in the relationship between the Ottoman government and the Armenian community in the nineteenth century. On one hand, Ottoman Armenians' communal matters tended to assume a non-religious aspect because of the expansion of community institutions; on the other, their religious issues had political significance due to the international political situation. These developments sometimes conflicted with the interests of the upper echelons of the Ottoman government, who were intent on expanding their sphere of direct control over society but had to be cautious about how their relationships with the European Great Powers might be affected.

Previous studies that have analysed the case of Orthodox Christians have assumed that this type of conflict surfaced in the 1880s and associated it with the Islamist tendency of Sultan Abdülhamit II.[1] The experiences of Armenians show that similar conflicts, albeit on a smaller scale, occurred in the 1860s and 1870s. This and the following chapters demonstrate that these conflicts were rather products of the activism of non-Muslims and the state's push for civil and political integration regardless of religion. To this end, this chapter considers three cases: the prohibition of non-religious *takrir*s (official reports), the Armenians' demand for reforms in the eastern provinces and the state's attempts to expropriate Armenian cemeteries in Beyoğlu, Istanbul.

As I will discuss below, both Muslim and Armenian actors became more attentive to the scope of the jurisdiction granted to non-Muslim communities in the 1860s. Muslim statesmen considered it important to draw a distinction between religious and political affairs as they attempted to limit the sphere of the Armenian community's control (and that of other non-Muslim groups) and achieve the broader political integration of its multireligious subjects, claiming that Armenians were going beyond the confines of religion. The Armenians, for their part, justified their activities by insisting on the inseparability of religion and politics or by claiming that their activities were not political but religious.

The Prohibition of Non-religious Takrirs

When the Tanzimat statesmen pushed for reforms in the mid-nineteenth century, their key objective was to create a centralised tax collection system through the reorganisation of provincial administration. In the eastern provinces, which contained the majority of Ottoman Armenians, they needed to remove semi-autonomous local rulers to achieve this. As I wrote in Chapter 2, the central government incorporated the eastern provinces into its direct authority by removing these rulers, but it was not very successful at maintaining control. This situation urged Armenians in the eastern provinces to seek aid by appealing to the central government. One of the channels they relied on was the intermediary role of the Istanbul Patriarchate.

In the nineteenth century, Armenian Patriarchs of Istanbul were allowed to present official reports called *takrir*s to the Ottoman government.[2] Until the 1840s, the petitions and *takrir*s submitted by the patriarchate largely dealt with such issues as the appointment or dismissal of clergymen and requests for non-interference in religious affairs. After the late 1840s, however, the number of *takrir*s on issues including complaints against local officials, tax collection and violence from nomadic tribes increased. *Takrir*s on these issues were the patriarchate's response to the petitions sent by distressed provincial Armenians.[3] In the same late 1840s, the appointment charters of the Armenian patriarch of Istanbul began to include a clause on the submission of *takrir*s.[4] In the 1860s, the Armenian elites in Istanbul increasingly began to face the challenge of dealing with such requests.

In 1866, while Armenian elites in Istanbul were preparing their approach to the election of the Echmiadzin Catholicosate, then-foreign minister Ali Pasha issued an order to non-Muslim religious authorities in Istanbul:

> The patriarchates sometimes deliver *takrir*s [to the Sublime Porte] for matters not related to religious cases but on other normal problems and customary rights. In terms of such issues, however, it is natural to appeal directly to the government here [Istanbul] and in the provinces. It is evident that doing so would not harm the vested rights of anyone. Therefore, it is obvious that any mediation or recommendation [by the patriarchates] would never be necessary and would lead to nothing but confusion. This note was written to inform [you]

> that, hereafter, there is no need to write and deliver *takrir*s on matters other than the issues related to the patriarchate, churches, monasteries, clergymen and other religious cases.

This order was transliterated into Armenian script and published by the Armeno-Turkish newspaper *Manzume-i Efkar*.[5] Interestingly, the Armenian newspaper *Masis* summarily framed this prohibition of non-religious cases as a prohibition of political cases, referring to the jurisdiction of the Ottoman government.[6]

The rhetoric distinguishing religious from non-religious (or political) issues was useful for Ali Pasha to circumscribe the jurisdiction of non-Muslim religious authorities. Although this order was addressed to all the religious authorities of non-Muslim religions in Istanbul, the circumstances (and later developments) suggest that the main addressee was the Armenian Patriarchate, and that the intent of the order was to stop this patriarchate's continuous submission of *takrir*s concerning problems in the provinces. The upper echelons of the government began to devote their attentions to provincial reforms in 1860, but their main concern was the Balkans; they did not have enough financial and human resources to extensively push forward reforms in the other areas.[7] Moreover, because many *takrir*s described the oppression of Christian Armenians by Muslim Kurds, openly acknowledging these might have prompted the European Great Powers to intervene in Ottoman politics.[8] State officials likely felt harried by the many *takrir*s submitted by the Armenian Patriarchate.

Furthermore, the government's acceptance of *takrir*s from non-Muslim religious authorities was one reason that some Muslim intellectuals criticised government policy in the late 1860s. According to İsmail Kara, they saw this as favouring non-Muslims. In articles published in Ottoman Turkish newspapers, these critics reported on this perceived unfairness, claiming that, although the government had promised equality between Muslims and non-Muslims with an eye to the inequality that favoured Muslims, there was also an inequality that favoured non-Muslims because they could take certain measures to remedy injustices that were unavailable to Muslims. One such measure was the option of appealing to a foreign consulate, and another was that of appealing to the central government by asking 'patriarchates with privileges' to submit *takrir*s.[9] A similar argument can be found in a pamphlet published in 1876 by a middle-ranking Muslim state official. The author depicted a state of inequality favouring Christians because of these two channels that only Christians could use.[10]

A Curtailing of Privileges?

The prohibition of non-religious *takrir*s invited responses from Armenians in Istanbul. Excerpts from Armenian newspapers present a glimpse into their reactions. *Masis* described rumours among Istanbul Armenians that the intent of the order was to curtail the privileges of non-Muslims.[11] Denying this rumour, Garabed Panosian claimed in his newspaper that the government's order for the revision of the Armenian National Constitution indicated that it did not intend to limit privileges because 'most of the rights and privileges included in the Constitution' could be understood as 'secular' (*cismani*). Moreover, the representative of the Protestant community – a layman – was still allowed to shoulder his secular duties (*sırf cismani olan memuriyyet*).[12] Panosian therefore rejected the idea of defining the jurisdiction of the Community Administration as merely religious. Associating religious privileges with the issue of equality between Muslims and non-Muslims, he added that he could reasonably assume that the order was not intended to curtail the patriarchate's privileges because it would have meant that non-Muslims could not run their churches and schools, and public order would deteriorate if they were left without these special privileges before the equality of Muslims and non-Muslims could be achieved.[13]

To silence the rumours, the Armenian Patriarchate made an official announcement that the patriarch had gone to see Ali Pasha to inquire about the intent of the order.[14] Ali Pasha informed the patriarch that the government would continue to focus on the preservation of religious privileges, and the order's only intention was to prevent possible absurdities caused by exceeding the limits of those privileges. This remark was based on his belief that religious matters should be separated from political integration. In a memorandum addressed to Sultan Abdülaziz following the Cretan revolt in the late 1860s, he wrote that 'the [social] fusion of all [the Ottoman] subjects ... with the exception of purely religious affairs' was the only way to remove the present danger and strengthen the Ottoman state.[15] As an advocate of Ottomanism, he proposed that the government exclude religious matters from the political integration of multireligious Ottoman subjects. In his request to achieve broader integration, he was against allowing non-Muslim communities (but not individuals) to step outside of religious affairs.

Ali Pasha did not fail to underline his perspective that the privileges guaranteed by the empire to non-Muslims were religious in nature, which was a striking contrast to Panosian's article. Ali Pasha added that the government would continue to accept the *takrir*s that were presented by the patriarchate, just as before. He carefully avoided assuming blame for any of the limitations of privileges for non-Muslims. He ensured that there would be no heavy-handed attitude, to avoid inviting intervention from the European powers on behalf of Ottoman Christian subjects. Instead, he laid the blame on the non-Muslims themselves, who, he asserted, were crossing the line; simultaneously, he assuaged the patriarch by assuring him that *takrir*s could continue to be presented as before. Ali Pasha's public stance weakened the effectiveness of the ban on non-religious *takrir*s.

Paul Werth argues that while Russian state officials believed that spiritual affairs fell under the jurisdiction of their respective non-dominant religious groups, they did not define which affairs were to be included in this category.[16] The Ottoman government likewise had no clear criterion for deciding what 'religious' meant or what was to be included under 'religious affairs'. This ambiguity, which applied to the government's intervention into Armenian communal affairs in the late 1860s, stimulated Istanbul Armenians to open an intra-communal discussion on the jurisdiction of the patriarchate after the prohibition of non-religious *takrir*s. For example, Oksen Khojasarian published an article in 1868 on the collection of communal taxes, in which he discussed whether the patriarchate would be able to use force to collect them. According to his argument, 'the duty of our [Community] Administration was derived from our religion' and the scope of its activity included 'our religion, our religious rights, community wealth, monasteries, churches, schools, etc'.[17] On this basis, Khojasarian could not justify the use of force to collect communal taxes because religion could not force anyone to pay taxes. The patriarchate could, however, accept voluntary donations.[18] An article published in *Manzume-i Efkar* introduced an argument for the collection of communal taxes. In opposition to the assertion that the jurisdiction of the Community Administration should be limited to religious affairs, some claimed that in practice the Armenian community should have the right to manage institutions other than churches and monasteries, and that Armenians possessed a unique nationality (*azkut'iwn*) in addition to their unique religion. The patriarchate needed communal taxes to support these institutions, including schools and hospitals.[19] This opinion thus justified tax collection, and in practice the government had previously tolerated these diverse aspects of the Armenian community.

At any rate, people on both sides of the debate were mindful that the Community Administration's jurisdiction should, in principle, be limited to religious matters, and they inferred their own conclusions as to what the government would allow to fall within the scope of that jurisdiction. An Armenian newspaper article dated 1868 manifestly argued this principle, clearly corresponding with the abovementioned argument of Ali Pasha. The article first referred to the dual spheres of state and community, describing the Armenians as 'citizens' (*k'aghak'ats'i*) of the Ottoman Empire who at the same time formed a 'religious community' (*grōnagan hasaragut'iwn*) because they embraced a religion different from that of the state. For non-Muslims, the Ottoman government admitted religious privileges and freedom of religion, which included non-interference by the government, on the condition that the freedom did not go beyond the confines of religion (*grōnk'i sahmanĕ*).[20] The problem was the gap that existed between this principle and reality, in which – as Panosian discussed – the Ottoman government allowed non-Muslims to deal with the non-religious affairs of their communities. There was thus room to negotiate the scope of their authority. In discussions about provincial Armenians in the early 1870s, Istanbul Armenians deliberately went beyond the borders of what was strictly religious into the political sphere.

Oppression in the Provinces

Beginning in the 1840s, the plight of Armenians in the eastern provinces gradually began to attract the attention of Istanbul Armenians. In the 1860s, concern about their coreligionists in the provinces grew tremendously as a result of calls from journalists.[21] A pamphlet published in 1865 warned Istanbul Armenian elites that the only recourse for some of their coreligionists in the eastern provinces was not the Ottoman government or the Istanbul Patriarchate but the Russian governor of Tiflis and the Echmiadzin Catholicosate.[22] The change in the Istanbul Armenians' position was expressed in an article published by Panosian in his newspaper in 1871. He argued that, previously, the ideas of nation, fatherland and Armenia had been mere words that could only be found in books and newspapers, but that recently, members of the General Assembly had become 'enthusiastic lovers of their nation', shouting 'Armenia, Armenia'. Their shouts resulted in a movement that sought a remedy for the plight of provincial Armenians.[23]

In 1870, the newly elected Patriarch Mgrdich Khrimian brought the issue to the General Assembly. Khrimian had been born and had made his career in the eastern provinces. Since the middle of the 1850s, he had devoted himself to educating provincial Armenians, opening schools and publishing journals in Van and Muş. He was one of the most popular clergymen of the time, both in Istanbul and the provinces.[24] In November 1870, Khrimian presented six petitions from provincial Armenians and proposed that they discuss what the Istanbul Patriarchate should do in place of presenting conventional *takrir*s (*sovoragan takrir*) to the Sublime Porte to demand case-by-case measures.[25] Under his initiative, the 'oppression in the provinces' (*kawaragan harsdaharut'iwn*) was placed on the assembly's agenda, and the phrase began to be used frequently in its meetings.

At an 1870 meeting, Khrimian remarked that

> When the considerate [Ottoman] government accepted the European enlightenment on the date of the Gülhane Rescript, it prepared a code of laws and named it *Düstur*. The government gave it to both brothers [Kurds and Armenians] and asked, 'Why do you behave hostilely towards each other? Worship the Quran in a mosque and the Bible in a church. Then, in your social life, obey this code of laws'. In doing this, the government fulfilled its duty. However, the Kurds never even read the cover of this code of laws, and thus the situation [in the eastern provinces] remains.

He added that 'when the principle of equality is enforced and the Kurds see that some among Christians … are promoted to the rank of provincial governor, then they will truly understand the essence of the code of laws and the government's order'.[26] In discussing the promotion of Christians to provincial governorships, Khrimian must have been thinking of the 1861 appointment of an Armenian Catholic as the governor of the semi-autonomous district of Lebanon following strife in the region between the Druze and the Maronites. Although the case of Lebanon was exceptional, the idea of Christians being promoted to provincial governorships probably seemed realistic in the atmosphere of the Tanzimat Reforms. Five years after the speech, *Masis* reported a rumour that the Ottoman government would soon begin to appoint Christian state officials, including Krikor Odian, as provincial governors.[27]

Before his election, Khrimian had been criticised for having a poor understanding of both politics and the Turkish language, but in his speech he invoked the achievements of the Tanzimat Reforms to analyse the causes of oppression in the eastern provinces and to propose the principle of equality as a panacea to Kurdish tribal violence.[28] Moreover, he bore in mind the dual spheres created by the Tanzimat Reforms: a religious community superintended by religious authorities according to sacred scripture, and social life regulated by state law.[29] At the same meeting, Bishop Eremia called for a survey on oppression in the provinces to be drawn up and submitted to the Ottoman government.[30] Eremia classified oppression in the provinces into two types: that from within the Armenian community and that from non-Armenians. He categorised the latter as an issue that Armenians could not deal with on their own but one that the Ottoman government should address. Although Armenian patriarchs had presented protests about oppression in the provinces to the government, these had been insufficient because they had neither clearly reported the entire situation nor dared to demand solutions. Eremia was well aware that the treatment of Christians bore closely on the international reputation of the Ottoman Empire in the eyes of high-ranking officials. He claimed that informing the government of the terrible situation in the provinces would not only aid the Armenian community but would also be an act of allegiance to the Ottoman state, adding that the tragic state of the provinces would harm the empire's international reputation if the world learned of it.

To prepare the report, the assembly created a committee to investigate 'oppression in the provinces' and elected four clergymen and six laymen (four of the latter, including Khojasarian and Utujian, were journalists) to the committee. The head of the committee was Bishop Nerses Varjabedian.[31] According to one member of the assembly, these individuals learned of the state of affairs in the provinces either by visiting the region themselves or through journalistic channels.[32] Giving examples of the types of problem, the committee requested all provincial dioceses to submit a report on the problems faced by Armenians and their solutions.[33] They also evaluated all *takrir*s that the patriarchate had submitted to the Ottoman authorities since 1849. In October 1871, the committee presented a report to the Armenian Assembly, consisting of two parts: the first summarised the complaints, and the second proposed solutions.[34] After a discussion in the assembly, the report was published in *Masis*.[35] Later, the patriarchate presented the report to the government and requested that the reforms it proposed be put into effect.

One assembly member opposed the idea of recommending solutions to the government. His remarks and those of several other members suggest that it was unconventional for non-Muslim communities to propose comprehensive (rather than case-specific) solutions to be carried out by the state. However many other members of the assembly (including Krikor Odian) supported the idea of including the recommendations in the report, pointing out that the government was eager to accelerate reforms in the provinces and collect information on the situation.[36] Believing that the ends would justify their means, the assembly members thus assigned themselves the role of Tanzimat reformers.

Indeed, the government did accelerate the pace of its reforms in the provinces during the 1860s, and some Armenian state officials were involved in this work. Following defeat in the Crimean War, the main Russian justification for interfering in Ottoman politics was the alleged oppression of Christian Ottoman subjects in the provinces, and other European Great Powers joined in to pursue their own interests. In 1860, after the Russian Empire demanded the dispatch of a commission from Europe to investigate the alleged oppression of Serbian Christians, the Ottoman government warded off this demand by creating an investigation commission of their own headed by Grand Vizier Kıbrıslı Mehmet Emin Pasha. Among the members of this commission were four Christian state officials, including Harutyun Dadian, an Armenian official in the Ministry of Foreign Affairs.[37] Later that decade, the government sent inspectors to the Balkan and Anatolian provinces to investigate the situation there. Among these inspectors were also several Armenian officials, including Sarkis Aghapegian, a future member of the State Council (*Şura-yı Devlet*).[38] In 1864, Midhat Pasha, the new governor of the Danube province, implemented a number of reforms as a test case for a future empire-wide provincial reorganisation, which was accomplished in 1867 as the general law for the provincial system.[39] Krikor Odian assisted Midhat Pasha in implementing administrative reforms as the chief foreign affairs officer for the Danube province.[40]

In Istanbul, Dadian, Aghapegian and Odian were leading figures in the Armenian General Assembly.[41] They involved themselves in the provincial reforms both as Ottoman officials and as Armenians. High-ranking Muslim state officials tended to employ Christian officials in provincial reforms out of consideration for the watchful eyes of the European Great Powers. They needed to demonstrate that the Tanzimat Reforms improved the status of Ottoman Christians, that the promise of religious equality enabled Christians to play an active part in the state apparatus and that the Ottoman government was fairly carrying out provincial reforms. Therefore, they welcomed non-Muslims taking part in the provincial reforms as individual state officials. Nevertheless, as will be discussed, they were still reluctant to allow them to do so as a religious community.

The 1871 Survey Report

The final report found that the Armenian Patriarchate submitted 539 *takrir*s to the Ottoman government from 1849 to 1869.[42] A majority of these related to petitions from the eastern provinces: 158 were from Diyarbakır, 136 from Erzurum and 83 from Sivas.[43] The largest number of *takrir*s were related to violence against Armenians (210), followed by complaints against local officials (122) and problems related to tax collection (76). Others dealt with religious problems: disputes with Catholics and Protestants (38), the forced conversion of women and children (32), the obstruction of church construction or summons to prayer (26) and disturbances of religious rites (13). Using these *takrir*s and newly collected information from provincial dioceses, the committee that prepared the report classified oppression in the provinces into four categories: injustices related to taxation, injustices conducted by state officials, the unheard testimonies of non-Muslims and specific violent acts.

Interestingly, the committee devoted only a few pages to specifically religious problems in the survey report, probably because they felt it was less important to include these matters. According to the report, the distinction between religious and non-religious affairs influenced the response of the central government. When Armenians in the provinces complained to the central government through *takrir*s, *takrir*s with a 'religious appearance' (*grōnagan gerbarank'*) generated positive results where others did not.[44] It was also found that when provincial officials refused to hear complaints brought by Armenian clergymen from the provinces, they employed an argument similar to that expressed by Ali Pasha, namely, that Armenian clergymen should 'be involved merely with spiritual issues [*hokewor kordzer*] … Your place is the church and your job is to preach your religion. Thus, you should not intervene in governmental affairs'.[45]

Most of the complaints described in the report echoed the same concerns that had been expressed in *takrir*s since the 1840s. For example, the report gave substantial space to discussions of the insufficient implementation of the new Tanzimat taxation system, including the tax in lieu of military service and the taxes on property and income. These complaints did not contest the new taxes themselves but instead criticised how they were being assessed and collected.[46] Meanwhile, the survey report devoted surprisingly little space to violence against Armenians, one of the main topics of the *takrir*s.[47]

Because it was unconventional to propose solutions to the government, the committee considered it necessary to justify their doing so. They described it as their attempt to confirm the duty and loyalty of the General Assembly to the Ottoman government, writing that they wished to combat injustices that went against the laws and the principle of equality proclaimed by the sultan. They then framed their right to propose solutions as part of the privileges accorded to non-Muslim communities and the clause in the Reform Edict that called on each community to discuss a plan of reform as necessitated by the demands of the time and to submit it to the government.[48] The members of the committee adopted this clause, which was originally intended to promote reforms to the administration of the community, to claim that their action was within the scope of the Reform Edict.

The report proposed that some of the achievements of the Tanzimat Reforms should be utilised or modified to improve the social status of provincial Armenians. For example, it demanded a public reassessment of taxable property and income. As for complaints against provincial officials, while the report apologised for dealing with these issues, admitting that these belonged to 'the jurisdiction of the Imperial Government' (*Gayseragan Gaṛavarut'ean tsernhasut'iwnĕ*), it nevertheless proposed that the selection of these officials should be improved and that inspectors should be independent from provincial governments. Moreover, it recommended that Armenians bring commercial, criminal and property-related cases to the newly organised Nizamiye courts (which heard cases according to state law) instead of the traditional sharia courts. It also proposed that the orders of the Sublime Porte be promulgated through the official gazette of the provinces, which was published not only in Ottoman Turkish but also in local languages, and that the code of laws be translated (presumably into Kurdish, Armenian and/or Armeno-Turkish). Finally, the report suggested that the election procedures for the local administrative councils be reformed so that Armenian candidates could be approved by the Armenian councils of their respective regions.[49]

Military Conscription

The most striking proposals were those related to military service. In 1855, the Ottoman government had decided to subject non-Muslim males to military conscription as a step towards establishing their equality with Muslims. In practice, however, the government imposed a tax on non-Muslims in lieu of military service. The committee report proposed that the Armenian community provide men to the Ottoman army to eliminate the unequal tax.

Julia Phillips Cohen aptly demonstrates that showing willingness to serve in the military was one of the measures that Jewish leaders took to favourably impress their non-Jewish compatriots (especially Muslims) and to make Jews 'counted and esteemed'.[50] Behind this effort was the negative response that many Muslims had to the fact that the Ottoman government had promised equality to non-Muslims without also imposing military duties on them.[51] The Armenian committee members also recognised the importance of showing their willingness to serve in the military. They asserted that their proposal was based on the text of the Reform Edict and was founded on their opinion that Armenians needed to show a 'spirit of honour and citizenship' and a willingness to spill their blood 'for the Fatherland and the State' (*Hayreneats' u Dērut'ean hamar*) alongside their Muslim compatriots.[52] In other Armenian writings from this period, 'fatherland' most often referred to the Armenian national fatherland – that is, the eastern Ottoman provinces.[53] The committee's proposal, however, used the word to describe the Ottoman Empire, for which Armenians, as Ottoman citizens, should not hesitate to spill their own blood alongside Muslims. The dual spheres of state and community enabled Ottoman Armenians to claim two fatherlands: one Armenian and one Ottoman.[54]

It is worth noting that Muslim inhabitants of Istanbul were exempted from military service in this period.[55] This meant that when the committee members called for male Armenian military conscription, they and their sons would never be compelled to enter the army and fight; rather, they were proposing the conscription of their coreligionists in the provinces. This may have been due to a recollection of how, at the beginning of the Crimean War in 1853, the Armenian patriarch had been the first of the non-Muslim religious authorities to propose that men from his community be provided to the Ottoman army and how the Ottoman government had praised this Christian display of allegiance in its official gazette.[56]

The call for conscription met with a stormy response in the assembly. The representatives who supported it were largely also members of the report committee, such as Sdepan Papazian, who expressed his optimism by invoking the principle of the Tanzimat Reforms. He asserted that, as Armenians proved their readiness to take on the same military duties that were shouldered by their 'Ottoman compatriots' (*Ōsmants'i hayrenagits'*), Muslims would accept them as 'compatriots with equal rights' (*hawasar irawants' dēr hayrenagts'ut'iwn*). Furthermore, if provincial Armenians could learn from their military training how to defend their property, honour and family, the violence inflicted on them by Kurdish nomads might cease.[57] This conscription proposal was thus promoted as a partial solution to Armenian oppression by nomads, whom the report described as armed rebels who neither paid taxes nor faced conscription. By contrast, Armenians were taxpaying subjects who were willing to serve as full-fledged citizens of the Ottoman Empire.[58]

Another member of the assembly who invoked the ideology of Ottoman nation-building during the conscription debate was Garabed Utujian, a member of the committee and the editor of *Masis*, which published editorials in support of the proposal. One such editorial argued that if Armenians were to demand the enforcement of equal rights from the government, according to the Reform Edict's promise, they first needed to fulfil their equal duties through military service. In this argument, those who were not willing to spill their blood to defend their country had no claim to a fatherland and should not be allowed to demand equal rights as citizens.[59]

A larger number of representatives opposed the proposal, however, arguing that it was too soon for Armenians to begin to serve in the military (or for the government to allow them to do so). Several representatives, including Aghapegian, implied that the members of the committee had failed to understand the wishes of provincial Armenians, who would not agree to conscription. Although Patriarch Khrimian admitted that the conscription of Armenians might provide an effective solution to Kurdish violence, he, too, insisted that Armenians in the provinces were not ready to serve in the military.[60] Like the supporters of the proposal, those who opposed it invoked the language of the Tanzimat. One lay representative asserted that the military conscription of Armenians was impossible because while the 'Tanzimat [Reform] Edict' had announced the introduction of conscription of non-Muslims, it had also announced the conferral of privileges, and these had not yet been realised. He argued that the government should perform its duties before Armenians were required to perform theirs, insisting that when the time came, the government – not the Armenian Assembly – should be the one to institute conscription.[61]

Panosian's argument reflected the ongoing discussion about the jurisdiction of the patriarchate. While the duties of the General Assembly included affairs that had been 'publicly known since days of yore' – that is, the preparation of regulations for improving the state of churches, schools and the poor – it had no authority over conscription. Any amelioration to the provincials' lot would be the duty of the state. Although the patriarchate was allowed to make a proposal to the government, this was meant to be done informally, not through a 'formal assembly' (*bir resmi meclis*).[62] The assembly thus decided to exclude the clause related to military service in the final report submitted to the Ottoman government.[63]

The discussion of conscription in the assembly demonstrates that Armenian community elites were deeply concerned about equality between Muslims and non-Muslims and the negative response Muslims might have to it. Even though most assembly members opposed the immediate conscription of Armenians, their discussion assumed that conscription would be a future reality on the grounds that equal rights as Ottoman citizens would need to be accompanied by equal duties. The argument concerned whether the Armenian community or the government should fulfil its duties first. Papazian optimistically expected that the Armenians' conscription initiative would hasten Muslim acceptance of non-Muslims' equality. Even though many representatives – including several state officials – argued that equality could help solve Kurdish violence, they cautioned that the government required time to let Muslim subjects accept the equality of non-Muslims and that provincial Armenians were not ready to perform military service.

In March 1872, the General Assembly approved the revised version of the report, which included proposals for the solutions that the Ottoman government should implement in the provinces. Khojasarian, who was a member of the report preparation committee, lauded the document, saying that in it, 'Armenians were calling attention for the first time to a political issue [*k'aghak'agan khntir*] in the [General] Assembly'.[64] He (and probably other assembly members) recognised that proposing solutions was an unconventional venture beyond the limits traditionally assigned to non-Muslim communities.

We should note that this project was exceptional for the assembly. When they discussed the intervention of the Echmiadzin Catholicosate into the relationship between Istanbul Armenians and the Sis Catholicosate later that same year, Hampartsum Ipekjian (who was originally from the Russian Empire and had moved to the Ottoman Empire in 1868) claimed that the Russian government was behind this episode. Responding to this, Dikran Yusufian – the assembly chairman and a state official – intervened to suppress this statement on state politics. Another lay member asked, 'Do we have the liberty of making such remarks?'[65] Another lay member said that it was dangerous to criticise the Ottoman or Russian Empire because the Armenians were a 'subject nation' (*hbadag azk*), and the great majority of Armenians were under the protection of these empires.[66] The responses of assembly members in this case show that they still shared a commitment to non-intervention in state politics. Meanwhile, Muslim state officials had their own responses to the Armenians' ground-breaking proposal.

The Second Prohibition of Non-religious Takrirs

Patriarch Mgrdich Khrimian submitted the assembly's report to Grand Vizier Mahmut Nedim Pasha in April 1872.[67] Four months later, Khrimian visited Midhat Pasha, the new grand vizier, to deliver further reports on outstanding issues and to remind him of the survey report. Khrimian was invited to a room where Midhat Pasha was meeting with European guests. *Masis* reported that Midhat Pasha came to Khrimian's side and asked to deliver documents through Krikor Odian.[68] This remark suggests that Midhat Pasha was not happy to have received a report like this from the patriarchate so openly, as it might attract the attention of the Great Powers and lead to intervention. Rather, he preferred such problems to be managed under the table, channelled through lay non-Muslim elites.

A few weeks later, the government orally instructed non-Muslim religious authorities in Istanbul that *takrir*s delivered to the Sublime Porte should be restricted to those 'on purely religious matters but not regarding secular issues'. Although the government had issued a similar ban in 1866, the patriarchate was able to continue submitting *takrir*s as it had done before because of Ali Pasha's emphasis on public stance. The Armenian patriarch refused to accept the 1872 prohibition and claimed that important notices such as this should not be delivered orally but in writing.[69] The government official responded that the order had already been delivered in a written document and added that the ecumenical patriarch of the Orthodox Church had accepted it without complaint.[70] The fact that a similar ban was issued again in the 1880s suggests that the patriarchate continued to submit *takrir*s on non-religious matters despite the ban.[71]

Masis published arguments for the reasons why provincial Armenians needed to deliver *takrir*s on non-religious problems to the patriarchate. First, it emphasised the inseparability of religion and politics, justifying the patriarchate's involvement in issues that were not strictly religious and adding that religious differences played an important role in the political affairs in the provinces. *Masis* then claimed that the situation in the provinces prevented Armenians from addressing problems locally and summarised the points of the survey report. According to the newspaper, the testimonies of non-Muslims were not respected by the courts in the provinces, provincial Armenians were not generally familiar with state law and, moreover, law and order were not robustly enforced. Furthermore, provincial Armenians – unlike the Christian communities who shared a religion with European Great Powers – could not count on help from foreign consuls because the latter did not wish to be involved with Armenians belonging to the Armenian Church. This may have been a response to the abovementioned Muslim belief that there was inequality favourable towards Christians, an opinion that neglected the differences between Christian sects. *Masis* concluded that Armenians in the provinces had no choice but to deliver their petitions to their bishops, and these, in turn, had no remedy but to deliver the petitions to the Istanbul Patriarchate, which was then expected to appeal to the central Ottoman government.[72] Thus, the newspaper justified the presentation of non-religious *takrir*s by blaming local officials who, according to the newspaper, were unable (or unwilling) to help their Armenian populations.

Notably, both the unnamed state official mentioned above and *Masis* referred to other non-Muslim communities. The state official demanded that the Armenian patriarch obey the order, implying that the patriarch should do so because other non-Muslim religious authorities already had. This argument was founded on the understanding that the same rules should apply to every non-Muslim community. *Masis*, on the other hand, drew attention to the uniqueness of the Armenian position, indicating that it was less favourable than that of other Christian communities because the Armenians did not have recourse to the support of foreign consuls.

Therefore, unlike other Christian communities, they were entitled to affirmative action, and the government should permit them to present political questions through their patriarchate.

The Ottoman government, which enforced a strict censorship of the press during the late Tanzimat period, considered this article problematic. *Masis* reported the oral warning that its editor received from a state official:

> The privileges of the patriarchs are not political but religious and thus [the patriarchs] do not have any rights or privileges to intervene in political issues. They are out of their jurisdiction. Political issues belong only to the government. The subjects of the state have to deliver communal and religious issues to the patriarchate but political issues directly to the government. The responsibility of provincial bishops to the patriarchate is also purely religious. Politically, they are responsible to the government, not to the patriarchate.[73]

The official had then threatened the editor of *Masis*, stating that any Armenian newspaper that published an article on the issue would be shut down.

Religious Peculiarities

While Armenians were reluctant to separate religious from non-religious issues in *takrir*s, they took advantage of the same distinction on other occasions. Their response to the expropriation of their cemetery presents a good example, showing that this separation had implications for urban society and promoted popular activism. It furthermore demonstrates that not only did the Ottoman government violate its own principle of religious and non-religious separation when it suited the state, but that Armenians applied the same tactic against the government in defence of their communal interests.

During the nineteenth century, greater Istanbul experienced a significant population growth and urban expansion. The expansion was mainly in the Galata and Beyoğlu districts on the northern shore of the Golden Horn, which grew until the residential area surrounded several cemeteries previously located on the city's outskirts. These districts were also areas where Western European cultures were widely introduced and the Ottoman government had first implemented urban infrastructure reforms.[74] As the expansion combined with the government's orientation towards reforms and the need for hygiene measures in response to the cholera epidemic, Ottoman officials planned for the relocation of cemeteries in Beyoğlu so that the newly available land could be used for other purposes.[75] In the nineteenth century, two large cemeteries were located in Beyoğlu at both ends of the Grand Rue de Pera (today's İstiklal Caddesi), namely the Petit Champ des Morts and the Grand Champ at the southern and northern ends, respectively. The former was assigned to Muslims, while the latter was divided into several lots according to religion and denomination, including Islam, Orthodox Christian, Armenian, Catholic and Protestant.[76]

Among these, the Catholic cemetery was chosen as the first to be relocated in 1853 to build 'a recreation site for the people'.[77] This relocation sparked rumours that the Ottoman government intended to expropriate the neighbouring Armenian cemetery and build another recreation site in its place. *Masis* contradicted this in September 1853 based on the evidence that the government had recently re-guaranteed the privileges and freedom of non-Muslims, invoking the edict promulgated three months before.[78] In the following years, however, the government opened negotiations several times with Orthodox Christian and Armenian Patriarchates to relocate their cemeteries from this area. Although burials were prohibited in the Beyoğlu cemeteries after the cholera epidemic of 1865 and the government assigned each religious community several sites on the outskirts of Istanbul for new cemeteries, Armenians kept hold of their Beyoğlu cemetery.[79] After all, it contained the tombs of 'Catholicoses [*sic*], Patriarchs as well as several martyrs for their faith', which were the 'objects of pilgrimage for Armenians from all parts of the world'.[80]

In December 1872, a government official again demanded that the Armenian Patriarchate transfer the site of the Armenian cemetery in Beyoğlu to the government. An Armenian newspaper reported that the government wished to create a new parade ground, uniting the site with the public park that had been opened in 1870 on the grounds of the former Catholic cemetery, so they could then open a larger park on the old parade ground.[81] According to *Manzume-i Efkar*, this demand 'invited the interest and attention of almost all Armenians'. The newspaper implied that the patriarchate should not allow it, noting that Orthodox Christians had refused to relinquish their much smaller cemetery to the government, thus justifying themselves with reference to the response of another religious community.[82]

On 26 December, the vice patriarch told Foreign Minister Halil Şerif Pasha that the patriarchate had rejected the demand because they considered cemeteries to be 'holy places and unroofed churches'. Halil Şerif Pasha explained that it was his intention to turn the cemetery into a public park and that everyone, including the Armenians, would be pleased with the results, justifying the expropriation on the basis of public benefit.[83] *Manzume-i Efkar* reported that Halil Şerif Pasha had urged the vice patriarch to accept the offer, stating that he had already ordered the municipality to force the Armenians to remove corpses from the site. This heavy-handed action prompted hundreds of Armenians to ask the patriarch to approach the Sublime Porte to discuss the issue, which Khrimian did, protesting that the government was violating the religious rights and privileges of the community.[84] Halil Şerif Pasha claimed that the issue was merely political and had no religious meaning. He threatened the patriarch, saying that he had already ordered the bones to be removed from the cemetery by force if the Armenians would not cooperate.[85]

Halil Şerif Pasha's response prompted more than 100 clergymen and 1,500 Istanbul Armenians to go to the Dolmabahçe Palace and petition the sultan. They claimed that the government was 'about to violate their rights and privileges, spiritually as well as materially'. Several petitioners subsequently erected tents on the Beyoğlu cemetery site, affixed crosses to the tops of the tents, and stationed guards. Khrimian visited Yusuf Kamil Pasha, the chairman of the State Council, and requested his help, which he received. The next day, the Sublime Porte informed the patriarch that the plan to expropriate the cemetery had been abandoned.[86]

After this successful appeal, the editor of *Masis* explained the logic behind the Armenians' refusal.[87] First, he quoted Jesus's famous instruction to 'Give to Caesar what is Caesar's and to God what is God's'. With this saying, which is often still used today as a justification for the separation of religion and politics, the editor – who had hitherto advocated the inseparability of religion and politics in the context of the discussion of non-religious *takrir*s – now implied that the state had no right to intervene in Armenian's religious affairs. He argued that, as a reward for the Armenians' loyalty to the Ottoman state, the government had guaranteed their freedom of religion through its own edict, thus making the cemetery as sacred and inviolable as a church. He asserted that the expropriation of their cemetery would therefore have contradicted the government's policy of religious freedom. Furthermore, Halil Şerif Pasha came in for criticism: namely, that he was ignorant of this logic and wrongly regarded the cemetery problem merely as a political matter. The Armenian community – especially the patriarchate – should thus help officials understand that the problem was of a religious nature.

To defend their cemetery, *Masis* and other Armenian voices asserted that religion was an inviolable sphere. We can see this logic underlying the acts of the Armenian petitioners, who affixed crosses to the tops of their tents as they guarded the cemetery. It is likely that the petitioners adopted the rhetoric employed in the negotiations between the patriarch and the foreign minister with the intention of expressing the religiousness of their act. The foreign minister's denial of the religious nature of the issue indicates that he in fact did share the same logic of religious and political distinction, albeit with different conclusions. An aspect of the issue noted in the Ottoman Turkish newspaper *Hadika* is interesting in this context: as part of its criticism of the Armenian resistance, the newspaper stated that, 'Strangely, non-Muslim groups in our country perceive every problem as religious'. *Hadika* further described the Armenian attitude as 'fanatical' (*taassubla*), contrasting it with the attitude of Muslims, who had made no complaint about sacrificing a part of their own cemetery.[88]

Susan Gilson Miller argues that Muslims in Tangier had created 'new geographies of holy space' to resist European encroachment into the city beginning in the mid-nineteenth century.[89] Similarly, assigning their cemetery an explicitly religious significance was, for the Istanbul Armenians, a means of combatting the Ottoman government's attempts at encroachment into their communities. During the 1865 cholera epidemic, the Armenian community had built a small wooden church in their Beyoğlu cemetery. This new church faced the former site of the Catholic cemetery, where the government was then installing the new public park. Three Armenians (Sdepan Aslanian, Serovpe Vichenian and Feruhan, an army surgeon) with strong connections to high-ranking Muslim officials had obtained permission from the government to build the church.[90] In its criticism, *Hadika* asserted that the Armenians were now refusing to relinquish the cemetery under the pretext that there was 'a chapel or a small church' on the site.[91]

Several months before the Armenians had constructed their church, the Orthodox Christians had also obtained permission to build a church on the site of their old cemetery in Beyoğlu.[92] The Ecumenical Patriarchate of the Orthodox Church had previously agreed to transfer part of the cemetery to the government to allow it to use the land to widen the adjacent street. Although the remaining cemetery was small, the patriarch nevertheless faced further demands for land from the government. Some state officials had the idea of erecting walls around the surplus land that remained after the construction and to build a public park there. The patriarch protested, claiming that this contradicted the terms of the agreement between the government and the Orthodox Christians. Eventually, the park idea was also abandoned.[93] Instead, twenty-two years after the initial permission was granted, Orthodox Christians opened a large church on the cemetery grounds, where they also built a girls' school.[94]

The attitude of the Orthodox Christian Patriarchate suggests that the Armenians were not the only religious community to make claims against the government based on the idea of religion as an inviolable sphere. In fact, a copy of a document sent to the Orthodox Christian Patriarchate demonstrates this. When the patriarchate protested the government's decision to appoint an exarch to the Bulgarian Orthodox Christians and separate them from the Orthodox Christian community in 1870, the patriarchate criticised the government's decision to intervene in 'purely ecclesiastical issues' (*sırf ruhani olan umur*). State officials agreed that non-intervention in 'purely religious issues' (*sırf umur-ı diniye*) was a principle that had been maintained until then and would therefore not be abandoned. Meanwhile, they invoked their own concern for order and concluded that it would not be acceptable to neglect matters that could harm public security, even if such matters involved intervention in non-Muslims' religious issues.[95]

To return to the Armenian cemetery, *Hadika* was not the only newspaper to criticise the Armenians' stance. *Manzume-i Efkar* cited criticism from *Le Phare du Bosphore*, a French newspaper published in Istanbul, which claimed that the Catholic and Protestant residents of Istanbul were making sacrifices for 'the benefit of the public' (*umumun fayidesi*), while the Armenians did not. Furthermore, it made the harsh judgement that the Armenians, unlike other religious communities, were living in 'old barbarism'.[96] Thus, *Le Phare du Bosphore* both compared the Armenians' response to those of other religious groups and used a binary opposition (in this case, civilisation versus barbarism) to criticise it. Responding to these attacks, Panosian issued a detailed justification of the Armenians' attitude in *Manzume-i Efkar*. A major part of his argument was the observation that each religious group had its own peculiarities and that it was not always appropriate to apply the same rules to all religious groups. For example, contrasting Armenians with Catholics (*Frenk*), he wrote, 'we are not *Frenk*s, our confessions are different, our customs are different, our feelings are different'.[97] A similar justification – also founded on religious peculiarity – can be observed in an article in *Masis*, which claimed that Armenians had a different understanding of the meaning of a cemetery: 'for Armenians, church and cemetery are the same, and both are sacred and both are inviolable'.[98] This claim was based on the understanding that Armenians were entitled to special treatment in religious affairs because each religion or confession had a different understanding of what was properly understood to be 'religious' and what was not.

An International Problem

Despite the reluctance of high-ranking Muslim state officials, in 1874 the Armenian Patriarchate presented the government with a report similar to the one it submitted in 1872.[99] It was later noted in the Armenian General Assembly that the government had formed a committee to investigate instability in the eastern provinces.[100] However, the state's ability to implement reforms was limited by its financial constraints, and it suffered an additional setback in the deaths of Tanzimat leaders Fuat Pasha in 1869 and Ali Pasha in 1871. In 1875, the situation deteriorated further as Christians revolted in Bosnia and Herzegovina. This invited something that Ottoman state officials had feared for decades. By the end of 1875, Austria-Hungary, Germany and Russia had intervened in the turmoil in Bosnia and Herzegovina, demanding that the Ottoman government implement a reform programme prepared by the Austro-Hungarian foreign minister. Following this intervention, there was another uprising in Bulgaria in April 1876.[101]

With the empire in turmoil, the Armenian elites considered it necessary to demonstrate their allegiance. In the Armenian General Assembly in May 1876, Patriarch Nerses Varjabedian declared in a long speech that 'we Armenians' would remain inseparable 'from the Ottoman nation' (*Ōsmanean azkēn*). The assembly members responded to this declaration by repeating the word 'yes'.[102] Demonstrations of allegiance were not limited to the assembly. Armenians, Orthodox Christians and Jews in Istanbul, Bursa, Salonica and İzmir came forward to volunteer for military service.[103] Elite Armenian women established an association to provide aid for the soldiers who 'fought against the enemies of the Ottoman state'. Many members of this 'humanitarian and patriotic' (*martasiragan ew hayrenasiragan*) association were the wives of high-ranking Armenian officials, including Odian, Abro and Aghapegian.[104]

The turmoil in the Balkans might have affected how Armenian Assembly members viewed the plight of provincial Armenians. They had previously referred to 'oppression in the provinces' but, following the disturbances in the Balkans, they began to use a new phrase: 'oppression in Armenia' (*Hayasdani harsdaharut'iwn, Hayasdani mēch kordzuadz harsdaharut'iwn*).[105] With the Great Powers demanding that the Ottoman government implement reforms in particular provinces in the Balkans but not the rest of the empire, the Armenian Assembly found it necessary to focus on their national fatherland when appealing for reforms in the eastern provinces. Khojasarian went further, suggesting that Armenians needed support from the Great Powers to pressure the Ottoman government on this front. Since Christians in the Balkans had gained the support of the European Great Powers by using violence, he impatiently stated that those who were living peacefully in the Asian part of the Ottoman Empire deserved to be protected in the same way as those in the European part.[106]

Although the necessity of foreign support was not frequently alluded to in the assembly, some members insisted that the right to demand reforms should be a reward for their continued allegiance.[107] This opinion was voiced more clearly after the outbreak of the Ottoman-Russian War in 1877, when the government required that the patriarchate provide soldiers under the principle of equality that was guaranteed by the new Constitution. While the Ottoman government delayed implementing the conscription of non-Muslims to avoid confusion, the Armenian patriarch promised certain high-ranking state officials that even if he could not send untrained men to the front, Armenians would still serve their fatherland.[108] After the government said that it would conscript non-Muslims for garrisons, Madteos Izmirlian, a clerical representative and future patriarch, insisted that, although the Ottoman Constitution (promulgated a year earlier) declared Armenians to be Ottomans (*ōsmants'i*) under the law of equality, this principle had not yet been realised. Believing full equality to be a solution to the injustices in the provinces, he argued that if the government had the right to demand Armenians be soldiers, Armenians had the right to demand equality in all aspects.[109]

Under British pressure, the Russian Empire accepted the truce offered by the Ottoman Empire and signed the Treaty of San Stefano in 1878. The European Great Powers later convened a congress in Berlin to review the settlement, which seemed to them to be overly favourable to Russia. Prior to this congress, Armenian delegates, including Mgrdich Khrimian, the former Istanbul patriarch, had visited European officials in Paris, London and Berlin to request their assistance in pressuring the Ottoman government to implement administrative reforms in the eastern Ottoman provinces. As a result, an article was inserted into the Treaty of Berlin that mandated that the Ottoman government implement reforms demanded by 'local requirements' in Armenian-inhabited provinces.[110]

The Ottoman Constitution

As the empire fell into turmoil due to the revolts in the Balkans, in December 1876 the Ottoman government promulgated a new constitution to prove to the representatives of the European Great Powers – who had gathered in Istanbul to discuss possible solutions – that it was willing to pursue reform.[111] The Constitution of the Ottoman Empire acknowledged the duality of state and religious community in a more explicit way. It stipulated that all people of Ottoman nationality were to be called 'Ottoman' (*Osmanlı*), regardless of the religion they professed or the denomination to which they belonged. Previously, in the Tanzimat period, the term 'Ottoman' had been synonymous with Muslims living in the Ottoman mainland. The drafters deliberately expanded this term's scope to subsume the multireligious, multiethnic and multilingual subjects of the empire under the category of a single Ottoman nation. The Constitution allowed all Ottomans, regardless of their religion, to enter the newly established parliament, which was to represent the entire country. In addition, the Constitution repeated the principle of equality by stipulating that 'all Ottomans were equal in their rights and duties in front of the law except for religious affairs'.[112]

Clause Eleven of the Constitution stipulated the special status of Islam as the state religion. This was accompanied by a proclamation of the freedom of religion, which the Constitution inherited from the Reform Edict of 1856. Because the religious sphere was separated from the political sphere, the Ottoman state left its subjects' religion up to them, at least in principle. However, the drafters limited this freedom to 'all religions known in the Ottoman domains'. This created a delimited category of 'religions officially recognised by the state'.[113]

Clause Eleven also included an explicit guarantee of religious privileges to non-Muslims. This clause indicated that religious privileges were to be granted not to religious authorities but to non-Muslim communities (*cemaat-i muhtelife*).[114] Traditionally, the Ottoman Empire had granted charters of investiture to individual high clergy rather than to a particular church or institution and approved their rights and exemptions as imperial favours. Following this custom, the Privileges Edict of 1853 that had redefined the rights and exemptions as religious privileges had been addressed to the religious authorities of each confessional group. By contrast, the Ottoman Constitution officially stated that the privileges belonged to the non-Muslim communities themselves.

The drafters also found it necessary to temper the scope of religious freedom and privileges by adding a proviso that public order must not be disturbed over these issues. This was a reminder of the debate over the independence of Bulgarian Orthodox Christians from the Orthodox Christian Patriarchate. The proviso was especially meaningful given that political movements could sometimes be conducted under the guise of religion. As will be discussed in Chapter 6, the spheres of religion and politics would commonly become inseparable in the subsequent history of the empire.

Conclusion

In the 1860s, Muslim statesmen were inclined to limit the sphere of the control of non-Muslim communities to achieve the broader integration of the empire's multireligious subjects. To do so, they foregrounded the logic of distinguishing between religious and non-religious (or political) affairs. Nevertheless, the line between these remained flexible and unclear. This allowed non-Muslims to negotiate with the imperial authorities over the scope of their privileges. The discussions among Armenians and their negotiations with Muslim officials show how we can understand the changes that occurred in the relationship between the Ottoman state and non-Muslim communities in the mid-nineteenth century.

First, although the formal representatives of non-Muslim communities remained their respective religious authorities in Istanbul, Muslim state officials preferred using informal channels to conduct quiet negotiations with and exert control over non-Muslim communities. They frequently depended on non-Muslim lay elites to help manage their relationships with these non-Muslim communities. To them, Armenians who entered the state bureaucracy represented a reliable intermediary. This channel had existed before the guarantee of religious privileges in 1853, but its importance only grew as the necessity of dealing with issues 'under the table' increased. Second, horizontal relationships among non-Muslim communities or those between Muslims and non-Muslims acquired greater significance for the vertical relationships between the state and non-Muslim communities. Muslim officials, in general, demanded the Armenians accept the same treatment as other groups. The Armenians sometimes agreed, but at other times emphasised their peculiar situation. In any case, when discussing the scope of the Armenians' privileges, both Muslim officials and Armenian actors referred to the responses and statuses of other religious communities to justify their own claims. As will be discussed in the next chapter, these horizontal relationships among religious groups in the empire would take on increasing importance during the reign of Abdülhamit II.

Notes

1. This issue will be discussed in Chapter 6.
2. The documents submitted by the Armenian patriarchs came to be called *takrir* in the first half of the nineteenth century.
3. Masayuki Ueno, '"For the Fatherland and the State": Armenians Negotiate the Tanzimat Reforms', *International Journal of Middle East Studies* 45, no. 1 (2013): 96–8.
4. BOA, A.DVNS.GMC.d 9, p. 54–5. Based on information from secondary literature, Talin Suciyan claims that the same clause was included in earlier charters. *Outcasting Armenians*, 27. However, this claim could not be confirmed from copies of the charters recorded in the registers in the Ottoman archives.

5. *Manzumēi Ēfk'ear*, no. 18.
6. *Masis*, no. 731 (24 March 1866).
7. Davison, *Reform in the Ottoman Empire*, chap. 5.
8. Ueno, '"Fatherland and the State"', 96–8.
9. İsmail Kara, 'Müsâvat yahut Müslümanlara Eşitsizlik: Bir Kavramın Siyaseten/Dinen İnşası ve Dönüştürücü Gücü', in *Osmanlı Devleti'nde Din ve Vicdan Hürriyeti*, ed. Azmi Özcan (Istanbul: Ensar Neşriyat, 2000), 307–9.
10. The pamphlet, which was written to support the Constitution, was reprinted in Süleyman Paşazade Sami, *Süleyman Paşa'nın Muhakemesi* (Istanbul: Erkan-ı Harbiye-i Umumiye Onuncu Şubesi, 1928), vol. 1, 60; Tarık Zafer Tunaya, 'Osmanlı Anayasacılık Hareketi ve "Hükumet-i Meşruta"', *Boğaziçi Üniversitesi Dergisi* 6 (1978): 235.
11. *Masis*, no. 735 (21 April 1866).
12. Unlike other non-Muslim religious groups, the head of Ottoman Protestants – called a *vekil* (representative) – was selected from among the laymen. BOA, A.DVNSMHM.d 258, p. 5, no. 8.
13. *Manzumēi Ēfk'ear*, no. 24 (13 April 1866).
14. *Masis*, no. 735.
15. Roderic H. Davison, 'Turkish Attitudes Concerning Christian-Muslim Equality in the Nineteenth Century', *The American Historical Review* 59, no. 4 (1954): 851; Akarlı, *Belgelerle Tanzimat*, 16. Previous researchers who have dealt with this remark (and similar remarks) have argued that it reflected Ottomanism. See Safrastjan, 'Ottomanism in Turkey I', 76–7. In this discussion, however, they have not paid sufficient attention to the fact that Ali Pasha admitted the necessity of the exceptional treatment for the religious affairs of non-Muslims.
16. Werth, *Tsar's Foreign Faiths*, 67–9.
17. The word *harsdut'iwnner* (wealth) might be a misspelling of *hasdadut'iwnner* (institutions).
18. *Ōrakir Dziln Awarayrioy*, 1st ser., nos. 51 (3 August 1868), 52 (4 August 1868).
19. *Manzumēi Ēfk'ear*, no. 642 (27 April 1868).
20. *Manzumēi Ēfk'ear*, no. 614 (21 March 1868).
21. For example, *Masis*, nos. 559 (8 November 1862), 568 (10 January 1863), 655 (10 September 1864), 684 (1 April 1865).
22. Aghapēkean, *Deghegakir Amenayn Hayots' Gat'oghigosut'ean*, 16.
23. *Manzumēi Ēfk'ear*, no. 1753 (18 November 1871). Panosian was sceptical about the sincerity of the assembly members. In the book he published in 1864, he complained that the terms 'love for the nation' (*Azkasirut'iwn*) or 'love for the fatherland' (*hayrenasirut'iwn*) had lost their gravity because of the marked increase of 'lovers of their nation' (*azkasēr*) among Istanbul Armenians, especially in younger generations. See Garabed H. P'anosean, *Asar-ı Kayseriye* (no place, 1864), 27. In his view, true lovers of their nation

were willing to help their destitute national fellows and promote school education.

24. Derderian, 'Mapping the Fatherland', 144–69; Ēmma Kostandyan, 'Mkrtich' A Vanets'i', in *K'ristonya Hayastan Hanragitaran* (Erevan: Haykakan Hanragitarani Glkhavor Khmbagrut'yun, 2002), 745–7.
25. *Adenakrut'iwnk'* (3 November 1870), 127–35.
26. *Adenakrut'iwnk'* (3 December 1870), 161–2.
27. *Masis*, no. 1754 (16 November 1875).
28. *Manzumēi Ēfk'ear*, no. 988 (10 August 1869).
29. The speech recalls the famous words uttered by Mahmut II in his later years, in which he allegedly mentioned that he did not see any difference among his multireligious subjects outside of the mosques, churches or synagogues, and that he saw all his subjects, regardless of religious affiliation, as his children. This speech was considered (perhaps too optimistically) the earliest recognition of equality between Muslims and non-Muslims. Reşat Kaynar, *Mustafa Reşit Paşa ve Tanzimat*, 2nd. ed. (Ankara: Türk Tarih Kurumu, 1985), 99–100; Bozkurt, *Gayrimüslim Vatandaşlarının Hukukî Durumu*, 41. While these studies refer to non-contemporary sources, similar words (with different nuances) attributed to Mahmut II were recorded by a contemporary in a speech conducted during his tour to the Balkans. Helmuth von Moltke, *Briefe über Zustände und Begebenheiten in der Türkei aus den Jahren 1835 bis 1839* (Berlin: Ernst Siegfried Mittler, 1841), 131.
30. *Adenakrut'iwnk'* (3 December 1870), 153–5.
31. *Adenakrut'iwnk'* (3 December 1870), 152–3; (9 December 1870), 175–8.
32. *Adenakrut'iwnk'* (3 November 1871), 497.
33. *Adenakrut'iwnk'* (20 October 1871), 468–9. Talin Suciyan presents a report sent from the diocese of Erzincan, which, as requested by the committee, contained not only problems but also solutions. *Outcasting Armenians*, 89–100.
34. The entire report was inserted in the minutes of the assembly. *Adenakrut'iwnk'* (20 October 1871), 468–83.
35. *Masis*, nos. 1158–62 (9–18 November 1871).
36. *Adenakrut'iwnk'* (3 November 1871), 498–9.
37. Cevdet Paşa, *Tezâkir 13–20*, ed. Cavid Baysun, 2nd ed. (Ankara: Türk Tarih Kurumu Basımevi, 1986), 100–1.
38. Davison, *Reform in the Ottoman Empire*, 105–8; *Masis*, nos. 617 (19 December 1863), 650 (6 August 1864), 797 (1 June 1867).
39. Davison, *Reform in the Ottoman Empire*, chap. 5.
40. *Masis*, no. 666 (26 November 1864); Petrov, 'Tanzimat for the Countryside', 103.
41. Artinian, *Armenian Constitutional System*, 69–71, 86.
42. *Adenakrut'iwnk'* (20 October 1871), 475–8. This number does not include *takrir*s on matters such as the appointment of clergymen, or the repair of religious facilities, or expressions of gratitude for fair treatment from provincial officials.

43. In addition, forty-four were from Aleppo, nineteen from Adana, fourteen from Trabzon, thirteen from Damascus, one from Aydın, twenty-one from Ankara, thirty-eight from Bursa, three from Kastamonu and nine from Rumeli.
44. *Adenakrut'iwnk'* (20 October 1871), 474.
45. Ibid., 475.
46. Ibid., 469–70.
47. Ibid., 473–4.
48. Ibid., 479.
49. Ibid., 479–81.
50. Cohen, *Becoming Ottomans*, 30–9.
51. On Muslims' negative attitudes towards equality with non-Muslims, see Kara, 'Müsâvat yahut Müslümanlara Eşitsizlik', 307–9; Masami Arai, *Osuman Teikoku wa Naze Hokaishita noka* (Tokyo: Seidosha, 2009), 79–83, 146–60.
52. *Adenakrut'iwnk'* (20 October 1871), 479. This phrase derives from the phrase 'the State and the Fatherland', which was used in the government's announcement of the conscription of non-Muslims. Heinzelmann, *Cihaddan Vatan Savunmasına*, 144–5, 247–8.
53. For example, *Manzumēi Ēfk'ear*, no. 1753.
54. Şemsettin Sami Frashëri, a Muslim Albanian intellectual and state official, employed a similar discourse. See George W. Gawrych, 'Tolerant Dimensions of Cultural Pluralism in the Ottoman Empire: The Albanian Community, 1800–1912', *International Journal of Middle East Studies* 15, no. 4 (1983): 524.
55. Heinzelmann, *Cihaddan Vatan Savunmasına*, 155.
56. BOA, İ.HR 5001 (6 October 1853); *Takvim-i Vekayi'*, no. 494.
57. *Adenakrut'iwnk'* (3 November 1871), 502–3.
58. *Adenakrut'iwnk'* (20 October 1871), 481.
59. *Masis*, no. 1161 (16 November 1871).
60. *Adenakrut'iwnk'* (3 November 1871), 500–5.
61. Ibid., 500, 504.
62. *Manzumēi Ēfk'ear*, no. 1767 (2 December 1871).
63. *Adenakrut'iwnk'* (10 November 1871), 510–12; (1 March 1872), 593–8.
64. *Adenakrut'iwnk'* (1 March 1872), 591–2.
65. *Adenakrut'iwnk'* (20 December 1872), 771–4.
66. *Adenakrut'iwnk'* (28 February 1873), 814–15.
67. *Masis*, no. 1226 (27 April 1872).
68. *Masis*, no. 1273 (22 August 1872).
69. *Manzumēi Ēfk'ear*, no. 1980 (11 September 1872); *Masis*, no. 1282 (13 September 1872).
70. *Masis*, no. 1285 (19 September 1872).
71. Gerard Libaridian, 'The Ideology of Armenian Liberation: The Development of Armenian Political Thought before the Revolutionary Movement (1639–1885)' (PhD diss., University of California Los Angeles, 1987), 180.

72. *Masis*, no. 1282.
73. *Masis*, no. 1291 (3 October 1872).
74. For the urban reforms, see Steven Rosenthal, *The Politics of Dependency: Urban Reform in Istanbul* (Westport, CT: Greenwood Press, 1980).
75. N. Işık Demirakın, 'Expropriation as a Modernizing Tool in the Nineteenth-Century Ottoman Empire: The Case of Cemeteries in Beyoğlu', *International Journal of Turkish Studies* 18, no. 1–2 (2012): 1–15.
76. Hans-Peter Laqueur, *Hüve'l-Baki: İstanbul'da Osmanlı Mezarlıkları ve Mezar Taşları*, trans. Selahattin Dilidüzgün (Istanbul: Tarih Vakfı Yurt Yayınları, 1997), chap. 2; Pars Tuğlacı, *İstanbul Ermeni Kiliseleri* (Istanbul: Pars Yayın, 1991), 217–28.
77. BOA, A.MKT.NZD 121/59 (27 March 1853); *Masis*, no. 62 (13 April 1853).
78. *Masis*, no. 83 (7 September 1853).
79. Behind this treatment was the new concept of public hygiene. According to Demirakın, the government 'prohibited as "a great threat to public health", burials in Muslim and non-Muslim cemeteries closer than 500 *zirâ*s [approximately 379 metres] to living areas'. Demirakın, 'Expropriation as a Modernizing Tool', 10. On this occasion, non-Muslims obtained land for their new cemetery, the largest of which still exists in the middle of the Şişli district. Today, due to the expansion of the urban area, this cemetery is now completely surrounded by residential and commercial buildings.
80. *The Levant Times* (11 January 1873); Demirakın, 'Expropriation as a Modernizing Tool', 10; BOA, İ.MVL 25997 (13 October 1867).
81. *Masis*, no. 1321 (14 December 1872). This park, called a 'national garden' (*millet bağçesi*) or 'public garden' (*bağçe-i umumi*, *umum bağçesi*), attracted the interest of many Istanbulites. Zeynep Çelik, *The Remaking of Istanbul: Portrait of an Ottoman City in the Nineteenth Century* (Seattle: University of Washington Press, 1986), 69–70. In 1879, after the failed expropriation of the Armenian cemetery, the government decided to open another park in the Muslim cemetery in Tepebaşı with the expectation that 'the public demand for the national garden in Taksim would drop'. BOA, İ.DH 63659 (23 July 1879); ŞD 282/17 (11 March 1880).
82. *Manzumēi Ēfk'ear*, no. 2050 (21 December 1872).
83. *Masis*, no. 1326 (28 December 1872); *Manzumēi Ēfk'ear*, no. 2057 (28 December 1872).
84. *Manzumēi Ēfk'ear*, no. 2060 (1 January 1873); *Masis*, no. 1328 (2 January 1873).
85. *Masis*, no. 1329 (4 January 1873); *Manzumēi Ēfk'ear*, no. 2062 (3 January 1873). It is likely that Halil Şerif Pasha took an initiative in the expropriation, suggesting a plan that was abandoned or suspended. In an open letter published in an English newspaper, an Armenian clergyman explained the Armenian view on this cemetery issue. In so doing, he attributed all the problems to Halil Şerif Pasha, who was originally from Egypt and had spent

much of his career in foreign embassies, and (according to the author) was therefore ignorant of the Ottoman way of treating non-Muslims, unlike the grand viziers in the previous decades. *The Levant Times* (11 January 1873). Halil Şerif Pasha – who had studied in Paris and was well known for his excessive fondness of the Parisian lifestyle – must have had close connections with the social circle of Beyoğlu's European residents, who desired a public park in the area. Masayuki Ueno, 'Urban Politics in 19th-century Istanbul: The Case of the Armenian Cemetery in Beyoğlu', in *Human Mobility and Multiethnic Coexistence in Middle Eastern Urban Societies 1: Tehran, Aleppo, Istanbul, and Beirut*, ed. Hidemitsu Kuroki (Tokyo: ILCAA, 2015), 95–6.

86. *Manzumēi Ēfk'ear*, no. 2063 (4 January 1873); *Masis*, no. 1329. *Manzume-i Efkar* referred to the importance of the Yusuf Kamil Pasha's help. Interestingly, this high-ranking official, who established his career in Egypt under the governorship of Mehmet Ali Pasha but transferred to Istanbul after his death, shared an Egyptian connection with Halil Şerif Pasha. Both married one of Mehmet Ali's descendants (Yusuf Kamil married Mehmet Ali's daughter and Halil Şerif married his great-granddaughter). Ueno, 'Urban Politics', 96–7.
87. *Masis*, no. 1329.
88. *Hadika*, no. 40 (19 January 1874). The depiction of the Muslims' attitude was not completely correct. Some Muslims in Istanbul had also criticised the government for the destruction of cemeteries during the urban reorganisation, calling it a 'disrespectful treatment of the dead'. Grand Vizier Fuat Pasha responded by arguing that the 'constructive work would surely please the souls of the dead'. Çelik, *The Remaking of Istanbul*, 61–2.
89. Susan Gilson Miller, 'Apportioning Sacred Space in a Moroccan City: The Case of Tangier, 1860–1912', *City & Society* 13, no. 1 (2001): 73–6.
90. Mardiros Hanēsean, *Hariwr K'san ew Hink Ameay Hopelean Perayi S. Errortut'iwn Egeghets'woy 1807–1932* ([Istanbul]: Dbaran Sēlamēt', 1932), 292.
91. *Hadika*, no. 40.
92. BOA, İ.HR 12251 (2 March 1865).
93. BOA, İ.MVL 21687 (14 December 1862); Demirakın, 'Expropriation as a Modernizing Tool', 1, 2, 5–7.
94. Ahmet Mülayim, 'Rum Okulları', in *Dünden Bugüne İstanbul Ansiklopedisi* (Istanbul: Kültür Bakanlığı ve Tarih Vakfı, 1994), vol. 6, 348; Zafer Karaca, 'Taksim Ayia Trias Kilisesi', *İstanbul* 52 (2005): 56–7.
95. BOA, Y.PRK.A 6/2 ([1870]).
96. *Manzumēi Ēfk'ear*, no. 2069 (10 January 1873). The idea of building a public park was probably appealing to the target readership of *Le Phare du Bosphore* (namely, Istanbul's residents of European origin). They wanted public parks like those in European cities, believing that these would bring the lifestyle of their home countries to the Ottoman capital. Panosian also

claimed that another French newspaper continually supported the expropriation of the Armenian cemetery. *Manzumēi Ēfk'ear*, no. 2068 (9 January 1873).

97. *Manzumēi Ēfk'ear*, no. 2067 (8 January 1873). Panosian first published his response to the criticism and later the translation of *Le Phare du Bosphore*.
98. *Masis*, no. 1329.
99. *Masis*, nos. 1226, 1574 (8 September 1874).
100. *Adenakrut'iwnk'* (22 September 1876), 174–6.
101. Leften S. Stavrianos, *The Balkans since 1453* (New York: Rinehart & Company, 1958), 396–401.
102. *Adenakrut'iwnk'* (19 May 1876), 6–7.
103. *Manzumēi Ēfk'ear*, nos. 3180 (17 July 1876), 3183 (20 July 1876); *Masis*, no. 1852 (22 July 1876); Cohen, *Becoming Ottomans*, 30–4.
104. *Masis*, nos. 1847 (11 July 1876), 1848 (13 July 1876); *Manzumēi Ēfk'ear*, no. 3175 (12 July 1876).
105. For example, see *Adenakrut'iwnk'* (7 June 1876), 38–42; (8 September 1876), 153; (22 September 1876), 174–86.
106. *Adenakrut'iwnk'* (22 September 1876), 185–6.
107. Ibid., 180–4.
108. *Adenakrut'iwnk'* (3 August 1877), 150–1.
109. *Adenakrut'iwnk'* (7 December 1877), 309–10, 317–18.
110. Richard G. Hovannisian, 'The Armenian Question in the Ottoman Empire, 1876–1914', in *The Armenian People from Ancient to Modern Times*, vol. 2: *Foreign Dominion to Statehood: The Fifteenth Century to the Twentieth Century*, ed. Richard G. Hovannisian (New York: St. Martin's Press, 1997), 206–12.
111. For the Ottoman Constitution, see Koçunyan, *Negotiating the Ottoman Constitution*.
112. *Kanun-ı Esasi*, 7–9.
113. This category was used to discuss the permissibility of the activities of Mormons and a foreign religious group called 'Seption'. For example, an undated document mentions that 'in the imperial domains, the freedom of ritual and religion is limited to and reserved for the communities appertaining to the religions and denominations officially recognised by the state'. (*Memalik-i Şahanede serbesti-yi ayin ve mezhep devletçe resmen malum olan edyan ve mezhebe mensup cemaatlere münhasır ve mahsus olup*). BOA, DH.TMIK.M 67/5 (26 February 1897), 102/48 (no date).
114. *Kanun-ı Esasi*, 8.

6

The Legacies of the Tanzimat Reforms

In the historiography of Ottoman Orthodox Christians, 'the Privileges Question' refers to the disputes between the Orthodox Christians and the Ottoman authorities over the privileges that their patriarchate in Istanbul possessed; these were first the subject of conversation in the 1880s and resurfaced in the early 1890s, and the discussion reached a climax in 1909–11. On all three occasions, Orthodox Christians protested that the Ottoman authorities were violating their privileges and then were able to re-negotiate the scope of the privileges.[1] These disputes were grounded, as our discussion in previous chapters has already suggested, in the redefinition of the favours and exemptions that non-Muslim religious authorities had enjoyed and in the application of this terminology to determine the foundations and extents of these favours. Indeed, it was suggested in a state document that Orthodox Christians had taken earlier Armenian protests as a model for their own actions.[2] Nevertheless, Ottoman officials had a different attitude in the 1880s and 1890s: they became more wary of the Christian clergy and determined in their efforts to reduce their influence. To this end, they expanded the scope of civil integration at the expense of religious spheres while increasing their reliance on the lay elites in their relationship with non-Muslim communities and incorporating these elites as individuals into imperial governance. Responding to this shift of attitude, the Orthodox Christian Patriarchate adopted a different strategy than the Armenians: while the Armenian protests had been sporadic and arose in response to specific problems, the Orthodox Christians brought forth several issues at each protest. This led to the emergence of the collective expression 'the Privileges Question' in the 1880s.[3]

How did Ottoman Armenians respond to this new development in the 1880s and the 1890s? Did they take any part in the Orthodox Christians' movement? Were they unaware of the political actions of their fellow

Christians? Previous studies that have examined the Privileges Question for Orthodox Christians have neglected Armenian reactions, and even general studies on Ottoman Armenians tend not to discuss the Privileges Question or how it affected them.[4] This is in part because studies of late nineteenth-century Ottoman Armenians have generally focused on the plight of the Armenians in the eastern provinces, its possible remedies and the emergence of revolutionary parties who had the emancipation of the Armenians as their main goal. We should recall, however, that the maintenance of patriarchal privileges was among the reforms that the European Great Powers demanded on behalf of the Ottoman Armenians in 1895 after the situation in the eastern provinces seriously deteriorated.[5] Moreover, as I will discuss in this chapter, the Kumkapı Incident – the first major act of an Armenian revolutionary party within the Ottoman Empire – occurred while the patriarchate was negotiating with the government over religious privileges and seriously affected the course of the negotiations.

Chapter 6 takes a new look at the Privileges Question of the 1880s and the early 1890s during the early reign of Abdülhamit II. I will foreground the involvement of the Armenians to analyse how the Hamidian regime succeeded in continuing the legacy of the Tanzimat Reforms and how the regime modified this legacy. During the Tanzimat era, Armenians used two different justifications: the inseparability of religion and politics and the inviolability of the religious sphere. During the Hamidian era, Orthodox Christians and Armenians increased their reliance on the latter logic to protect their privileges. The re-examination of the Privileges Question in this chapter will contribute to our understanding of how non-Muslim groups observed and were influenced by the acts and position of their neighbours and how Ottoman actors came to regard different religions and religious groups – including Islam and Muslims – as comparable and equal.

Armenians and the Hamidian Regime

Addressing the situation of the Armenians in the eastern Ottoman provinces was a significant political agenda item for Armenian elites in Istanbul during the Hamidian period. The fact that the Balkan Christians had gained independence and autonomy by exercising violence and inviting the intervention of the European Great Powers inspired feelings of unfairness and anxiety in the Armenians. They considered themselves entitled to enjoy the fruits of reforms where they lived (for the most part) in the eastern provinces. They saw that region as their fatherland. Armenian lobbying in Western Europe only resulted in the inclusion in the 1878 Treaty of Berlin of a single article requiring reforms in Armenian-inhabited provinces.[6]

In spite of its lack of strength, this article raised expectations among Armenian elites in Istanbul. An ecclesiastical member of the Armenian General Assembly mentioned that this event was an 'unveiling' of 'the name of the Armenians', which 'for the first time is acquiring a political appearance' rather than 'a mere religious appearance'. It was through this 'great international treaty [that] the Armenian Problem is turning into an international problem'.[7]

The Treaty of Berlin certainly expressed the augmented concern of the Great Powers (especially of Britain) about the state of the Ottoman Armenians. There was talk of putting the administration of the eastern provinces under a European protectorate, although such efforts never went beyond requiring the Ottoman Empire to alter governance in those areas.[8] No matter how much they were pushed, however, financial and manpower constraints still restrained the Ottoman state, and it could not completely implement the required reforms. Three years before the treaty was signed, the empire had effectively declared bankruptcy. In 1881, part of its financial affairs was entrusted to the Ottoman Public Debt Administration, which was controlled by European creditors. Moreover, the plight of the Armenians in the Ottoman Empire was only one of several issues within the Eastern Question for the European Great Powers, who, in the 1880s, had turned their attention to Africa and East Asia and away from the Ottoman Empire. They thus 'shelved the Armenian Question for fifteen years'.[9]

This lack of outside support forced Armenians in the eastern provinces to create local self-defence organisations. Although little is known of the activities or even the identities of most of these groups, the names of two early organisations have survived: the Defence of the Fatherland Society, founded in Erzurum in 1881, and the Armenagan Society, founded in Van in 1885. The Treaty of Berlin, followed by the inaction of the Great Powers, prompted concern among Russian Armenians. They began to take a more activist attitude that was intended to draw the attention of the Great Powers to the plight of their cousins on the other side of the border. Some made incursions into Ottoman territory, and others made donations to fund such activities.[10] In 1887, in Geneva, six Russian Armenians formed the Hunchakian Revolutionary Party, subsequently renamed the Social Democrat Hunchakian Party. From its base in Switzerland, the party developed a network of Russian and Ottoman Armenians. With the creation of an independent socialist state as its long-range objective, the party worked to liberate 'Western Armenia [that is, the eastern Ottoman provinces] through revolution'.[11] In response to the subsequent proliferation of small Armenian political groups, mainly within Russia, an umbrella organisation called the Federation of Armenian Revolutionaries was created in 1890 in Tiflis. This organisation, better known by its Armenian name, Dashnaktsutiwn, pursued the emancipation of the Armenians in the eastern provinces.[12]

In 1878, Abdülhamit II suspended parliament and the new constitution. He then worked to concentrate his political power instead of leaving it to the bureaucratic elites who had long dominated Ottoman politics or to representatives in parliament. The Yıldız Palace thus replaced the Sublime Porte as the centre of political decision making.[13] Abdülhamit's autocratic reign is often characterised as being centred on an Islamic ideology. His regime invoked Islamic symbolism and use religious vocabulary to gain support from its Muslim subjects, who had voiced discontent with the pro-Christian appearance of the Tanzimat policies. Behind this decision to focus on the Muslim subjects of the empire was the demographic shift that had taken place as the Ottoman Empire lost most of the large Christian populations of its Balkan territories in 1878 and a heavy influx of Muslim immigrants and refugees from the Russian Empire and the lost Balkan territories streamed into the empire. Abdülhamit acted as the caliph, the leader of all Sunni Muslims worldwide; in this capacity, he claimed a spiritual tie with Muslims worldwide, especially those who were under the colonial rule of the Great Powers. He used this claim to avoid war with the Great Powers, buying time to develop his empire economically and socially.[14]

This series of events has prompted researchers to conclude that the Hamidian regime deliberately alienated the non-Muslim subjects of the empire, which pushed them towards anti-regime movements. Nadir Özbek has challenged this view, however, drawing attention to the positive attitude of the Hamidian regime towards the voluntary activities of various social groups, including those of non-Muslims. He argues that while the regime regarded initiatives among non-Muslims with caution due to fears of separatism, Abdülhamit deliberately portrayed himself as a patron of philanthropy among non-Muslims and 'as the protector of Muslim and non-Muslim Ottomans alike'.[15] In fact, Abdülhamit extended paternalistic favours to his non-Muslim subjects, who still made up approximately 30 per cent of the empire's total population. He continued the custom of giving gifts to the representatives of non-Muslim religious communities to mark their religious feasts. For example, he granted 1,000 liras to the Ecumenical Patriarchate of the Orthodox Christians, 500 liras to the Armenian Patriarchate and 300 liras to the Chief Rabbinate on the joint occasion of the Christian Easter and Jewish Passover in 1889. An Armenian newspaper reported that the Armenian patriarch paid a formal visit to the Yıldız Palace to show his gratitude.[16] This was a ceremonial opportunity for the patriarch in his capacity as the official representative of the Ottoman Armenians to explicitly show the allegiance of the Armenians to the sultan and to publicly reconfirm the patron–client relationship they had with the state. It was also a good occasion for Abdülhamit to display his amicable relationship with non-Muslims to the European Great Powers.

The *tuğra*, or calligraphic signature of a sultan, was a symbolic object used to honour this relationship. An Armenian newspaper carried a detailed report of the first granting of the *tuğra* to the Istanbul Patriarchate in 1889, during a time when the Armenian revolutionary parties and their actions were beginning to draw attention from the upper echelons of the empire.[17] It was reported that a crowd gathered around the patriarchate on the day that the *tuğra* was due to arrive. Numerous policemen and gendarmes were waiting at the external door, and Armenian notables – both lay and clerical – arrived to attend the ceremony. Choristers sang a Turkish song dedicated to the sultan, and the gendarmes saluted when the *tuğra* arrived. The vice patriarch and members of lay and ecclesiastical councils received the *tuğra* at the external door, while the patriarch stood at the internal door wearing an Ottoman decoration, along with some clergy and the chair and members of the General Assembly. The patriarch respectfully kissed the *tuğra* and pronounced an address in both Turkish and Armenian to show his gratitude for the favour that the sultan had granted to his 'loyal Armenian subjects'. Finally, the participants cheered, 'Long live the Emperor, Sultan Abdülhamit!' and the choristers reprised their song. As Julia Phillips Cohen argues, although the Hamidian regime 'undoubtedly alienated non-Muslim individuals and collectives', 'a state's mobilization and public display of official religion did not always, or necessarily, prevent members of other faiths from identifying with that state'.[18]

Ultimately, the Hamidian regime could not remove the treatment of non-Muslims from its political agenda. Because it was a possible cause for dispute between the Ottoman Empire and the Great Powers, the survival of the empire depended on a careful handling of its relationship with non-Muslims. One of the foremost items on Abdülhamit's agenda was changing the imbalance of the Ottoman Empire's foreign relations – in which the Great Powers reserved the right to intervene in Ottoman internal politics on behalf of their coreligionists – to a relatively equal, mutual and balanced relationship between peers. The claim of caliphal protection for Muslims worldwide had the potential to help achieve this goal.

The Ottoman dynasty began to consolidate its caliphal claim after losing the Crimea in the late eighteenth century.[19] This territorial loss and the following annexation by Russia marked a turning point for the religious policies of the two empires. For Russia, the annexation of the Crimea and the partition of Poland led to a sudden increase in the number of its non-Orthodox Christian subjects (that is, Muslims, Catholics and Jews). This in turn required a new method of confessional administration. In 1788, the Russian Empire established a confessional administrative body to handle Muslims' religious affairs called the Orenburg Muslim Spiritual Assembly. This body's mandate bore a marked resemblance to the Ottoman treatment of non-Muslim religious groups and authorities. For the Ottoman Empire, the loss of Crimea meant the loss of a Muslim-dominant region. This increased the importance of its claim of continued ties with its former subjects there.[20] These parallel phenomena suggest that the confessional administration of non-dominant religious groups and the development and the claim of protection of coreligionist foreign populations were two sides of the same coin. This is also the perspective from which the pan-Islamist claims of Abdülhamit II must be understood.

Abdülhamit inherited this caliphal claim and radically strengthened it, displacing the Great Powers as the sole claimants of being the protectors of foreign coreligionists. Abdülhamit's claim was 'a defensive bargaining lever in the international arena, as a policy of destabilization against rival Christian powers who had Muslim subjects'.[21] It only increased in importance as the Great Powers expanded their colonial territories into parts of Asia and Africa that had large Muslim populations. France's conquest of the former Ottoman territory of Algeria was complete in 1847, and neighbouring Tunisia was made a protectorate in 1881. Britain instituted direct rule in India (which included today's Pakistan and Bangladesh) in 1858. Beginning in the 1860s, the Russian Empire gradually expanded its territory out into Central Asia. The Austro-Hungarian Empire meanwhile occupied Bosnia during the years of the Balkan turmoil in the 1870s and continued to administer it afterwards even though it was nominally under Ottoman sovereignty. To counteract Abdülhamit's spiritual influence over Bosnian Muslims, in 1882 the Austro-Hungarian Empire established its own confessional administrative position, the *Reis-ul-ulema*, along with an administrative body made up of a council of ulamas.[22]

Armenian State Officials

Although Abdülhamit suspended the Ottoman Constitution and the parliament in 1878 – a suspension that lasted for thirty years – he did not ultimately deny the fundamental principles of the Constitution or attempt to roll back the achievements of the Tanzimat Reforms: namely, the legal and political equality of all Ottomans, freedom of religion and guarantees of religious privileges for non-Muslims. While non-Muslims were still not subject to military conscription, they continued to be able to enter the state bureaucracy, which high-ranking Muslim officials of the Tanzimat period saw as the foremost means of integrating a multireligious empire.[23] They concluded that they would be able to unify the religiously and ethnically diverse Ottoman Empire by incorporating the top elites of its non-dominant religious groups and guiding them upwards into the state apparatus. During the Tanzimat period, Armenian lay elites in Istanbul, as I have already noted, generally preferred this career path, and they continued to do so in the Hamidian period. High-ranking Muslim officials in the Tanzimat period had cultivated personal ties with them and employed them as intermediaries with the Armenian community. Abdülhamit adopted this technique as part of his 'patronage system of rewarding loyalty in order to get things done'.[24] While he bypassed key sectors of government, he cultivated personal ties with notable figures of various social groups, including local elites, Kurdish tribal leaders, sheikhs of tariqas and lay (sometimes religious) leaders of non-Muslim communities.[25]

When the Armenian revolutionary groups caught his attention, Abdülhamit relied on Armenian state officials. On 21 January 1888, Grand Vizier Kamil Pasha, following Abdülhamit's orders, invited four Armenian notables – namely, Harutyun Dadian, Serovpe Vichenian, Vahan Efendi and Nurian Efendi – to discuss the matter. All were likely state officials. As shown in previous chapters, both Dadian and Vichenian began their careers during the late Tanzimat period. It is also highly likely that the Vahan Efendi in this case was the same man who served in the Ministry of Justice and Religious Affairs and that Nurian Efendi was a member of the State Council.[26] Kamil Pasha addressed these men on the subject of the recent rumours about 'revolutionary committees' (*heghap'okhagan masnazhogovner*) that had arisen among Armenians in Istanbul and elsewhere. The Armenian notables each confirmed in turn that the rumours were the 'invention of malicious people' who wanted to 'stain the centuries-old allegiance' of the Armenians to the Ottoman state. Kamil Pasha was satisfied with their response and stated that he would pass it on to the sultan. A few days later, the grand vizier brought up the rumours with the Armenian patriarch and received a similar answer.[27]

Although the upper echelons of the Ottoman Empire hoped to restrict the collective activities of non-Muslims, there was still a widespread belief among them that Armenians and other religious groups were jointly responsible to the empire as collective entities represented by lay and ecclesiastical elites. An Armenian newspaper article published in January 1891 provides us with an image of the symbolic position held by Armenian state officials during the Hamidian period. This article reported the occasion of Abdülhamit's grant of decorations to two Armenian officials.

In the nineteenth-century Ottoman Empire, this was often done to reconfirm the patron–client relationship between the sultan and notable subjects, especially state officials, but the measure took on additional meaning when the recipients were non-Muslims. Armenian newspapers frequently reported when Armenians were given decorations, and this was seen as a show of favour to the entire community at large. Although the two Armenians who received decorations on this occasion were merely minor officials in the telegraph and postal services, the growing suspicion of Armenians resulting from the activities of Armenian revolutionary parties encouraged the officials to write a special response. They sent a letter bearing 'signatures from various strata of Armenian people' to the sultan through a palace official. The palace then treated the letter as a collective appeal from 'all strata of Armenians' in Istanbul.[28]

The article provided an Armenian translation of the letter and the oral response that the Armenian officials had received from the palace. The letter itself began with a statement of sorrow about the 'illegal publications and activities' of Armenians who were 'trying to seduce simple-minded people' to 'harm the ties of allegiance that the Armenian community has with the Ottoman government'. It then claimed that 'these individuals constitute the smallest part of the Armenian community' and 'lack the quality and authority to act on behalf of the community'. The writers then celebrated the hitherto harmonious relationship between the empire and the Armenians. They praised 'the sublime protection of the August ancestors of Your Majesty' under which 'Armenian subjects have maintained their religion, language and nationality for more than 500 years'. They added that Abdülhamit had continually maintained the same generosity from the day of his accession and expressed confidence that Armenians would continue to merit the same favour. Finally, the letter asserted that the Armenians' centuries-old allegiance had so far kept them from straying off their course of love for and loyalty to the sultan, and that they would not serve any illegal cause. They concluded that the 'only desire of the Armenian subjects is to live entirely peacefully under the affectionate and justice-loving protection of the Ottoman government'.[29]

The oral response to this display of allegiance was as follows: they were told that the sultan was satisfied, having seen that 'Armenian subjects in my capital city rushed to reassert the allegiance they had' to him. It was also added that the Armenians had gained his trust because of their long history as subjects of the Ottoman Empire and that the sultan had never considered the Armenians to have strayed from their allegiance. The fact that some Armenians were 'insane' (as was also true among other nations) was merely a recent phenomenon, and their number was very small.[30]

Thus, public confirmation of the patron–client relationship took on even more importance during the Hamidian period, as the relationship between the regime and non-Muslims became increasingly fragile and the former increasingly criminalised the latter.

The Privileges Question, 1883–4

In the late 1870s to early 1880s, the Ottoman government became more wary of non-Muslim clergymen and increasingly determined to curb their influence over the flocks.[31] In June 1883, this shift resulted in a dispute over religious privileges between the patriarchate of the Orthodox Christians and the Ottoman authorities. The Orthodox Christian Patriarchate accused the authorities of infringing on its privileges, which the authorities denied. In contrast with the Armenians of the 1860s and 1870s, the Orthodox Christian Patriarchate brought three general issues before the government simultaneously: the legal treatment of clergymen, problems related to civil law and requests for permission to construct and restore churches and schools. The dispute reached a settlement in favour of the Orthodox Christians in May 1884. As in the Armenian case, the argument for a separate religious sphere was conspicuous here as well.

A detailed discussion of the claims put forward by the Orthodox Christians can be found in a copy of the document that Patriarch Yoakim III submitted to the Ottoman government in July 1883.[32] It was prepared as a response to a request from state officials, who wanted him to explain how he believed the government was infringing on the religious privileges of Orthodox Christians, and on what basis he made his claim. Before entering into the particulars, Yoakim enumerated the general grounds for Orthodox Christians' enjoyment of religious privileges. First, he invoked the foundation myth of the Istanbul Patriarchate, referring to Mehmet II's original appointment of an Orthodox Christian patriarch after the conquest of Constantinople. Then, his narrative passed over 400 years and arrived at the mid-nineteenth century. He quoted from the Privileges Edict of 1853, the Reform Edict of 1856 and the edict on the privileges of non-Muslims that Sultan Abdülaziz had issued during the turmoil in the Balkans in 1875. Yoakim also invoked Article Eleven of the Ottoman Constitution of 1876, which asserted the freedom of religion and guaranteed preservation for the religious privileges granted to non-Muslims. Interestingly, he stated that the Constitution, which had been promulgated three months after Abdülhamit's accession, was a symbol of the inheritance of the sultan's ancestors' policy towards non-Muslims (omitting the fact that the sultan had himself suspended the Constitution in 1878). He also referred to the correspondence that Ali Pasha and Fuat Pasha had with the European Great Powers in the 1850s and the 1860s, maintaining that this amounted to international confirmation that non-Muslims' religious privileges were to be preserved. In his discussion of these particular issues, Yoakim quoted from the charters of investiture granted to the patriarch and metropolitans, as well as the General Regulations of the Orthodox Christians, which the sultan had authorised in an edict in 1862 and were considered state laws (*nizamat-ı devlet*), along with several further orders issued by Ottoman authorities on the matter.

We can conclude from Yoakim's discussion that behind his protest were the judicial reforms that had been ongoing since the late Tanzimat period. Judicial reforms had been one important aspect of achieving civil integration in the multireligious Ottoman Empire. Previously, Muslims, Orthodox Christians, Armenians and Jews had their own religious judicial forum, while Muslims' sharia courts were also open to non-Muslims, albeit at some disadvantages.[33] In the course of the Tanzimat Reforms, the Ottoman government had codified penal and civil laws and created the Nizamiye courts, which adjudicated cases according to codified laws and were equally open to everyone: a step towards legal equality regardless of religion. However, while the creation of the Nizamiye courts reduced the jurisdiction of sharia courts and non-Muslim ecclesiastical courts, the Ottoman government allowed the latter two to continue functioning.[34] Thus, when Yoakim prepared his protest, a variety of judicial venues coexisted in the empire.

Modern researchers have foregrounded the pitfalls of using a binary contrast between sharia/religious law and state/secular law in the Ottoman judicial reforms. For Yoakim, however, this binary contrast was a tool for framing his argument. The coexistence of plural judicial systems allowed him to put forth the idea – in accordance with the idea of dual spheres promulgated by the Tanzimat Reforms – that the Ottoman Empire had a dual system: state law, which was used in Nizamiye courts and was applicable to all Ottoman subjects regardless of religion, and 'particular bodies of law' (*kavanin-i mahsusa*), which, in his argument, meant 'religious law' (*kavanin-i diniye, kavanin-i mezhebiye*). These were formulated and employed differently in the religious courts and councils of each religious group, including those of Muslims. Thus, Yoakim put sharia and non-Muslims' religious laws on the same footing.[35]

In the decades following the establishment of the Nizamiye courts, several changes, adjustments and reconfigurations were made in relation to the judicial sphere, some of which involved the treatment of non-Muslims. According to Yoakim, in the early 1880s, the Ottoman government had modified certain clauses in the appointment charters of the Orthodox Christian metropolitans to adapt them to the new justice system. The patriarchate protested this modification, and on 2 April 1883, the government replied that these were necessary to ensure conformity with the judicial reforms. The following month, the government sent out an official notice to the provinces to inform them of the new legal treatments of alimony and bequests for non-Muslims. With these changes, the state expanded the area of applicability of general law, thus increasing civil and political integration regardless of religion. This entailed the shrinking of the sphere of religious law, which prompted the patriarchate to protest the infringement of established religious privileges.

To return to the three general issues that the patriarch brought before the government, Yoakim first discussed two changes that were made in the charters of investiture regarding the legal treatment of metropolitans. The first change concerned the venues where cases against clergy members were heard. Previously, the charters had stipulated that these were only to be heard in Istanbul, regardless of the residence of the accused. The new charters, however, stipulated that cases against clergy would be heard in the sharia courts of the region in which the accused cleric resided. In Yoakim's interpretation, this meant that sharia court judges would have jurisdiction over Christian clergy, which was problematic. The second change he wanted to challenge related to the procedure of detaining, arresting and jailing accused clergy members. Previously, the detainment and imprisonment of clerics was entrusted to the relevant patriarchate in Istanbul or to the bishoprics in the provinces. In the new charters, however, accused clergymen were to be detained by the state instead. Yoakim claimed that these changes were a violation of existing ecclesiastical privileges.

Issues of civil law, including the treatment of disputes over alimony and bequest among Orthodox Christians, were also closely associated with the question of the scope of the religious sphere. In relation to alimonies following divorce, Yoakim criticised the government for ordering that 'decisions made by patriarchates [on alimony] would be in force as long as no objection arises', but that 'general courts' (*mahakim-i umumiye*, that is, Nizamiye courts) would hear and examine cases of alimony when objections arose to the patriarchates' decisions. He argued that this denied the final judicial power of the patriarchate over alimony, thus annulling the authority that the church courts had over marriages. Yoakim asserted that the charters of investiture granted the clergy jurisdiction over marriage, divorce and all issues related to them. Moreover, judges of other courts could not intervene in such questions. He claimed the Church's full authority over all issues related to marriage on the grounds that it was among the 'religious sacraments' (*esrar-ı diniye*) and asserted that the determination of alimony after a divorce was undoubtedly a marriage-related issue.

Yoakim's employment of the concept of religious particularism here recalls similar arguments made by the Armenians, as discussed in the previous chapter. Confronting the divided sphere of the judiciary, Yoakim asserted that alimony cases among Orthodox Christians should not be heard in Nizamiye courts, because 'no law [for alimony] that can be applied to everyone exists, and its creation is impossible'. Yoakim also denied the applicability of sharia to Orthodox Christians' marital issues, since sharia is a religious law applicable only to Muslims. Denying the universality of sharia, he neglected the fact that sharia had already been applied – and in some cases was still applied – to non-Muslim Ottomans. He also kept silent about the fact that the Ottoman civil code was created based on sharia.[36]

In Yoakim's argument, the ecclesiastical law of Orthodox Christians had equal footing with the sharia of Muslims as the laws of particular religions. This argument, which was made possible by the creation of the Nizamiye court system, allowed him to claim that Orthodox Christians' disputes over alimony should only be heard by their own religious councils. Thus, he wrote, 'marriage suits are fundamentally concerned with religion [*mezhebe müteallik*] and are subject to particular religious laws [*kavanin-i mahsusa-i mezhebiye*], and clearly none can interfere with them, because hearing them is permitted only in ecclesiastical councils'. The same logic was employed in his discussion of the treatment of bequests. The government ordered that Orthodox Christians' disputes on bequests should be entrusted to the Nizamiye courts if either side in a dispute requested it, but Yoakim argued that cases over bequests among Orthodox Christians should only be heard under ecclesiastical law.

Finally, Yoakim invoked the inviolability of the religious sphere in his discussion of churches and schools. The Ottoman government had previously taken a liberal attitude towards the construction and restoration of these buildings, but it had more recently begun to take a more severe approach. Yoakim argued that the construction and restoration of churches were among the articles of the freedom of religion, and that Orthodox Christians were thus entitled to permission to undertake such projects. He also emphasised that schools had a close tie with religion in the eyes of Orthodox Christians, reminding the government that schools were financially supported by the donations collected by the Church, that they were under the general supervision of patriarchates and metropolitanates and that each individual school was under the supervision of local church trustees.

Muslims in the Former and Privileged Ottoman Provinces

Interestingly, in his concluding remarks, Yoakim maintained that the recognition of religion as an exceptional sphere was 'an operative rule internationally confirmed' and not merely a custom of the Ottoman Empire. In his opinion, 'the sublime [Ottoman] government took pains to make holy sharia [courts] hear the cases that Muslims living in privileged or independent provinces had with their coreligionists according to their religious laws'.[37] The term 'privileged provinces' here referred to those provinces that had gained autonomy under Ottoman sovereignty. This was the product of Eurocentric international politics that preferred the survival of a weakened Ottoman Empire to maintain the balance among European powers.[38] Thus, when Yoakim wrote of 'Muslims living in privileged or independent provinces', the reference was to Muslims who were non-dominant in a territory that had gained autonomy or independence from Ottoman rule. To justify this, he underlined the parallelism between the treatment of Christians in the Ottoman Empire (on whose behalf the Christian Great Powers interfered in Ottoman politics) and the treatment of Muslims in former Ottoman lands (on whose behalf the Ottoman government engaged in comparable political intervention).

This parallelism is also evident in the instructions that the office of Şeyhülislam, the head of the empire's Islamic hierarchy, issued in July 1885, two years after Yoakim submitted his document.[39] These instructions related to the 'religious affairs' (*hususat-ı mezhebiye*) of Muslim inhabitants of former Ottoman territories in the Balkans (that is, Romania, Greece, Serbia, Montenegro and Bulgaria). Greece achieved its independence in 1830, and Romania, Serbia and Montenegro followed in 1878 under the Treaty of Berlin. This treaty also placed Bulgaria under Ottoman suzerainty. The independence or autonomy acquired by these regions made their Muslim inhabitants members of a non-dominant religious group in predominantly Christian countries. The 1885 instructions were intended to maintain religious ties between the Ottoman caliph and the Muslims in those territories. According to the instructions, the Ottoman caliph was to be considered the top of the Muslim hierarchical order, and Şeyhülislam acted as the liaison between the caliph and all other Muslims. Muftis represented each Muslim community in the aforementioned regions and would also act as judges.[40]

The instructions had 103 articles and mainly discussed the administration of Muslims' religious and communal affairs, including the election and appointment of religious functionaries (muftis, imams and preachers), the education of children, the administration of pious foundations and the treatment of orphans. In each district, a communal council (*cemaat meclisi*) would be formed, with branches in each town and village. The members of these councils would be elected by a general assembly (*meclis-i umumi*) consisting of ulamas, sheikhs, imams, headmen of neighbourhoods and villages, and guild representatives. This arrangement is reminiscent of those developed for the Armenian National Constitution and other regulations for Ottoman non-Muslims that had been stipulated in the 1860s, as well as the Spiritual Assembly of Russian Muslims. Thus, while the Ottoman government was struggling to curtail the sphere of communal autonomy of non-Muslims at home, it was endeavouring to create a similar sphere for Muslims in its former territories.

The Armenians' Response

Although the issues that Orthodox Christians problematised in their approach to the Privileges Question concerned the Armenians as well, they did not immediately follow suit. At the time, Patriarch Varjabedian was requesting approval from the Ottoman authorities for his resignation from his post but it was rejected for a period of several years.[41] Because Varjabedian was not working, the Armenians in Istanbul lacked leadership.[42] Moreover, they probably believed that this was not the right time to raise any issues, as the recent arrest of fifty-five Armenians in Erzurum – presumably members of the Defence of the Fatherland Society – had aroused suspicion of Armenians in government circles.[43] Nevertheless, the Armenians in Istanbul did not keep silent about the prolonged negotiations that the Orthodox Christians were having with the Ottoman authorities. The Armenian General Assembly briefly discussed the legal treatment of clergymen in criminal cases in September 1883, and the patriarchate raised the issue to the Ottoman government in a *takrir* on the 'question of our old religious privileges'.[44] Several months later, in January 1884, the Armenian Patriarchate submitted a more detailed *takrir* on the matter. An Armenian translation was recorded in the minutes of the General Assembly.[45] Although we do not have any information on the government's response, an examination of the method by which the Armenians sought to promote their claims can deepen our understanding of the extent and meaning of the Privileges Question in the 1880s.

Due to the patriarch's absence from duty, it fell to the general council of Armenian clergymen to deal with the Privileges Question. The members of the council felt it necessary to justify their deeds before the government, invoking an article of the Armenian National Constitution stipulating that important religious problems that went beyond the abilities of the ecclesiastical council would be entrusted to a general council of clergymen, which would be convened in the case of special necessity. Interestingly, the council members did not fail to mention that these issues could also be assigned to the Universal Catholicos (*Ěnthanragan Gat'oghigos*) of Echmiadzin if the general council considered it beyond their competence.[46] With this move, they likely were intimating to the government that the issue could develop into an international problem and, to avoid this possibility, the government should take a tolerant approach.

Although it is not clear whether the Armenian clergymen had any communication with the Orthodox Christian Patriarchate, the similarity between their *takrir* and the document submitted by Yoakim suggests that they were following his example by not restricting themselves to addressing issues on a case-by-case basis and instead addressing several issues at once. The Armenians' *takrir* had two sections, as had Yoakim's *takrir*. The first gave a general overview of the council's view of the Armenians' religious privileges, and the second dealt with the specific issues at hand. The grounds of the privileges discussed in the first sections of the two *takrir*s were also extremely similar. The council members first referred to the foundation myth to emphasise the similarity between the patriarchates of the Orthodox Christians and the Armenians, writing that Mehmet II wanted the Armenians to have a patriarchal seat in the Ottoman capital as the Greeks did. They likewise then jumped to the mid-nineteenth century, quoting from the edict of 1853 that guaranteed religious privileges, the Reform Edict, the edict of Abdülaziz and the Ottoman Constitution. In the discussion of specific issues, the council also invoked the charters of clergymen and the National Constitution of 1863.[47]

Most issues discussed in Yoakim's *takrir* were also found in the Armenians' document. Moreover, they also shared a justification: the inviolability of the religious sphere. While the Armenians were silent about the issue of court venues for cases against the clergy, they did address the procedures for the imprisonment of clergy. In addition, they discussed recent problems they had experienced as a community. One related to the obligation to respond to official requests for criminal information, which recent legislation on criminal procedures now required. The council maintained that the clergy should be exempt from this duty because they could not share certain confidential information, especially when it was obtained from the sacrament of confession. Therefore, the application of this obligation to clergymen 'was against the principles of our religious belief and Christian faith'.[48] The other concerned the dismissal of clergy from their positions. Referring to the recent treatment of Armenian clergy in the eastern provinces – namely, in Muş, Arapgir and Bulanık – the council claimed that provincial officials were forcing the dismissal of Armenian clergymen by accusing them of crimes and sending them to civil courts (*k'aghak'ayin adeanner*) in Istanbul, which the council held was 'an intervention in our religious affairs'.[49] The names of the specific places mentioned suggest that these protests probably stemmed from political suspicions of recent movements among Armenians in the eastern provinces.

In reference to alimony and bequest disputes, the council repeated Yoakim's assertion that the religious sphere was inviolable.[50] They maintained that disputes over alimony could not be entrusted to sharia courts or Nizamiye courts because they would judge not according to Christian law but according to the 'principles of the sharia of the Islamic religion', an arrangement that absolutely collided with 'our religion'.[51] Thus, like Yoakim, the Armenian council members neglected the fact that, in some cases, sharia was still applied to non-Muslims as well. A document written by a Muslim state official a few years later makes a clear contrast with this argument. To deny an Armenian claim opposing the applicability of sharia to an inheritance case, the Muslim official confidently asserted that 'the law of inheritance is sharia in our country'.[52]

Armenian clergymen also referred to Ottoman treatment of Muslim disputes over alimony and other marital issues, asserting that such disputes were entrusted to sharia courts in all provinces of the Ottoman Empire, including privileged provinces. The members of the Armenian council and Yoakim thus made the same argument: that Christians in the Ottoman Empire were entitled to the same treatment as Muslims, equating Muslim sharia courts with Christian religious ones.[53] This argument deserves our attention. Previously, in the 1860s and 1870s, the Armenians had claimed to be entitled to the same treatment as Orthodox Christians, taking equality among non-Muslim groups as a given. However, they did not expect the same treatment that Muslims received. When the Armenian General Assembly members discussed military conscription in 1871, for example, they admitted that the achievement of equality between Muslims and non-Muslims in Ottoman society would be a difficult and prolonged question, and that Armenians needed to be patient with the slow pace of change in Muslim attitudes.[54] By the 1880s, however, three decades after equality between Muslims and non-Muslims had been promised, Armenians had begun to argue that they were now entitled to equal treatment. This attitude led them to analogise Christianity to Islam, even though the empire had attached special status to Islam and reconfirmed it by declaring it to be the state religion in the Ottoman Constitution.[55]

In their discussion of the necessity of special treatment for clergy in cases of imprisonment, then, the members of the council declared that, 'like the ulamas, sheikhs, preachers and imams among the Muslims, our clergymen could not be exposed to public infamy'.[56] They therefore justified their claim by disregarding the particularities of the individual religions. This does not mean, however, that they had abandoned their demand for special treatment exclusive to their own religion. This type of double reasoning appears in the *takrir*s of both Orthodox Christians and Armenians.

The logic of the inviolability of religious affairs is also observable in the discussion of disputes over inheritance, which they saw as being inherently religious. The council members argued that although the judges in sharia courts intervened in the treatment of Christians' inheritance, following the Law on Heritage promulgated in the Hijri year of 1278 (1861/2), this did not conform with the 'principles and laws of Christian religion'.[57] Thus, the Armenian council found this occasion an opportunity to claim exclusive authority over all marital and inheritance issues in their community. The claims they put forward were not limited to the preservation of religious privileges. Instead, opportunities were sought to negotiate the scope of communal autonomy.[58]

In addition to references to the dismissal of clergy and their legal obligations, the originality of the Armenians' *takrir* lay in the insertion of issues related to education and censorship, both of which were under the jurisdiction of the Ministry of Public Education. Although these issues troubled Orthodox Christians as well, Yoakim had not raised them in his own *takrir*.[59] Education, along with justice, was the field in which the Tanzimat government had the greatest leeway to pursue its policy of civil integration. Meanwhile, as discussed in Chapter 3, censorship was an arena in which the jurisdictions of state and community leaders collided. The government began to expand its control over the schools of non-Muslims after the enactment of the Law of Public Education in 1869, which restricted the scope of the autonomy of non-Muslim communities.[60] In the early 1880s, the Ministry of Public Education began to enhance its supervision over Armenian schools, calling on the Armenian Patriarchate to submit the textbooks and curriculums that were being used in these schools.[61] The Armenians' *takrir* also claimed that the state ordered the closure of some Armenian schools in the provinces and protested that this intervention in their communal schooling was a deviation from Ottoman tradition.

The Views of Muslim State Officials

As previous studies have noted, the Ottoman government 'announced its full compliance with the "ancient regime"' in May 1884, which appeased the Christians with regard to the Privileges Question.[62] Nevertheless, this announcement was merely the general expression of a willingness to compromise, lacking any specifics. The bones of contention thus never truly disappeared. Christian clergymen closely examined the measures passed by the government for any signs of infringement of their privileges or any opportunities to expand their influence.[63] The government, meanwhile, did not avert its vigilant eye from political movements among Christians, which were a regular source of trouble following the Treaty of Berlin. A memorandum written in 1888 by Mustafa Ziver, head of the Directorate of Religious Affairs and thus in charge of the government's relationship with non-Muslim religious authorities, can help us to understand their view.[64]

According to his curriculum vitae, Mustafa Ziver entered the Directorate of Religious Affairs in 1863 at age twenty. He was promoted to its head in 1870 and remained in this post for several decades.[65] This gave him an exceptional degree of practical experience in the religious affairs of non-Muslims. Regarding the memorandum in question, Mustafa Ziver expressed a negative view of recent movements among 'Orthodox Christian, Bulgarian, Armenian and Catholic' clergy in the provinces. He argued that these movements were beyond their original duties, which – according to him – were limited to 'arranging the merely spiritual and religious necessities and conduct of non-Muslim subjects'. Some clergy were endeavouring to rescue Christians who had been arrested for criminal offences, while others involved themselves in land disputes, tax issues and the settlement of Muslim refugees and immigrants, all of which Ziver collectively called 'secular affairs' (*umur-ı dünyeviye*). It should be noted that he admitted the recent judicial reforms had reduced the involvement of the clergy in these issues. Nevertheless, they had not yet abandoned their 'malicious desires'. As he wrote: 'Today, the first preoccupation of the religious authorities is political affairs'. They were thus inciting 'national feelings' (*kavmiyet ve cinsiyet hissiyatı*) among the people and suspected of conducting secret negotiations with the ambassadors and consuls of foreign countries.[66]

Interestingly, Ziver thought it appropriate to analogise Christian clergymen to Muslim ulamas when denying that exceptional treatment was necessary for the former. He used the same reasoning as the Armenian clergy, except in support of the opposite conclusion. When the government tried to punish clergymen, the patriarchates in Istanbul protested, claiming that this amounted to an infringement of their privileges and demanding special treatment for their clergy in criminal cases. Ziver denied these requests, stating that because judicial decisions fell under the general law, this must be applied to everyone, including both Christian clerics and Muslim ulamas. He argued that if the government allowed exceptional treatment for Christian clergy, sharia and judicial law would be corrupted.[67] Ulamas were generally understood to be learned scholars but on an equal footing with Muslims in general before God, while Christian clergy were given a different standing from that of laymen on account of their ordination. Ziver would therefore have been justified in drawing a distinction between the way these two groups were to be treated. Ottoman authorities in the early modern period had treated the two groups differently, and the Tanzimat state had also chosen to give special treatment to non-Muslim clergymen by granting religious privileges to them alone. Ziver, however, disregarded any difference in status between Muslim ulamas and Christian clerics.[68] He supported the expansion of civil integration under the principle of equality, even though this sacrificed some of the inviolability of the religious sphere. Any rule that would apply to Muslims, in his view, must be applied to non-Muslims as well. The principle of equality thus overshadowed the particularism of each religion.

Ziver also saw the expansion of civil integration as an effective measure for weakening the secular influences of clergymen on their flocks and limiting their ability to incite Christians against the government. He expounded on this idea by using the example of clerics issuing the identity certificates necessary for the transfer of property or obtaining travel documents.[69] This role, which the government had entrusted to the clergymen of non-Muslim religions, augmented their secular influence. Although the Ministry of Justice and Religious Affairs had attempted to transfer this role to local municipalities nine years previously, the ministry was unable to complete this restructuring because the patriarchates had opposed it, claiming that the government needed to compensate them for the financial loss that this reform would cause them. In Ziver's view, however, this was a mere pretext disguising their real motive. According to him, the patriarchates opposed the reform because they did not want to lose the secular influence that the role gave them; the financial aspect was merely secondary.[70]

Furthermore, Ziver noted that he was considering turning Christian clergymen into government employees, thus transforming the financial difficulties that the patriarchates would have into an opportunity. According to this plan, the government would require clergymen to submit curricula vitae just as had been required of state officials since 1879. This idea, which Ziver proposed in 1888, was in keeping with the application of the system to ulamas, which was put in place in 1892.[71] His reference to the financial difficulties of the patriarchates suggests that the government would have paid the salaries of the Christian clergymen had this measure been implemented. State control of religious affairs would 'easily prevent the malicious behaviours' that were suspected among non-Muslims.[72]

The Resurgence of the Privileges Question

The Privileges Question resurfaced in late 1889 and reached its climax in September 1890. On this occasion, it did not simply result in a negotiation between the government and religious authorities but was accompanied by a public protest and a strike. Russia intervened in this issue in support of the Orthodox Christian Patriarchate, urging the Ottoman government to accede to its request. Importantly, the movements of the Orthodox Christian and Armenian Patriarchates were more closely linked than they had been on the previous occasion. The large number of surviving Ottoman documents related to this matter are excellent sources for the patriarchates' precise movements and the responses of the Ottoman authorities.

It is difficult to say how this resurgence of the question began. An Armenian newspaper reported in November 1889 that the Orthodox Christian Patriarchate was not satisfied with the response of the Sublime Porte to a document that the patriarchate had recently submitted on 'the question of ecclesiastical privileges' and that it had therefore decided to submit another.[73] This may have been one of the first signs of renewed interest in this area, and it immediately spurred Armenians to follow suit. An Ottoman document showed that the following month, the government was informed that the Armenian ecclesiastical council was preparing to submit an item for the discussion of three main issues: the incomplete observance of the Privileges Edict, the refusal of permission to publish certain books and the appointment of Armenian governors in the eastern provinces. The government was later informed that the Armenian clergy had decided to withdraw the third item.[74] On 28 February 1890, the grand vizierate prepared a response to the document that the ecclesiastical general council had prepared and that the Armenian Patriarchate had submitted on the 'old ecclesiastical permissions and privileges'.[75] Thereafter, negotiations over privileges continued between the state and the two patriarchates.

Cevdet Pasha, minister of justice and religious affairs until May 1890, claimed that behind the rise of the Privileges Question in the 1890s was the problem of the charters granted to the Bulgarian metropolitans in Skopje and Ohrid. Responding to the accusation that he was responsible for the renewed rise and development of the Privileges Question, Cevdet Pasha wrote a detailed explanation of the response of the Ottoman government to this issue at its earlier stage.[76] After issuing state approval for the independence of Bulgarians from the Orthodox Christian Patriarchate of Istanbul, the government granted charters of investiture to several Bulgarian metropolitans in the provinces. When two metropolitanates were left vacant during the war with Russia in 1878, the Bulgarian exarch petitioned the government for charters to appoint new metropolitans there, which invited protest from the Orthodox Christian Patriarchate. As the government postponed the resolution of this issue, the Bulgarian exarch petitioned the Sublime Porte in spring 1890 for permission to dispatch a metropolitan to consecrate the churches. The Sublime Porte allowed this, and the Orthodox Christian Patriarchate, which was simultaneously (both officially and unofficially) negotiating with the government over other requests, was angered.

Underlying the submission of the Armenian protest, meanwhile, was the state of affairs for Armenians in the eastern provinces. According to Erhan Ramazan Güllü, certain Armenian political groups had been threatening Patriarch Ashkian since 1888, demanding that he support the improvement of the situation for provincial Armenians.[77] Given the political character of these problems, Ashkian probably considered it appropriate to frame his request for reforms as religious affairs, thus limiting his points to those related to clergymen and churches. Moreover, the rise of Armenian political groups resulted in the upper echelons of the empire having a growing mistrust of Armenians, which in turn led to a shift in Muslim state officials' attitudes towards the Armenian community. During the disputes around the Privileges Question, the Armenian Patriarchate argued that issues such as searches for weapons in churches and schools in the eastern provinces, the dismissal of clergy and unnecessarily severe censorship were proof that 'there was suspicion and distrust of the Armenian community in the government'.[78] These government actions had been prompted by the activities of Armenian revolutionaries. For example, Derevank, an Armenian monastery close to Kayseri, was used as 'a center of [the] Hunchakian party's activities', and a priest at the monastery even participated, thereby convincing 'many peasants in the region to join the Hunchak Party'.[79] Muslim state officials likely believed that Armenians were engaging in anti-regime political activities under the guise of religion.[80]

The demands of the two patriarchates were discussed in numerous documents.[81] While in the 1890s both patriarchates covered the same issues that had already been discussed in 1883 and 1884, each also added new points. The legal treatment of the clergy and judicial jurisdiction over Christians' disputes over alimony and bequests were again shared concerns, and the matter of the clerics' judicial oaths was added to this. The Armenian Patriarchate claimed that although the Nizamiye courts had entrusted them with these oaths, this exceptional treatment had recently been abandoned and both patriarchates requested its reinstatement. Additionally, the Orthodox Christians problematised the intervention of the state in their communal education as Armenians had done previously during the 1880s discussion of their privileges. The Orthodox Christians also brought up the issue of the charters of investiture granted to Bulgarian metropolitans. The protests of the Armenians were more diverse. They raised the question of state intervention in the dismissal of clergy and the severity of the censorship of their publications. In addition, they put forward new issues, including the treatment of the conversion of minors to Islam, the treatment of children with one Christian parent and one who had converted to Islam, the state's requirements for permission to print donation receipts, the state's granting of permission for the construction and restoration of churches and schools without the consent of the patriarchate and searches for weapons in churches and monasteries in the eastern provinces.

A Convergence of Issues

Ashkian's protest did not reduce the pressure from one Armenian political group. On 27 July 1890, several members of the Hunchakian Party interrupted a mass conducted in a church in Kumkapı – the district where the patriarchate was situated – and conducted a procession from there to the Yıldız Palace to demand reforms in the eastern provinces. They forced Ashkian to join their procession. This resulted in a skirmish, several deaths and numerous injuries, and became known as the Kumkapı Incident.[82]

On this occasion, the presence of numerous Orthodox Christians among the Armenian crowds attracted the attention of the palace. Moreover, some Orthodox Christians spread the rumour that 'the Orthodox Christian Patriarchate will come to confusion because of the question of the charters of the Bulgarian metropolitans' and that the Orthodox Christian patriarch and all metropolitans would resign when the government issued charters of investiture. Fearing that a similar disturbance like the Kumkapı Incident might occur within the Orthodox Christian Patriarchate, on the following day, Abdülhamit ordered the government to take precautions to prevent it. Although Kamil Pasha assured the sultan that Orthodox Christians merely happened to be present at the incident as bystanders, he promised to take every precaution. The parallelism of the movements of Orthodox Christians and Armenians in the 1890s clearly alarmed Abdülhamit and state officials, who feared that the European Great Powers might be behind their actions.[83] After the Kumkapı Incident, they gradually became inclined to deal with the requests of two groups as a single question.

A report written by Kamil Pasha in October allows us to see how he – and probably other Muslim state officials and the sultan – saw the relations between the two patriarchates. In October, the Orthodox Christian Patriarchate decided to restrict Orthodox clergy from conducting their religious duties to express their dissatisfaction with the government's treatment of their requests. The patriarchate ordered all churches to be closed and forbade the conclusion of marriage contracts. It was even reported that corpses were left unburied for days. Kamil Pasha wrote of a rumour that the Armenians would soon follow this example. He explained his perception of the relationship between the two groups as follows:

> Although the same thing is motivating both the Orthodox Christians and the Armenians, they are rivals. While each has different aims and acts separately, the Armenians are expecting to gain whatever the Orthodox Christians will acquire in their religious affairs [*umur-ı mezhebiyede Rumlar her ne ki kazanırlar ise Ermeniler de andan istifade etmek intizarında bulunduklarıı*].[84]

Other documents suggest that what is described here as 'motivating both' groups refers to incitement from the Great Powers, although it is not clear whether this had actually occurred.[85] Kamil Pasha rather recognised that a rivalry between the two groups caused their parallel movements, supporting the argument that non-Muslims in the late Ottoman Empire were mindful of their relative positions in comparison with other non-Muslim groups. This perspective is also supported by a later development. When the Armenian Patriarchate protested to the government in relation to the assertion of its privileges that was sent to the provinces in March 1891, it claimed that although there could be no 'differences in or exceptions to the benefit of the glorious permissions and privileges' granted by the sultan, there were some differences between the decisions that the government made for the Orthodox Christians and those made for the Armenians.[86]

Documents from early August suggest that the higher echelons of the Ottoman Empire felt pressure to reach a compromise with the two patriarchates after the Kumkapı Incident.[87] It was necessary to avoid any further aggravation of the issue and especially to avoid the intervention of the Great Powers. A document sent to Abdülhamit about the international attention pointed out that *Le Figaro*, a newspaper widely read in France, had published an article on 14 August that reported on the issue of the charters for Bulgarian bishops, comparing this with the Armenian problem.[88] Nevertheless, the two patriarchates were not ready to make an immediate agreement. Both patriarchs had expressed their intention to resign in early August.[89] *Punch* reported that Abdülhamit had ordered Hagop Pasha Kazazian, the Minister of Finance and a man of Armenian origin, to invite Patriarch Ashkian to his house in Beyoğlu. Two other Armenian state officials, Harutyun Pasha Dadian (the undersecretary of the Foreign

Ministry) and Vahan Efendi (the undersecretary of the Ministry of Justice and Religious Affairs), also attended this meeting.[90] Abdülhamit likely wanted trustworthy Armenian officials to persuade Ashkian to stay in his position. After his terrible experience in the Kumkapı Incident, however, Ashkian had stopped fulfilling his patriarchal duties.[91] In early September, the government decided to form a committee under the chairmanship of the minister of justice and religious affairs to investigate the requests of the two patriarchates. The cabinet decided to include several Muslim officials in this committee, but Abdülhamit specifically ordered that two Christian state officials be included. One of these was Sava Pasha, an Orthodox Christian who had previously served as governor of the Archipelago and foreign minister, and the other was Harutyun Dadian. Abdülhamit ordered that the committee complete its work within eight to ten days to circumvent 'malicious publications in the European press'.[92]

In his later report to Abdülhamit, Harutyun Dadian declared the limits of the committee's competence for addressing the complexities of the Privileges Question.[93] He wrote that although the committee had invited the two patriarchs (or their deputies) to its meeting to provide oral testimony, neither had attended. The Orthodox Christian patriarch informed the committee that he could not participate because he had already resigned. The Armenian patriarch, for his part, had expressed his intention to resign because of his inability to perform his duty under 'provocations and threats from malicious Armenian groups'. Harutyun Dadian argued that as the two patriarchs had declined their invitations, the committee could not persuade them to keep silent. Moreover, this would likely provide the European press with a pretext for gossip. To explain this, he invoked the old division between religious and non-religious affairs:

> the abovementioned requests are concerned with Christian religious affairs, and therefore, their discussion belongs exclusively to clergymen (*rahipler*). Thus, even if the explanations that Sava Pasha and the humble servant [that is, Harutyun Dadian himself] give are correct, they will be insufficient to refute the claims that can be brought forward in the future mentioning that there was no hearing of the patriarchates' statements.

As discussed, there were two main aspects to the division between religious and non-religious affairs in the nineteenth-century Ottoman Empire. In the relationship between the state and non-Muslim communities, 'religious affairs' was the sphere of the non-Muslim community that was exempt from government interference. However, in the relationship between clergymen and laymen within the Armenian community, 'religious affairs' meant the sphere of clergymen alone, which in turn was exempt from the intervention of laymen. Harutyun Dadian, who mediated between the state and the Armenian community and worked to avoid being caught between them, introduced this nuance into his discussions of state politics.

With due consideration for Dadian's opinion, the palace soon formed another committee composed exclusively of Muslim state officials: Rıza Pasha, the minister of justice and religious affairs; Cevdet Pasha, the former minister; Zihni Pasha, the minister of pious foundations; Rauf Efendi, a senior staff member of the grand vizierate; and Mustafa Ziver.[94] This committee presented a report to the cabinet. Abdülhamit had repeatedly urged the prompt resolution of the Privileges Question, concerned that any delay could prompt foreign intervention. He also put forward his own understanding of the question: while the patriarchates related all of their requests to religion, both 'political' and 'religious' goals appeared within them. The true aims of the patriarchates were thus found in its political requests, but they put the religious ones forward instead to 'incite Christian commoners who could not distinguish good and evil' while proclaiming that 'their religious rules' were being infringed. Abdülhamit also argued that foreign intervention would not leave the issue within 'the scope of religious requests' and would force the empire to do 'some political favours' (*bazı müsaadat-ı siyasiye*), which, he noted, could endanger the survival of the empire. The empire thus needed to silence the patriarchates by consenting to their religious requests.[95] Religious and political affairs were inextricably intertwined.

The Limits of Power

In October, the government prepared an announcement to the two patriarchates concerning its decision, but it took some time for the patriarchates to assert their consent.[96] Nevertheless, the question seemed mostly resolved. It was not until 1909, after the Young Turk Revolution, that the Privileges Question returned to the fore.[97] The rest of Abdülhamit's reign witnessed domestic troubles and multiple interventions by the Great Powers and neighbouring countries. Among these troubles was the work of the Hunchakian Party in Istanbul, Anatolia and the eastern provinces.

As I have already discussed, religious privileges allowed the patriarchate and the Armenian elites in Istanbul to negotiate with the imperial authorities and make requests. Meanwhile, because the status and power of the lay and ecclesiastical elites were firmly embedded in the Ottoman governance, only peaceful and legal measures seemed a viable option for them.[98] The Hunchakians saw the elites as unwilling to pursue substantial remedies for the plight of Armenians in the eastern provinces.

With their orchestration of the Kumkapı Incident, the Hunchakians criticised Patriarch Ashkian for his lack of eagerness and began to challenge the Armenian elites in Istanbul. The limitations on the capabilities of these elites became increasingly apparent. As the situation in the eastern provinces deteriorated, the Hunchakians organised more demonstrations in diverse places across the empire, and their introduction of violence as a strategy changed the rules of negotiation between the Ottoman state and Armenians.[99]

In the summer of 1894, tensions between the Armenians, local Ottoman authorities and nomadic Kurds exploded into anti-Armenian violence in Sasun, which invited the attention of the European Great Powers.[100] In this emergency, Madteos Izmirlian, who had newly assumed the Patriarchate of Istanbul, submitted *takrir*s to the central government in January and February 1895. In these, he reported the plight of Armenians in the eastern provinces and protested the non-fulfilment of the promises regarding religious privileges. He added that the Armenians in the eastern provinces were 'not able to freely conduct their religion', claiming that the government was violating their religious rights. His *takrir*s produced no positive response. In 1895, as negotiations between the Ottoman Empire and the Great Powers continued, the Hunchakian Party staged a demonstration in Istanbul. Izmirlian tried to appease the protesters, saying that the government would not allow the demonstration to march to the Sublime Porte, and offered to deliver the petition instead, but this was in vain.[101] Meanwhile, developments in Istanbul heightened fears among Muslims of possible revolts by their Armenian neighbours, inspiring further distrust between these groups. The news about Abdülhamit's acceptance of the reforms that the Great Powers required then excited considerable confusion, resulting in widespread violence that claimed countless Armenian lives.[102]

Notes

1. Haris Exertzoglou, 'To "Pronomiako" Zitima', *Ta Istorika* 16 (1992): 65–84; Vangelis Kechriotis, 'The Modernization of the Empire and the Community "Privileges": Greek Orthodox Responses to the Young Turk Policies', in *The State and the Subaltern: Modernization, Society and the State in Turkey and Iran*, ed. Touraj Atabaki (London: I. B. Tauris, 2007), 53–70; Fujinami, 'Privileged but Equal'; Denis Vovchenko, 'A Triumph of Orthodoxy in the Age of Nationalism: The Ecumenical Patriarchate, the Sublime Porte, Russia, and Greece (1856–1890)', *Modern Greek Studies Yearbook* 28/29 (2012/2013): 255–66; Fujinami, 'Legal Pluralism'. See also Dimitris Stamatopoulos, 'The Christian Orthodox Family in Crisis: The Ecumenical Patriarchate's Courts and the Reconstruction of the

Private Sphere in Southeast Europe in the Nineteenth and Early Twentieth Centuries', in *Problems of Crime and Violence in Europe, 1780–2000*, ed. Efi Avdela, Shani D'Cruze and Judith Rowbotham (Lewiston: Edwin Mellen Press, 2010), 91–118.

2. BOA. Y.EE 38/107 (undated). This Ottoman document, which was written while Aleksandr Nelidov was stationed in Istanbul as Russian Ambassador (between 1883 and 1897), states that 'Following the example of the Armenian Patriarchate (*Ermeni patrikhanesinden örnek alarak*), the Orthodox Christian Patriarchate also complained that some of the privileges they had were not respected'.
3. In 1883, Safvet Pasha had already employed the term 'Privilege Question' (*imtiyaz meselesi*) to discuss the Orthodox Christians' protest against the violation of their privileges. BOA, Y.EE 44/151 (19 June 1883).
4. The sole (but important) exception is the article written by Ramazan Erhan Güllü, which discusses the development of Privileges Question in the early 1890s. His contribution, however, lacks insight into the developments of the previous decades and fails to grasp the significance of the events in the 1890s. 'İstanbul'da Ermeni-Rum Kiliseleri Krizi ve Ermenilere Tanınan Yeni İmtiyâzlar (1890–1891)', *OTAM* 38 (2015): 31–53.
5. Jeremy Salt, *Imperialism, Evangelism and the Ottoman Armenians 1878–1896* (London: Frank Cass, 1993), 84.
6. Hovannisian, 'The Armenian Question', 203–12.
7. *Adenakrut'iwnk'* (22 November 1878), 214.
8. Salt, *Imperialism, Evangelism*, chap. 4.
9. Hovannisian, 'Armenian Question', 212.
10. Stephan B. Riegg, 'Imperial Challengers: Tsarist Responses to Armenian Raids into Anatolia, 1875–90', *The Russian Review* 76, no. 2 (2017): 253–71.
11. Hovannisian, 'Armenian Question', 214.
12. Libaridian, 'Ideology of Armenian Liberation', chap. 6; Hovannisian, 'Armenian Question', 212–18.
13. François Georgeon, *Abdülhamid II: le sultan calife (1876–1909)* (Paris: Fayard, 2003), chap. 7; Jens Hanssen, '"Malhamé-Malfamé": Levantine Elites and Transimperial Networks on the Eve of the Young Turk Revolution', *International Journal of Middle East Studies* 43, no. 1 (2011): 25–48.
14. Deringil, 'Legitimacy Structures'. See also the stimulating analysis of caliphal protection by Lâle Can in 'Protection Question' and *Spiritual Subjects: Central Asian Pilgrims and the Ottoman Hajj at the End of Empire* (Stanford: Stanford University Press, 2020).
15. Nadir Özbek, 'Philanthropic Activity, Ottoman Patriotism, and the Hamidian Regime, 1876–1909', *International Journal of Middle East Studies* 37, no. 1 (2005): 66.
16. *P'unch*, no. 2147 (4 May 1889).

17. *P'unch*, no. 2140 (16 March 1889).
18. Cohen, 'Between Civic and Islamic Ottomanism', 239–40.
19. Tufan Buzpınar, *Hilafet ve Saltanat: II. Abdülhamid Döneminde Halifelik ve Araplar* (Istanbul: Alfa, 2016), 49–55.
20. Georgeon, *Abdülhamid II*, chap. 9; Crews, 'Empire and the Confessional State'; Werth, *Tsar's Foreign Faiths*.
21. Deringil, 'Legitimacy Structures', 350.
22. Yoneoka, 'Hapusuburuku Teikokuka', 89–107.
23. Akarlı, *Belgelerle Tanzimat*, 14–15.
24. Hanssen, '"Malhamé-Malfamé"', 33.
25. Georgeon, *Abdülhamid II*, chap. 7; Hanssen, '"Malhamé-Malfamé"'.
26. BOA, Y.PRK.AZN 3/14 (26 December 1887).
27. *P'unch*, no. 2081 (28 January 1888).
28. *P'unch*, no. 2234 (3 January 1891).
29. Ibid.
30. Ibid.
31. Ueno, 'Laicized Urban Administration'.
32. BOA, Y.A.HUS 176/2 (16 July 1883).
33. On non-Muslims' use of sharia courts, see Ronald C. Jennings, 'Zimmis (Non-Muslims) in Early 17th Century Ottoman Judicial Records: The Sharia Court of Anatolian Kayseri', *Journal of the Economic and Social History of the Orient* 21, no. 3 (1978): 225–93; Najwa al-Qattan, '*Dhimmīs* in the Muslim Court: Legal Autonomy and Religious Discrimination', *International Journal of Middle East Studies* 31, no. 3 (1999): 429–44; Sophia Laiou, 'Christian Women in an Ottoman World: Interpersonal and Family Cases Brought Before the *Shari'a* Courts during the Seventeenth and Eighteenth Centuries (Cases Involving the Greek Community)', in *Women in the Ottoman Balkans: Gender, Culture and History*, ed. Amila Buturović and İrvin Cemil Schick (New York: Palgrave Macmillan, 2007), 243–71. Ottomanist researchers who have studied the non-Muslims' usage of sharia courts sometimes doubt the existence of judicial system among non-Muslims. Eugenia Kermeli has refuted this scepticism using the example of Orthodox Christians. 'The Right to Choice: Ottoman Justice vis-à-vis Ecclesiastical and Communal Justice in the Balkans, Seventeenth-Nineteenth Centuries', in *Studies in Islamic Law: A Festschrift for Colin Imber*, ed. Andreas Christmann and Robert Gleave (Oxford: Oxford University Press, 2007), 165–210. See also Antonis Anastasopoulos, 'Non-Muslims and Ottoman Justice(s?)', in *Law and Empire: Ideas, Practices, Actors*, ed. Jeroen Duindam et al. (Leiden: Brill, 2013), 275–92.
34. Rubin, *Ottoman* Nizamiye *Courts*; Jun Akiba, 'Sharī'a Judges in the Ottoman Nizāmiye Courts, 1864–1908', *Osmanlı Araştırmaları* 51 (2018): 209–37.
35. See also, Fujinami, 'Legal Pluralism'.
36. Rubin, *Ottoman* Nizamiye *Courts*, 30–2.

37. BOA, Y.A.HUS 176/2.
38. On the Privileged Provinces, see Fujinami, 'Sovereignty and Suzerainty'; Genell, 'Autonomous Provinces'; Kostopoulou, 'Armed Negotiations'.
39. The instruction was labelled 'The instruction that the office of Şeyhülislam prepared on the religious affairs of Muslims in Rumania, Greece, Serbia, Montenegro and Bulgaria'. *Düstur*, 1st series, vol. 5 (Ankara: Başvekâlet Matbaası, 1937), 274–91.
40. In 1882, the Greek government had already created a law that enabled state authorities to appoint muftis for the Muslim communities in Greece. Stefanos Katsikas, *Islam and Nationalism in Modern Greece, 1821–1940* (New York: Oxford University Press, 2021), 79–80.
41. Güllü, *İstanbul Ermeni Patrikhanesi*, 86–9.
42. This opinion was clearly voiced in the General Assembly by a lay member. *Adenakrut'iwnk'* (20 January 1884), 427.
43. Güllü, *İstanbul Ermeni Patrikhanesi*, 90–4.
44. *Adenakrut'iwnk'* (28 September 1883), 235–40.
45. *Adenakrut'iwnk'* (28 March 1884), 529–42.
46. Ibid., 530.
47. Ibid., 531–4.
48. Ibid., 536.
49. Ibid., 535.
50. Ibid., 536–8.
51. Ibid., 537.
52. BOA, Y.PRK.AZN 3/14 (1 December 1887).
53. *Adenakrut'iwnk'* (28 March 1884), 536–7.
54. For example, see the articles published in *Masis*, nos. 1161, 1168 (2 December 1871).
55. *Kanun-ı Esasi*, art. 11.
56. *Adenakrut'iwnk'* (28 March 1884), 535.
57. Ibid., 538.
58. Hamdi Çilingir, 'İmtiyâzât-ı Mezhebiyenin Sınırı: Şer^{c}iye Mahkemeleri ile Gayrimüslim "Mahkemelerinin" Görev Alanına Dair Bir Tartışma', in *Son Dönem Osmanlı Hukuk Düşüncesi: Meseleler Fikirler ve Kurumlar*, ed. Hamdi Çilingir and Hüseyin Önal (Istanbul: İlem Yayınları, 2021), 3–30.
59. Gerd, *Russian Policy*, 43–4.
60. Somel, 'Osmanlı Ermenilerinde Kültür Modernleşmesi', 71–92.
61. *Adenakrut'iwnk'* (4 January 1884), 410–16.
62. Kechriotis, 'Modernization of the Empire', 57.
63. BOA, Y.PRK.AZN 3/14 (26 December 1887).
64. BOA, Y.PRK.AZN 3/17 (28 January 1888).
65. BOA, DH.SAİD.d 4/268, 269. In his curriculum vitae, Ziver Bey claimed the ability to speak Arabic and French, both of which he learned from private tutors.
66. BOA, Y.PRK.AZN 3/17 (28 January 1888).

67. Ibid.
68. Starting in the 1890s, especially after the Young Turk Revolution, Ottoman intellectuals criticised ulamas by likening them to Christian clergymen in Europe. Amit Bein, *Ottoman Ulema, Turkish Republic: Agents of Change and Guardians of Tradition* (Stanford: Stanford University Press, 2011), 21–4.
69. Ueno, 'Laicized Urban Administration'. On the travel document system, see Nalan Turna, *19. Yüzyıldan 20. Yüzyıla Osmanlı Topraklarında Seyahat, Göç ve Asayiş Belgeleri: Mürûr Tezkereleri* (Istanbul: Kaknüs Yayınları, 2013); İlkay Yılmaz, *II. Abdülhamid Döneminde Güvenlik Politikaları, Mürur Tezkereleri, Pasaportlar ve Otel Kayıtları: Serseri, Anarşist ve Fesadın Peşinde* (Istanbul: Tarih Vakfı Yurt Yayınları, 2014); David Gutman, 'Travel Documents, Mobility Control, and the Ottoman State in an Age of Global Migration, 1880–1915', *Journal of the Ottoman and Turkish Studies Association* 3, no. 2 (2016): 347–68.
70. BOA, Y.PRK.AZN 3/17 (28 January 1888).
71. Jun Akiba, 'The Practice of Writing Curricula Vitae among the Lower Government Employees in the Late Ottoman Empire: Workers at the Şeyhülislâm's Office', *European Journal of Turkish Studies* 6 (2007), pars. 2–4, https://journals.openedition.org/ejts/1503, accessed 3 May 2024. On the system of personal record registration, see Sarıyıldız, *Sicill-i Ahvâl Komisyonu'nun Kuruluşu.*
72. BOA, Y.PRK.AZN 3/17 (28 January 1888).
73. *P'unch*, no. 2176 (23 November 1889).
74. BOA, İ.DH 91013 (21 December 1889).
75. BOA, Y.PRK.A 6/2 (6 August 1890).
76. BOA, Y.EE 39/11 (17 October 1890).
77. Güllü, *İstanbul Ermeni Patrikhanesi*, 111–20.
78. BOA, Y.PRK.AZN 4/53 (7 September 1890).
79. Toygun Altıntaş, 'The Placard Affair and the Ankara Trial: The Hnchak Party and the Hamidian Regime in Central Anatolia, 1892–93', *Journal of the Ottoman and Turkish Studies Association* 4, no. 2 (2017): 321.
80. Contemporary Ottoman officials in the Balkans also observed the involvement of Christian clergymen in non-religious activities. Yosmaoğlu, *Blood Ties*, 186.
81. For the demands of the Orthodox Christian Patriarchate, see BOA, İ.MMS 4995 (2 November 1890); for the demands of the Armenian Patriarchate, see BOA, Y.PRK.AZN 4/48 (19 August 1890), Y.PRK.AZN 4/53 (7 September 1890).
82. Güllü, *İstanbul Ermeni Patrikhanesi*, 120–5; Güllü, 'Ermeni-Rum Kiliseleri Krizi', 33–4; Hovannisian, 'Armenian Question', 218.
83. BOA, Y.A.HUS 237/47 (28 July 1890).
84. BOA, Y.A.HUS 240/11 (16 October 1890).
85. BOA, Y.A.HUS 237/47 (28 July 1890), Y.A.RES 52/8 (6 September 1890).

86. BOA, Y.MTV 49/101 (18 April 1891).
87. See the documents in BOA, Y.PRK.A 6/2 (6 August 1890). See also BOA, Y.A.HUS 237/47 (28 July 1890), Y.A.RES 52/8 (6 September 1890).
88. BOA, İ.DH 93344 (19 August 1890), Y.A.HUS 238/23 (20 August 1890).
89. *Arewelk'*, nos. 1954 (2 August 1890), 1957 (6 August 1890).
90. *P'unch*, no. 2214 (16 August 1890).
91. *P'unch*, no. 2215 (23 August 1890).
92. BOA, Y.A.RES 52/8 (6 September 1890).
93. BOA, Y.PRK.HR 13/70 (21 September 1890).
94. BOA, İ.DH 93656 (16 September 1890).
95. BOA, İ.DH 93678 (27 September 1890).
96. *P'unch*, nos. 2223 (18 October 1890), 2239 (7 February 1891), 2240 (14 February 1891); *Arewelk'*, no. 2029 (1 November 1890). As I have already mentioned, the Armenian Patriarchate protested about the difference in the responses that the government gave the two patriarchates. BOA, Y.MTV 49/101 (18 April 1891).
97. Fujinami, 'Privileged but Equal'; Kechriotis, 'Modernization of the Empire'.
98. In this respect, Lâle Can's argument is instructive. In her article on the status of Central Asians in the Ottoman Empire, she called researchers' attention to the necessity of understanding the limits of the 'power to negotiate', recognising how plural legal orders not only allowed people to exploit 'competition over foreign protection, legal jurisdiction, and spheres of sovereignty' but also 'constrained rights and opportunities'. Can, 'Protection Question', 681, 693.
99. Altıntaş, 'Placard Affair'; Varak Ketsemanian, 'The Hunchakian Revolutionary Party and the Assassination Attempts against Patriarch Khoren Ashekian and Maksudzade Simon Bey in 1894', *International Journal of Middle East Studies* 50, no. 4 (2018): 735–55.
100. On the violence in Sasun, see Miller, 'Sasun 1894'.
101. Güllü, *İstanbul Ermeni Patrikhanesi*, 229–31, 253.
102. There has recently been an upsurge of work on the Hamidian massacres; see Jelle Verheij, 'Diyarbekir and the Armenian Crisis of 1895', in *Social Relations in Ottoman Diyarbekir, 1870–1915*, ed. Joost Jongerden and Jelle Verheij (Leiden: Brill, 2012), 85–145; Jelle Verheij, '"The Year of the Firman": The 1895 Massacres in Hizan and Şirvan (Bitlis Vilayet)', *Études arméniennes contemporaines* 10 (2017): 125–59; Sipahi, 'At Arm's Length', chap. 10; Gölbaşı, 'Official Conceptualization'; Selim Deringil, '"The Armenian Question is Finally Closed": Mass Conversions of Armenians in Anatolia during the Hamidian Massacres of 1895–1897', *Comparative Studies in Society and History* 51, no. 2 (2009): 344–71.

Conclusion: Rediscovering the Religious Privileges

Today, the site where Istanbul Armenians staged a sit-in protest in 1872 to protect their cemetery's land from state expropriation is dominated by luxury hotels and cafés. No trace of the old cemetery remains above ground; it was completely removed when, as a large plot of valuable land near the new city centre, it fell within the boundaries of an exploitation project during the early period of the newly formed Turkish Republic. In 1931, the municipal government of Istanbul demanded that ownership of the old Armenian cemetery land be transferred to the city. Municipal Law No. 1580, promulgated in 1930, stipulated that 'abandoned and desolated cemeteries' would be transferred to their respective municipalities. Due to Armenian resistance, however, the legal dispute between municipal Istanbul and the Istanbul Armenians continued for eight years. The issue was ultimately decided in favour of the city, which duly expropriated 50,000 square metres of land in 1939, leaving only about 6,000 square metres to the Armenians.[1] The church that the Armenians had established in the cemetery in 1865 was also demolished. The tomb of Catholicos Hagop, which had been the object of 'pilgrimage for Armenians from all parts of the world', was moved to the Armenian Church in Beyoğlu.[2]

Both Tanzimat and early Republican statesmen had attempted to expropriate the same Armenian cemetery land but with different results. This difference reflects the changing position of Armenians. The Armenians of the Tanzimat period were able to exert their negotiating powers by invoking religious privileges. In contrast, the concept of religious privileges ceased to be a legitimate reason for any kind of exemption under the Republic of Turkey. From the birth of this new state, it rejected the inheritance of the imperial legacy, including the privileges of non-Muslims. When the new Turkish government signed the Treaty of Lausanne with the Allies in 1923, religious privileges and the privileges of foreigners (also known as capitulations) were abolished.[3] For the Turkish political elite, these privileges were a headache that made foreign intervention possible and from which the new republic should be liberated. The treaty did grant Christian and Jewish citizens a special status as a minority, committing the Turkish government to maintaining their religious and linguistic rights and their right of self-governance in their own community affairs. However, this official status did not extend to the provision of any allowance for the Armenians in Istanbul to keep hold of their cemetery land. Moreover, Turkish political elites were not entirely willing to fulfil their commitment; they saw the granting of minority status as 'privileges' for Christian and Jewish citizens that the Allies had forced them to guarantee. They had to allow the Orthodox Christian and Armenian Patriarchates to remain, but these institutions would 'be deprived of all political, administrative and judicial power and would only deal with religious matters'.[4]

The number of Armenians and Orthodox Christians in Anatolia and the eastern provinces was already much smaller than it had been when the Ottoman Empire officially collapsed. The atrocities of the 1890s had caused countless deaths and triggered a process of gradual emigration followed by the Adana Massacre of 1909, which claimed many Armenian lives.[5] The final catastrophe that took place during World War I, now known as the Armenian Genocide, almost eliminated all the Armenians of Anatolia and the eastern provinces.[6] These areas were also the only part of the empire left to non-Arab Muslims – especially Turkish-speaking Muslims – as war accelerated the empire's dissolution. During World War I in 1915, the Ottoman government started to eliminate the Armenians from the region by ordering their deportation. Some managed to reach Syria, Lebanon and Palestine, where a few were able to survive. Others saved themselves by fleeing the empire entirely or through abduction into Muslim households and conversion to Islam. However, the overwhelming majority of Ottoman Armenians were simply massacred or died of hunger or other causes during the desperate, chaotic and ill-prepared wartime deportations. Most Orthodox Christians in Anatolia left their homeland by the end of 1922, and the remainder were to be displaced through the Turkey–Greece population exchange.[7] The large-scale reconfiguration of the area triggered by the collapse of the empire was thus accompanied by a large-scale demographic transformation.

The Ottoman government did not leave Armenian elites in Istanbul or the patriarchate untouched during the genocide of the 1910s. Their first targets were the elites, who, it was feared, might protest and thus had to be silenced before the mass deportations could begin. On 24 April 1915, hundreds of Armenian elites – including members of the Ottoman parliament – were arrested and deported to the Anatolian towns of Ayaş and Çankırı. Later, more than half of them were killed.[8] In 1916, the Ottoman government implemented its final attempt to deprive the Armenian religious authorities of their political influence. To achieve this goal, the government prepared its Law on the Armenian Catholicosate and Patriarchate, nullifying the Armenian National Constitution of 1863. Furthermore, the four religious authorities of the Armenian Church in the Ottoman Empire were merged into a single catholicosate–patriarchate, which was to be the sole religious authority for all Ottoman Armenians, thereby severing the Ottoman Armenians' relationship with the Catholicosate of Echmiadzin. The catholicos–patriarch would have his seat in the Armenian Patriarchate of Jerusalem and have jurisdiction only over religious affairs. The government chose Sahag, the catholicos of Sis, for this depoliticised position. The General Assembly in Istanbul was abolished, and an ecclesiastical council and a mixed council were formed in Jerusalem. The ecclesiastical council, composed of twelve high clergymen, would manage the religious affairs of Ottoman Armenians. The mixed council, composed of four clergymen and eight laymen, would manage the financial affairs of the community. Zaven, the Armenian patriarch of Istanbul, lost his position and was sent to Baghdad. After the Armistice of Mudros in 1918, the Patriarchate of Istanbul and the Armenian National Constitution were restored.[9]

As noted in the Introduction, Alford Carleton proposed the *millet* system in 1937, shortly after the final collapse of the Ottoman Empire. This argument was widely accepted by scholars in the mid-twentieth century, leading them to mistakenly assume that the term *millet* had an institutional meaning during the Ottoman period. Revisionist scholarship inherited this assumption, arguing either that the Ottomans began to use *millet* in the nineteenth century or that it gained institutional meaning in that period, assuming that recognition as a *millet* was a sign of approval for the community status of a non-Muslim group within the framework of the late Ottoman Empire.[10] One of the achievements of the present book has been to challenge these long-standing assumptions by bringing due attention to the fact that the term that mattered to Ottoman actors was not *millet* but privileges. This is not just a matter of terminology. *Millet* symbolised Ottoman tolerance and was associated with the assumption that the empire gave clergymen the authority to manage the affairs of their community autonomously, while privileges indicated the desire of Ottoman statesmen to limit the influence of clergymen and lessen the non-Muslims' area of activity as a community.

As we have discussed, privileges became the established term for discussing the approved status of the patriarchates after the Ottoman government redefined the favours and exemptions that had individually been granted to non-Muslim clergymen as religious privileges in 1853. For Ottoman statesmen, the question of how to create an equal Ottoman nation was accompanied by the question of how to deal with the religious diversity of the empire and, more specifically, the accumulated favours and exemptions that had been granted to non-Muslim clergymen, who, along with lay elites, oversaw not only religious services but also education, mutual aid, reconciliation, medical treatment and the operation of the facilities used for these activities. Simply abolishing favours and exemptions was not a choice, as doing so would have caused mass confusion among non-Muslim subjects as well as their fierce resistance. Moreover, it would have endangered the government's relationship with the European Great Powers. Instead, Ottoman statesmen redefined the favours as religious privileges and removed religious matters from the scope of political and civil integration.

Their plan for achieving a religiously different but politically equal Ottoman nation – a move that would align with contemporary multiculturalism – had a next step. Ottoman statesmen saw curbing the power of clergymen as crucial. Despite being derived from early modern Ottoman arrangements, the power of the clergy seemed excessive and their religious networks, extending beyond the borders of the empire, could be used as a pretext for foreign intervention. In the early nineteenth century, after the Great Powers agreed to adopt the Concert of Europe as the principle of their foreign relations and to maintain the balance of power, their dependence on soft power tactics led to the politicisation of religion in European dealings with the Ottoman Empire. In short, the Great Powers used the treatment of Christian subjects to justify their intervention in Ottoman politics. Religious ties not necessarily linked to modern states' territoriality gained importance in international politics. Ottoman Armenian religious affairs also necessarily assumed a political character due to the existence of the Catholicosate of Echmiadzin under Russian rule and Russia's desire to obtain support from Ottoman Armenians by using this religious authority. Thus, as religion and politics became increasingly intertwined, it became increasingly necessary to maintain a distinction between them in relations between Ottoman state officials and non-Muslim religious communities. For Ottoman statesmen, the privileges of non-Muslim clergy needed to be reduced to 'purely religious' ones.

The statesmen of the Tanzimat period tended to be seen as having favoured non-Muslims. They indeed were willing to incorporate non-Muslims into imperial governance as individuals. However, they also hoped to reduce the favours and exemptions that had been granted to the clergy and thereby limit their collective activities. Their failure to achieve this makes their policies seem permissive in hindsight. Non-Muslims – lay and ecclesiastical Armenian elites in particular – did not sit back and watch as their privileges were reduced. Rather, they sought opportunities to protect and even expand the scope of these privileges and their own arenas of jurisdiction through the promises that the government had made during the Tanzimat Reforms. They defined their actions as within the scope of these privileges, invoked the principle of non-interference in religious affairs and negotiated with the state over the hazy boundary between the religious and the political. When the Ottoman state shifted from a relationship with non-Muslims mediated by religious institutions towards one that instead incorporated individual non-Muslim laymen into imperial governance, Armenian lay elites did not merely participate as individuals in the imperial bureaucracy and other state services. They eagerly involved themselves in the protection and expansion of their collective rights and carved out a space for their religious/communal activities within the multireligious empire. They chose to find their place in the empire as both individuals and members of a religious community. In this way, they doubly embedded themselves in the empire, not foreseeing a future in which its Muslim leadership would deny them a place in it.

Notes

1 Armaveni Miroğlu, 'Tarihi 16. Yüzyıla Uzanan Pangaltı Ermeni Mezarlığı (Surp Hagop Mezarlığı)', *Toplumsal Tarih* 187 (2009): 34–8.
2. *The Levant Times* (11 January 1873); *Masis*, no. 1324 (24 December 1873); Pamukciyan, *Biyografileriyle Ermeniler*, 236.
3. Seyfeli, *İstanbul Ermeni Patrikliği*, 162–5; Alexis Alexandris, 'Lozan Konferansı ve İstanbul Rum Patrikhanesi'nin Ekümenik Boyutu: 10 Ocak 1923 Tarihli Tutanağın Önemi', in *Tarihî, Siyasi, Dinî ve Hukuki Açıdan Ekümenik Patrikhane*, ed. Cengiz Aktar (Istanbul: İletişim, 2011), 77–119.
4. Lerna Ekmekçioğlu, *Recovering Armenia: The Limits of Belonging in Post-Genocide Turkey* (Stanford: Stanford University Press, 2016), 97, 104–5.
5. On the Adana massacres, see Bedross Der Matossian, *The Horrors of Adana: Revolution and Violence in the Early Twentieth Century* (Stanford: Stanford University Press, 2022); Tetsuya Sahara, *What Happened in Adana in April 1909? Conflicting Armenian and Turkish Views* (Istanbul: Isis Press, 2013).
6. On the 1915 genocide, see Raymond Kévorkian, *The Armenian Genocide: A Complete History* (London: I. B. Tauris, 2011); Taner Akçam, *Young Turks' Crime against Humanity: The Armenian Genocide and Ethnic Cleansing in the Ottoman Empire* (Princeton: Princeton University Press, 2012); Ronald

Grigor Suny, *"They Can Live in the Desert but Nowhere Else": A History of the Armenian Genocide* (Princeton: Princeton University Press, 2015).

7. On the legal aspect of the population exchange, see Umut Özsu, *Formalizing Displacement: International Law and Population Transfers* (Oxford: Oxford University Press, 2015).
8. For the deportation of Armenian elites from Istanbul, see Nesim Ovadya İzrail, *24 Nisan 1915: İstanbul, Çankırı, Ayaş, Ankara* (Istanbul: İletişim, 2013).
9. Güllü, *İstanbul Ermeni Patrikhanesi*, 469–96. For the history of Armenians and the patriarchate in Republican Turkey, see Talin Suciyan, *The Armenians in Modern Turkey: Post-Genocide Society, Politics and History* (London: I. B. Tauris, 2016).
10. See the discussion in the Introduction.

Bibliography

Archives

T.C. Cumhurbaşkanlığı Osmanlı Arşivi (BOA), Istanbul

A.AMD	Sadaret Amedi Kalemi Evrakı
A.DVN	Sadaret Divan Kalemi Evrakı
A.DVN.MHM	Sadaret Divan Mühimme Evrakı
A.DVNS.GMC.d	Bab-ı Asafi Divan-ı Hümayun Sicilleri Gayr-i Müslim Cemaatler
A.DVNSMHM.d	Bab-ı Asafi Divan-ı Hümayun Sicilleri Mühimme Defterleri
A.MKT.MHM	Sadaret Mektubi Mühimme Kalemi Evrakı
A.MKT.NZD	Sadaret Mektubi Kalemi Nezaret ve Devair Evrakı
A.MKT.UM	Sadaret Mektubi Kalemi Umum Vilayet Evrakı
AE.SAMD.III	Ali Emiri Ahmed III
AE.SMHD.I	Ali Emiri Mahmud I
AE.SMST.II	Ali Emiri Mustafa II
AE.SMST.III	Ali Emiri Mustafa III
C.ADL	Cevdet Adliye
D.PSK	Bab-ı Defteri Piskoposluk Kalemi Evrakı
DH.İD	Dahiliye Nezareti İdare Evrakı
DH.SAİD.d	Dahiliye Nezareti Sicill-i Ahval Defterleri
DH.TMIK	Dahiliye Nezareti Tesri-i Muamelat ve Islahat Komisyonu
HR.İD	Hariciye Nezareti İdare
HR.MKT	Hariciye Nezareti Mektubi Kalemi Evrakı
HR.TO	Hariciye Nezareti Tercüme Odası Evrakı
İ.DH	İrade Dahiliye
İ.HR	İrade Hariciye
İ.MMS	İrade Meclis-i Mahsus
İ.MSM	İrade Mesail-i Mühimme

İ.MVL	İrade Meclis-i Vala
İE.DH	İbnülemin Dahiliye
İE.ML	İbnülemin Maliye
KK.d	Kamil Kepeci
MŞH.ŞSC.d	Meşihat, Şeriye Sicilleri Defterleri
ŞD	Şura-yı Devlet Evrakı
TS.MA.E	Topkapı Sarayı Müzesi Arşivi Evrakı
Y.A.HUS	Yıldız Sadaret Hususi Maruzat Evrakı
Y.A.RES	Yıldız Sadaret Resmi Maruzat Evrakı
Y.EE	Yıldız Esas Evrakı
Y.MTV	Yıldız Mütenevvi Maruzat Evrakı
Y.PRK.A	Yıldız Perakende Evrakı Sadaret Maruzatı
Y.PRK.AZN	Yıldız Perakende Evrakı Adliye ve Mezahib Nezareti Maruzatı
Y.PRK.HR	Yıldız Perakende Evrakı Hariciye Nezareti Maruzatı

İstanbul Şeriye Sicilleri (İŞS)

Matenadaran, Kat'oghikosakan Divan (KD)

Papers of the American Board of Commissioners for Foreign Missions Unit 5 (ABCFM)

Published Primary Sources

PERIODICALS

Adenakrut'iwnk' Azkayin Ĕnthanur Zhoghovoy
Arewelk'
Arshaloys Araradean
Ceride-i Havadis
Hadika
Hayasdan
Jamanag
The Levant Times
Manzumēi Ēfk'ear
Masis
Masis Ōrat'ert'
Meghu
Miwnadiyi Ērjiyas
Ōrakir Dziln Awarayrioy
P'unch
Salname[-i Devlet-i Aliye-i Osmaniye]
Takvim-i Vekayi'

Books

Aghapēkean, Margos. *Deghegakir Amenayn Hayots' Gat'oghigosut'ean Ayzhmean Vijagin vray*. Istanbul: Dbakrut'iwn Aramean, 1865.

Aristarchi. *Législation ottomane: Recueil des lois, règlements, ordonnances, traités, capitulations, et autres documents officiels de l'empire ottoman*, 5 vols. Istanbul: Bureau du journal Thraky, 1873–88.

Awetik'ean, H. G. et al. *Nor Bargirk' Haykazean Lezui*, 2 vols. Venice: Tparan Srboyn Ghazaru, 1836–7; repr. Erevani Hamalsarani Hratarakch'ut'yun, 1979–81.

Ayppenaran ew K'risdonēagan. Istanbul: n.p., 1740.

Azkayin Sahmanatrut'iwn Hayots'. Istanbul: Azkayin Dbaran Surp P'rgch'i, 1860.

Azkayin Sahmanatrut'iwn Hayots'. Istanbul: Dbaran H. Miwhēndisean, 1863.

Baghdasar. *Grt'ut'iwn K'risdonēagan*. Istanbul: n.p., 1742.

Deghegakir Hamaraduut'ean Dndesagan Khorhrtoy aṛ Azkayin K'aghak'agan Zhoghovn Getronagan Varch'ut'ean. Istanbul: Dbakrut'iwn Ō. Khōjasarean, 1872.

Deghegakir Kordzatir Hantsnazhoghovoy Azkayin Sahmanatrut'ean Nergayats'eal Handean Ěnthanur Zhoghovoy Azkayin Eresp'okhanutean i 20 Sebdemper Amsoy 1863. Istanbul: Dbakrut'iwn Hovhannu Miwhēndisean, 1863.

Düstur, 1st series, vols 1–4 and 4 suppls. Istanbul: Matbaa-i Amire, 1872–85.

Düstur, 1st series, vols 5–8. Ankara: Başvekâlet Devlet Matbaası, 1937–43.

Dwight, H. G. O. *Christianity in Turkey: A Narrative of the Protestant Reformation in the Armenian Church*. London: James Nisbet, 1854.

Erewants'i, Simeōn. *Jambr*. Vagharshapat: Tparan Srboy Kat'ughike Ējmiatsni, 1873.

İbrahim Hakkı. *Hukuk-ı İdare*. 1st edition, 2 vols. Istanbul: Karabet Matbaası, 1889/90–1890/1.

Kanun-ı Esasi. Istanbul: Karabet Matbaası, 1908/9.

La Motraye, Aubry de. *Travels through Europe, Asia, and into Part of Africa*. 2 vols. London: printed for the Author, 1723.

Moltke, Helmuth von. *Briefe über Zustände und Begebenheiten in der Türkei aus den Jahren 1835 bis 1839*. Berlin: Ernst Siegfried Mittler, 1841.

P'anosean, Garabed H. *Asar-ı Kayseriye*. No place, 1864.

———. *Ēfk'earě Mukhayyērē*. Istanbul: Hovhannēs Miwhēndisean T'abkhanēsi, 1863.

———. *Miwst'ēdiyi Sahmanatrut'iwn*. [Istanbul]: Miwhēndisean T'abkhanēsi, 1861.

Pērpērean, Awetis. *Patmut'iwn Hayots': Skseal i 1772 Amē P'rkch'in Minch'ew Hamn 1860*. Istanbul: Tpagrut'iwn Pōghosi K'irishchean, 1871.

Polozhēnia: Bardzragoyn Kargadrut'iwn Haghags Karavarut'ean Gortsots' Lusaworch'akan Hayots' Ekeghets'woy i Rusastan. Echmiadzin: n.p., 1836.

Sahman Azkayin Zhoghovoy. Istanbul: n.p., 1830.
Sahman Azkayin Zhoghovoyn. Istanbul: n.p., 1826.

Edited Primary Sources

Akarlı, Engin Deniz ed. *Belgelerle Tanzimat: Osmanlı Sadrıazamlarından Ali ve Fuad Paşaların Siyasi Vasiyyetnameleri*. Istanbul: Boğaziçi Üniversitesi Yayınları, 1978.

[Altınay], Ahmet Refik. *Hicrî On İkinci Asırda İstanbul Hayatı (1100–1200)*. Istanbul: Enderun Kitabevi, 1988.

Bournoutian, George A. ed. *Russia and the Armenians of Transcaucasia, 1797–1889: A Documentary Record*. Costa Mesa: Mazda Publishers, 1998.

Cevdet Paşa. *Tezâkir 1–12*, edited by Cavid Baysun. 2nd edition. Ankara: Türk Tarih Kurumu Basımevi, 1986.

———. *Tezâkir 13–20*, edited by Cavid Baysun. 2nd edition. Ankara: Türk Tarih Kurumu Basımevi, 1986.

———. *Tezâkir 21–39*, edited by Cavid Baysun. 2nd edition. Ankara: Türk Tarih Kurumu Basımevi, 1986.

———. *Tezâkir 40–Tetimme*, edited by Cavid Baysun. 2nd edition. Ankara: Türk Tarih Kurumu Basımevi, 1986.

Çolak, Hasan and Elif Bayraktar-Tellan. *The Orthodox Church as an Ottoman Institution: A Study of Early Modern Patriarchal Berats*. Istanbul: Isis Press, 2019.

Correspondence Respecting the Rights and Privileges of the Latin and Greek Churches in Turkey: Presented to Both Houses of Parliament by Command of Her Majesty. London: Harrison and Son, 1854.

Süleyman Paşazade, Sami. *Süleyman Paşa'nın Muhakemesi*. Istanbul: Erkan-ı Harbiye-i Umumiye Onuncu Şubesi, 1928.

Secondary Sources

Abou-El-Hajj, Rifa'at. *Formation of the Modern State: The Ottoman Empire, Sixteenth to Eighteenth Centuries*. Syracuse: Syracuse University Press, 2005.

Akçam, Taner. *Young Turks' Crime against Humanity: The Armenian Genocide and Ethnic Cleansing in the Ottoman Empire*. Princeton: Princeton University Press, 2012.

Akiba, Jun. 'The Practice of Writing Curricula Vitae among the Lower Government Employees in the Late Ottoman Empire: Workers at the Şeyhülislâm's Office'. *European Journal of Turkish Studies* 6 (2007).

———. 'Preliminaries to a Comparative History of the Russian and Ottoman Empires: Perspectives from Ottoman Studies'. In *Imperiology: From Empirical Knowledge to Discussing the Russian Empire*, edited by Kimitaka Matsuzato, 33–47. Sapporo: Slavic Research Center, 2007.

———. 'Sharīʻa Judges in the Ottoman Nizāmiye Courts, 1864–1908'. *Osmanlı Araştırmaları* 51 (2018): 209–37.

Aksan, Virginia H. 'Ottoman Political Writing, 1768–1808'. *International Journal of Middle East Studies* 25, no. 1 (1993): 53–69.

Akyıldız, Ali. *Tanzimat Dönemi Osmanlı Merkez Teşkilâtında Reform (1836–1856)*. Istanbul: Eren, 1993.

Albōyajean, Arshag A. 'Azkayin Sahmanatrut'iwnĕ: Ir Dzakumĕ ew Girạrut'iwnĕ'. In *1910 Ĕntartsag Ōrats'oyts' S. P'rgchean Hiwantanots'i Hayots'*, 76–528. Istanbul: Dbakrut'iwn H. Madt'ēosean, 1910.

———. *Badmut'iwn Hay Gesarioy: Deghakragan, Badmagan, ew Azkakragan Usumnasirut'iwn*. 2 vols. Cairo: Hradaragut'iwn Gesarioy ew Shrchagayits' Hayrenagts'agan Miut'ean Kahirēi Varch'ut'ean, 1937.

Alexandris, Alexis. 'Lozan Konferansı ve İstanbul Rum Patrikhanesi'nin Ekümenik Boyutu: 10 Ocak 1923 Tarihli Tutanağın Önemi'. In *Tarihî, Siyasi, Dinî ve Hukuki Açıdan Ekümenik Patrikhane*, edited by Cengiz Aktar, 77–119. Istanbul: İletişim, 2011.

Altıntaş, Toygun. 'The Placard Affair and the Ankara Trial: The Hnchak Party and the Hamidian Regime in Central Anatolia, 1892–93'. *Journal of the Ottoman and Turkish Studies Association* 4, no. 2 (2017): 309–37.

Anagnostopulu, Athanasia. 'The "Nation" of the *Rum* Sings of Its Sultan: The Many Faces of Ottomanism'. In *Economy and Society on Both Shores of the Aegean*, edited by Lorans Tanatar Baruh and Vangelis Kechriotis, 79–105. Athens: Alpha Bank Historical Archives, 2010.

Anastasopoulos, Antonis. 'Non-Muslims and Ottoman Justice(s?)'. In *Law and Empire: Ideas, Practices, Actors*, edited by Jeroen Duindam, Jill Diana Harries, Caroline Humfress and Hurvitz Nimrod, 275–92. Leiden: Brill, 2013.

Antaramian, Richard Edward. *Brokers of Faith, Brokers of Empire: Armenians and the Politics of Reform in the Ottoman Empire*. Stanford: Stanford University Press, 2020.

———. 'In Subversive Service of the Sublime State: Armenians and Ottoman State Power, 1844–1896'. PhD diss., University of Michigan, 2014.

Arai, Masami. *Isuramu to Kindaika: Kyowakoku Toruko no Kuto*. Tokyo: Kodansha, 2013.

———. '"Osuman Shimin" no Jiyu to Byodo: Midohato Kempo kara 1924 Nen Kempo he'. In *Kokumin Kokka to Shimin: Hosetsu to Haijo no Shoso*, edited by Hirotaka Tateishi and Taku Shinohara, 141–64. Tokyo: Yamakawa Shuppansha, 2009.

———. *Osuman Teikoku wa Naze Hokaishita noka*. Tokyo: Seidosha, 2009.

Aral, Guillaume. 'La Juridiction du Saint-Siege de Rome sur les Armeniens Catholiques (XVIIe–XIXe siècle)'. PhD diss., Université de Nice, 2001.

Artinian, Vartan. *The Armenian Constitutional System in the Ottoman Empire 1839–1863: A Study of Its Historical Development*. Istanbul: n.p., 1988. (Enlarged edition in Turkish, *Osmanlı Devleti'nde Ermeni Anayasası'nın Doğuşu 1839–1863*, translated by Zülal Kılıç. Istanbul: Aras Yayıncılık, 2004.)

Bibliography

Asad, Talal. *Formations of the Secular: Christianity, Islam, Modernity*. Stanford: Stanford University Press, 2003.

———. *Genealogies of Religion: Discipline and Reasons of Power in Christianity and Islam*. Baltimore: Johns Hopkins University Press, 1993.

Aslanian, Sebouh David. *Early Modernity and Mobility: Port Cities and Printers across the Armenian Diaspora, 1512–1800*. New Haven: Yale University Press, 2023.

———. 'The "Great Schism" of 1773: Venice and the Founding of the Armenian Community in Trieste'. In *Reflections of Armenian Identity in History and Historiography*, edited by Houri Berberian and Touraj Daryaee, 83–131. [Irvine]: UCI Jordan Center for Persian Studies, 2018.

———. '"Prepared in the Language of the Hagarites": Abbot Mkhitar's 1727 Armeno-Turkish Grammar of Modern Western Armenian'. *Journal of the Society for Armenian Studies* 25 (2016): 54–86.

Astourian, Stephan H. 'On the Genealogy of the Armenian–Turkish Conflict, Sultan Abdülhamid and the Armenian Massacres'. In *Collective and State Violence in Turkey: The Construction of a National Identity from Empire to Nation-State*, edited by Stephan H. Astourian and Raymond H. Kévorkian, 13–55. New York: Berghahn, 2021.

Atamian, Sarkis. *The Armenian Community: The Historical Development of a Social and Ideological Conflict*. New York: Philosophical Library, 1955.

Augustinos, Gerasimos. *The Greeks of Asia Minor: Confession, Community, and Ethnicity in the Nineteenth Century*. Kent, OH: The Kent State University Press, 1992.

Ayalon, Yaron. 'Rethinking Rabbinical Leadership in Ottoman Jewish Communities'. *Jewish Quarterly Review* 107, no. 3 (2017): 323–53.

Aymes, Marc. *Un grand progrès sur le papier: Histoire provinciale des réformes ottomanes à Chypre au XIXe siècle*. Leuven: Peeters, 2010.

Balcı, Sezai. 'Bir Osmanlı-Ermeni Aydın ve Bürokratı: Sahak Abro (1825–1900)'. In *Osmanlı Siyasal ve Sosyal Hayatında Ermeniler*, edited by İbrahim Erdal and Ahmet Karaçavuş, 105–38. Istanbul: IQ Kültür Sanat, 2009.

Bardakjian, Kevork B. 'The Rise of the Armenian Patriarchate of Constantinople'. In *Christians and Jews in the Ottoman Empire: The Functioning of a Plural Society*, edited by Benjamin Braude and Bernard Lewis, vol. 1, 89–100. New York: Holmes & Meier Publishers, 1982.

Barkey, Karen. 'Aspects of Legal Pluralism in the Ottoman Empire'. In *Legal Pluralism and Empires, 1500–1850*, edited by Lauren Benton and Richard J. Ross, 83–107. New York: New York University Press, 2013.

———. *Empire of Difference: The Ottomans in Comparative Perspective*. Cambridge: Cambridge University Press, 2008.

Barkey, Karen and George Gavrillis. 'The Ottoman Millet System: Non-Territorial Autonomy and Its Contemporary Legacy'. *Ethnopolitics* 15, no. 1 (2016): 24–42.

Barsoumian, Hagop Levon. 'The Armenian *Amira* Class of Istanbul'. PhD diss., Columbia University, 1980.

Başaran, Betül. *Selim III, Social Control and Policing in Istanbul at the End of the Eighteenth Century: Between Crisis and Order*. Leiden: Brill, 2014.

Bayraktar Tellan, Elif. 'The Patriarch and the Sultan: The Struggle for Authority and the Quest for Order in the Eighteenth-Century Ottoman Empire'. PhD diss., Bilkent University, 2011.

Bebiroğlu, Murat. *Tanzimat'tan II. Meşrutiyet'e Ermeni Nizamnameleri*. Istanbul: Orhan Matbaacılık, 2003.

Bein, Amit. *Ottoman Ulema, Turkish Republic: Agents of Change and Guardians of Tradition*. Stanford: Stanford University Press, 2011.

Bērbērean, Hayg. 'G. Bolsoy Hay Badriark'ut'ean Himnargut'iwnĕ'. *Hantēs Amsōreay* 78, no. 7–9 (1964): 337–50; no. 10–12: 497–510.

Berkes, Niyazi. *The Development of Secularism in Turkey*. Montreal: McGill University Press, 1964; repr. New York: Routledge, 1998.

Beydilli, Kemal. *Recognition of the Armenian Catholic Community and the Church in the Reign of Mahmud II. (1830)*. Cambridge, MA: The Department of Near Eastern Languages and Civilizations, Harvard University, 1995.

Beylérian, Arthur. 'Krikor Odian (1834–1887): Un haut fonctionnaire ottoman, homme des missions secretes'. *Revue du monde arménien moderne et contemporain* 1 (1994): 45–86.

Boogert, Maurits H. van den. *The Capitulations and the Ottoman Legal System: Qadis, Consuls and* Beratlıs *in the 18th Century*. Leiden: Brill, 2005.

———. 'Millets: Past and Present'. In *Religious Minorities in the Middle East: Domination, Self-Empowerment, Accommodation*, edited by Anne Sofie Roald and Anh Nga Longva, 27–45. Leiden: Brill, 2012.

Bozkurt, Gülnihâl. *Alman-İngiliz Belgelerinin ve Siyasî Gelişmelerin Işığı Altında Gayrimüslim Osmanlı Vatandaşlarının Hukukî Durumu (1839–1914)*. Ankara: Türk Tarih Kurumu Basımevi, 1989.

Braude, Benjamin. 'Foundation Myths of the Millet System'. In *Christians and Jews in the Ottoman Empire*, vol. 1, 69–88.

Bruinessen, Martin van. *Agha, Shaikh and State: The Social and Political Structures of Kurdistan*. London: Zed Books, 1992.

Buzpınar, Tufan. *Hilafet ve Saltanat: II. Abdülhamid Döneminde Halifelik ve Araplar*. Istanbul: Alfa, 2016.

Can, Lâle. 'The Protection Question: Central Asians and Extraterritoriality in the Late Ottoman Empire'. *International Journal of Middle East Studies* 48, no. 4 (2016): 679–99.

———. *Spiritual Subjects: Central Asian Pilgrims and the Ottoman Hajj at the End of Empire*. Stanford: Stanford University Press, 2020.

Carleton, Alford. 'The Millet System for the Government of Minorities in the Ottoman Empire'. PhD diss., Hartford Seminary, 1937.

———. 'Near Eastern Aspects of the Problem of Church and State'. *The Moslem World* 28 (1938): 279–84.

Clements, Henry. 'Documenting Community in the Late Ottoman Empire'. *International Journal of Middle East Studies* 51, no. 3 (2019): 423–43.

Cohen, Julia Phillips. *Becoming Ottomans: Sephardi Jews and Imperial Citizenship in the Modern Era*. Oxford: Oxford University Press, 2014.

———. 'Between Civic and Islamic Ottomanism: Jewish Imperial Citizenship in the Hamidian Era'. *International Journal of Middle East Studies* 44, no. 2 (2012): 237–55.

Cora, Yaşar Tolga. 'Transforming Erzurum/Karin: The Social and Economic History of a Multi-ethnic Ottoman City in the Nineteenth Century'. PhD diss., The University of Chicago, 2016.

———. 'Why was Pastırmacı Khachatur Efendi Killed? The Life of an Ottoman-Armenian Elite in Mid-19th-Century Erzurum/Karin'. In *Ottoman Armenians: Life, Culture, Society* 1, edited by Vahé Tachjian, 64–87. Berlin: A Houshamadyan Publication, 2014.

Cora, Yaşar Tolga, Dzovinar Derderian and Ali Sipahi eds. *The Ottoman East in the Nineteenth Century: Societies, Identities and Politics*. London: I. B. Tauris, 2016.

Crews, Robert. 'Empire and the Confessional State: Islam and Religious Politics in Nineteenth-Century Russia'. *The American Historical Review* 108, no. 1 (2003): 50–83.

———. *For Prophet and Tsar: Islam and Empire in Russia and Central Asia*. Cambridge, MA: Harvard University Press, 2006.

Çadırcı, Musa. *Tanzimat Döneminde Anadolu Kentleri'nin Sosyal ve Ekonomik Yapısı*. Ankara: Türk Tarih Kurumu Basımevi, 1997.

Çark, Y. G. *Türk Devleti Hizmetinde Ermeniler, 1453–1953*. Istanbul: Yeni Matbaa, 1953.

Çelik, Zeynep. *The Remaking of Istanbul: Portrait of an Ottoman City in the Nineteenth Century*. Seattle: University of Washington Press, 1986.

Çilingir, Hamdi. 'İmtiyâzât-ı Mezhebiyenin Sınırı: Şer^{c}iye Mahkemeleri ile Gayrimüslim "Mahkemelerinin" Görev Alanına Dair Bir Tartışma'. In *Son Dönem Osmanlı Hukuk Düşüncesi: Meseleler Fikirler ve Kurumlar*, edited by Hamdi Çilingir and Hüseyin Önal, 3–30. Istanbul: İlem Yayınları, 2021.

Çolak, Hasan. *The Orthodox Church in the Early Modern Middle East: Relations between the Ottoman Central Administration and the Patriarchates of Antioch, Jerusalem and Alexandria*. Ankara: Türk Tarih Kurumu, 2015.

Davison, Roderic H. *Reform in the Ottoman Empire 1856–1876*. Princeton: Princeton University Press, 1963; repr. New York: Gordian Press, 1973.

———. 'Turkish Attitudes Concerning Christian-Muslim Equality in the Nineteenth Century'. *The American Historical Review* 59, no. 4 (1954): 844–64.

Demirakın, N. Işık. 'Expropriation as a Modernizing Tool in the Nineteenth-Century Ottoman Empire: The Case of Cemeteries in Beyoğlu'. *International Journal of Turkish Studies* 18, no. 1–2 (2012): 1–15.

Demirel, Fatmagül. *II. Abdülhamid Döneminde Sansür*. Ankara: Bağlam, 2007.

———. *Adliye Nezareti: Kuruluşu ve Faaliyetleri (1876–1914)*. Istanbul: Boğaziçi Üniversitesi Yayınevi, 2008.

Dennis, Brad Ronald. 'Explaining Coexistence and Conflict in Eastern Anatolia 1800–1878'. PhD diss., University of Utah, 2015.

Dēr Bedrosean, Hovhannēs. *Grt'agan Sharzhumě T'rk'ahayots' Mēch 1600–1900*. Cairo: Hay Azkayin Himnatram, 1983.

Der Matossian, Bedross. *The Horrors of Adana: Revolution and Violence in the Early Twentieth Century*. Stanford: Stanford University Press, 2022.

———. *Shattered Dreams of Revolution: From Liberty to Violence in the Late Ottoman Empire*. Stanford: Stanford University Press, 2014.

Derderian, Dzovinar. 'Mapping the Fatherland: Artzvi Vaspurakan's Reforms through the Memory of the Past'. In *Ottoman Armenians: Life, Culture, Society* 1, 144–69.

———. 'Nation-Making and the Language of Colonialism: Voices from Ottoman Van in Armenian Print Media and Handwritten Petitions (1820s to 1870s)'. PhD diss., University of Michigan, 2019.

———. 'Orders and Disorders of Marriage, Church, and Empire in Mid-Nineteenth-Century Ottoman Armenia'. *International Journal of Middle East Studies* 56, no. 1 (2024): 75–90.

Deringil, Selim. '"The Armenian Question is Finally Closed": Mass Conversions of Armenians in Anatolia during the Hamidian Massacres of 1895–1897'. *Comparative Studies in Society and History* 51, no. 2 (2009): 344–71.

———. 'Legitimacy Structures in the Ottoman State: The Reign of Abdülhamid II (1876–1909)'. *International Journal of Middle East Studies* 23, no. 3 (1991): 345–59.

———. *The Well-Protected Domains: Ideology and the Legitimation of Power in the Ottoman Empire 1876–1909*. London: I. B. Tauris, 1998.

Dipratu, Radu. *Regulating Non-Muslim Communities in the Seventeenth-Century Ottoman Empire: Catholics and Capitulations*. London: Routledge, 2022.

Dressler, Markus. 'Tracing the Nationalisation of *Millet* in the Late Ottoman Period: A Conceptual History Approach'. *Die Welt des Islams* 62, no. 3–4 (2022): 360–88.

Ekmekçioğlu, Lerna. *Recovering Armenia: The Limits of Belonging in Post-Genocide Turkey*. Stanford: Stanford University Press, 2016.

Eldem, Edhem. 'Capitulations and Western Trade'. In *The Cambridge History of Turkey*, vol. 3, edited by Suraiya N. Faroqhi, 281–335. Cambridge: Cambridge University Press, 2006.

Ĕntartsag Ōrats'oyts' Azkayin Hiwantanots'i. Istanbul, 1900–1910.

Ercan, Yavuz. *Kudüs Ermeni Patrikhanesi*. Ankara: Türk Tarih Kurumu Basımevi, 1988.

Eryılmaz, Bilal. *Osmanlı Devletinde Gayrimüslim Teb'anın Yönetimi*. Istanbul: Risale, 1990.

———. *Osmanlı Devleti'nde Millet Sistemi*. Istanbul: Ağaç Yayıncılık, 1992.

Etmekjian, James. *The French Influence on the Western Armenian Renaissance 1843–1915*. New York: Twayne Publishers, 1964.

Evered, Emine Ö. *Empire and Education under the Ottomans: Politics, Reform, and Resistance from the Tanzimat to the Young Turks*. London: I. B. Tauris, 2012.

Exertzoglou, Haris. 'To "Pronomiako" Zitima'. *Ta Istorika* 16 (1992): 65–84.

Fairey, Jack. 'The Great Game of Improvements: European Diplomacy and the Reform of the Orthodox Church'. PhD diss., University of Toronto, 2004.

———. *The Great Powers and Orthodox Christendom: The Crisis over the Eastern Church in the Era of the Crimean War*. Basingstoke: Palgrave Macmillan, 2015.

Faroqhi, Suraiya. 'Ottoman Guilds in the Late Eighteenth Century: The Bursa Case'. In *Making a Living in the Ottoman Lands 1480 to 1820*, edited by Suraiya Faroqhi, 93–112. Istanbul: Isis Press, 1995.

Findley, Carter V. *Bureaucratic Reform in the Ottoman Empire: The Sublime Porte, 1789–1922*. Princeton: Princeton University Press, 1980.

Fortna, Benjamin C. *Imperial Classroom: Islam, the State, and Education in the Late Ottoman Empire*. Oxford: Oxford University Press, 2002.

Fotić, Aleksandar. 'Tracing the Origin of a New Meaning of the Term *Re'āyā* in the Eighteenth-century Ottoman Balkans'. *Balcanica* 48 (2017): 55–66.

Frazee, Charles A. *Catholics and Sultans: The Church and the Ottoman Empire 1453–1923*. London: Cambridge University Press, 1983.

Fujinami, Nobuyoshi. 'Between Sovereignty and Suzerainty: History of the Ottoman Privileged Provinces'. In *A World History of Suzerainty: A Modern History of East and West Asia and Translated Concepts*, edited by Takashi Okamoto, 41–69. Tokyo: Toyo Bunko, 2019.

———. 'The Ecumenical Patriarchate in the Age of Ottoman Suzerainty'. In *A World History of Suzerainty*, 241–70.

———. 'The First Ottoman History of International Law'. *Turcica* 48 (2017): 245–70.

———. 'Georgios Streit on Crete: International Law, Greece, and the Ottoman Empire'. *Journal of Modern Greek Studies* 34 (2016): 321–42.

———. 'Legal Pluralism for Whose Sake? Ottoman Law, Greek Jurists, and Religious Privileges'. *Byzantine and Modern Greek Studies*. Advance online publication. doi: 10.1017/byz.2023.22

———. 'Privileged but Equal: The Privilege Question in the Context of Ottoman Constitutionalism'. In *Balkan Nationalism(s) and the Ottoman Empire*, vol. 3, edited by Dimitris Stamatopoulos, 33–59. Istanbul: Isis Press, 2015.

Gara, Eleni. 'Conceptualizing Interreligious Relations in the Ottoman Empire: The Early Modern Centuries'. *Acta Poloniae Historica* 116 (2017): 57–91.

Gawrych, George W. 'Tolerant Dimensions of Cultural Pluralism in the Ottoman Empire: The Albanian Community, 1800–1912'. *International Journal of Middle East Studies* 15, no. 4 (1983): 519–36.

Genell, Aimee M. 'Autonomous Provinces and the Problem of "Semi-Sovereignty" in European International Law'. *Journal of Balkan and Near Eastern Studies* 18, no. 6 (2016): 533–49.

Georgeon, François. *Abdülhamid II: le sultan calife (1876–1909)*. Paris: Fayard, 2003.

Gerd, Lora. *Russian Policy in the Orthodox East: The Patriarchate of Constantinople (1878–1914)*. Berlin: De Gruyter, 2014.

Gibb, H. A. R. and Harold Bowen. *Islamic Society and the West: A Study of the Impact of Western Civilization on Moslem Culture in the Near East*, vol. 1, 2 parts. London: Oxford University Press, 1950–7.

Girardelli, Paolo. 'Architecture, Identity, and Liminality: On the Use and Meaning of Catholic Spaces in Late Ottoman Istanbul'. *Muqarnas* 22 (2005): 233–64.

Gould, Andrew G. 'Lords or Bandits? The Derebeys of Cilicia'. *International Journal of Middle East Studies* 7, no. 4 (1976): 485–506.

Gölbaşı, Edip. 'The Official Conceptualization of the Anti-Armenian Riots of 1895–1897: Bureaucratic Terminology, Official Ottoman Narrative, and Discourses of Revolutionary Provocation'. *Études arméniennes contemporaines* 10 (2017): 33–62.

Gratien, Chris. *The Unsettled Plain: An Environmental History of the Late Ottoman Frontier*. Stanford: Stanford University Press, 2022.

Greene, Molly. *The Edinburgh History of the Greeks, 1453 to 1768: The Ottoman Empire*. Edinburgh: Edinburgh University Press, 2015.

Gutman, David. 'Travel Documents, Mobility Control, and the Ottoman State in an Age of Global Migration, 1880–1915'. *Journal of the Ottoman and Turkish Studies Association* 3, no. 2 (2016): 347–68.

Güllü, Ramazan Erhan. *Ermeni Sorunu ve İstanbul Ermeni Patrikhanesi (1878–1923)*. Ankara: Türk Tarih Kurumu, 2015.

———. 'İstanbul'da Ermeni-Rum Kiliseleri Krizi ve Ermenilere Tanınan Yeni İmtiyâzlar (1890–1891)'. *OTAM* 38 (2015): 31–53.

Gülsoy, Ufuk. *Osmanlı'nın Gayrimüslim Askerleri*. Istanbul: Timaş Yayınları, 2010.

Güngör, Ekrem. '1 Numaralı Kütahya Şer'iyye Sicili (II. Bölüm) Transkripsiyonu ve Kritiği'. Master's thesis, Dumlupınar University, 2006.

Hadjikyriacou, Antonis. 'Beyond the *Millet* Debate: Communal Representation in Pre-Tanzimat-Era Cyprus'. In *Political Thought and Practice in the Ottoman Empire: Halcyon Days in Crete IX A Symposium held in Rethymno 9–11 January 2015*, edited by Marinos Sariyannis, 71–96. Rethymno: Crete University Press, 2019.

Hamadeh, Shirine. *The City's Pleasures: Istanbul in the Eighteenth Century*. Seattle: University of Washington Press, 2004.

Hanēsean, Mardiros. *Hariwr K'san ew Hink Ameay Hopelean Perayi S. Errortut'iwn Egeghets'woy 1807–1932*. [Istanbul]: Dbaran Sēlamēt', 1932.

Hanley, Will. *Identifying with Nationality: Europeans, Ottomans, and Egyptians in Alexandria*. New York: Columbia University Press, 2017.

Hanssen, Jens. '"Malhamé-Malfamé": Levantine Elites and Transimperial Networks on the Eve of the Young Turk Revolution'. *International Journal of Middle East Studies* 43, no. 1 (2011): 25–48.

Hartmann, Elke. 'The "Loyal Nation" and Its Deputies: The Armenians in the First Ottoman Parliament'. In *The First Ottoman Experiment in Democracy*, edited by Christoph Herzog and Malek Sharif, 187–222. Würzburg: Ergon Verlag, 2010.
Haykakan Sovetakan Hanragitaran. 12 vols. Erevan: Haykakan SSH Gitut'yunneri Akademia, 1974–86.
Heinzelmann, Tobias. *Cihaddan Vatan Savunmasına: Osmanlı İmparatorluğu'nda Genel Askerlik Yükümlülüğü 1826–1856*, translated by Türkis Noyan. Istanbul: Kitap Yayınevi, 2009.
Hovannisian, Richard G. 'The Armenian Question in the Ottoman Empire, 1876–1914'. In *The Armenian People from Ancient to Modern Times*, vol. 2: *Foreign Dominion to Statehood: The Fifteenth Century to the Twentieth Century*, edited by Richard G. Hovannisian, 206–38. New York: St. Martin's Press, 1997.
Hyman, Paula E. *The Jews of Modern France*. Berkeley: University of California Press, 1998.
Inalcık, Halil. 'İmtiyazat, Osmanlı Dönemi'. In *Türkiye Diyanet Vakfı İslam Ansiklopedisi*, vol. 22, 245–52. Istanbul: Türkiye Diyanet Vakfı, 2000.
———. 'The Status of the Greek Orthodox Patriarch under the Ottomans'. *Turcica* 21–23 (1991): 407–36.
Isomae, Junichi. *Kindai Nihon no Shukyo Gensetsu to sono Keifu: Shukyo, Kokka, Shinto*. Tokyo: Iwanami Shoten, 2003.
Ivanova, Polina. 'Armenians in Urban Order and Disorder of Seventeenth-Century Istanbul'. *Journal of the Ottoman and Turkish Studies Association* 4, no. 2 (2017): 239–60.
İskit, Server. *Türkiyede Matbuat Rejimleri*. Istanbul: Ülkü Matbaası, 1939.
İzrail, Nesim Ovadya. *24 Nisan 1915: İstanbul, Çankırı, Ayaş, Ankara*. Istanbul: İletişim, 2013.
Jamgocyan, Onnik. 'Les finances de l'Empire ottoman et les financiers de Constantinople (1732–1853)'. PhD diss., Université de Paris I, 1988.
Jennings. Ronald C. 'Zimmis (Non-Muslims) in Early 17th Century Ottoman Judicial Records: The Sharia Court of Anatolian Kayseri'. *Journal of the Economic and Social History of the Orient* 21, no. 3 (1978): 225–93.
Kadı, İsmail Hakkı. *Ottoman and Dutch Merchants in the Eighteenth Century: Competition and Cooperation in Ankara, Izmir, and Amsterdam*. Leiden: Brill, 2012.
Kane, Eileen M. 'Pilgrims, Holy Places, and the Multi-Confessional Empire: Russian Policy toward the Ottoman Empire under Tsar Nicholas I, 1825–1855'. PhD diss., Princeton University, 2005.
Kara, İsmail. 'Müsâvat yahut Müslümanlara Eşitsizlik: Bir Kavramın Siyaseten/ Dinen İnşası ve Dönüştürücü Gücü'. In *Osmanlı Devleti'nde Din ve Vicdan Hürriyeti*, edited by Azmi Özcan, 307–47. Istanbul: Ensar Neşriyat, 2000.
Karabıçak, Yusuf Ziya. 'Local Patriots and Ecumenical Ottomans: The Orthodox Patriarchate of Constantinople in the Ottoman Configuration of Power, 1768–1828'. PhD diss., McGill University, 2020.

———. 'Ottoman Attempts to Define the Rebels during the Greek War of Independence'. *Studia Islamica* 114, no. 3 (2019): 316–54.

Karaca, Zafer. 'Taksim Ayia Trias Kilisesi'. *İstanbul* 52 (2005): 56–7.

Karmi, Ilan. *The Jewish Community of Istanbul in the Nineteenth Century: Social, Legal and Administrative Transformations*. Istanbul: Isis Press, 1996.

Karpat, Kemal H. '*Millet*s and Nationality: The Roots of the Incongruity of Nation and State in the Post-Ottoman Era'. In *Christians and Jews in the Ottoman Empire*, vol.1, 141–69.

———. *Ottoman Population 1830–1914: Demographic and Social Characteristics*. Madison: The University of Wisconsin Press, 1985.

Katsikas, Stefanos. *Islam and Nationalism in Modern Greece, 1821–1940*. New York: Oxford University Press, 2021.

Kaynar, Reşat. *Mustafa Reşit Paşa ve Tanzimat*. 2nd edition. Ankara: Türk Tarih Kurumu, 1985.

K'ēch'ean, Piwzant. *Badmut'iwn S. P'rgch'i Hiwantanots'in Hayots' i G. Bolis*. Istanbul: Db. K. Baghdadlean, 1887.

Kechriotis, Vangelis. 'The Modernization of the Empire and the Community "Privileges": Greek Orthodox Responses to the Young Turk Policies'. In *The State and the Subaltern: Modernization, Society and the State in Turkey and Iran*, edited by Touraj Atabaki, 53–70. London: I. B. Tauris, 2007.

Kenanoğlu, Macit. *Osmanlı Millet Sistemi: Mit ve Gerçek*. Istanbul: Klasik, 2004.

Kermeli, Eugenia. 'The Right to Choice: Ottoman Justice vis-à-vis Ecclesiastical and Communal Justice in the Balkans, Seventeenth-Nineteenth Centuries'. In *Studies in Islamic Law: A Festschrift for Colin Imber*, edited by Andreas Christmann and Robert Gleave, 165–210. Oxford: Oxford University Press, 2007.

Ketsemanian, Varak. 'The Hunchakian Revolutionary Party and the Assassination Attempts against Patriarch Khoren Ashekian and Maksudzade Simon Bey in 1894'. *International Journal of Middle East Studies* 50, no. 4 (2018): 735–55.

Kévorkian, Raymond. *The Armenian Genocide: A Complete History*. London: I. B. Tauris, 2011.

Kharatyan, A[lbert]. *Arevmtahay Parberakan Mamulě ev Grak'nnut'yuně Ōsmanyan T'urk'iayum*. Erevan: Haykakan SSH GA Hratarakch'ut'yun, 1989.

———. 'Arevmtahayeri Azgayin "Sahmanadrut'yuně" (1860–1863)'. *Patma-Banasirakan Handes* 136 (1992): 51–66.

———. 'Dardzyal Arevmtahayeri Azgayin Sahmanadrut'yan Masin'. *Patma-Banasirakan Handes* 178 (2008): 81–92.

———. *Kostandnupolsi Hay Gaght'ōjakhě (XV–XVII Darer)*. Erevan: Erevani Hamalsarani Hratarakch'ut'yun, 2007.

Kocabaşoğlu, Uygur. *Anadolu'daki Amerika: Kendi Belgeleriyle 19. Yüzyılda Osmanlı İmparatorluğu'ndaki Amerikan Misyoner Okulları*. Istanbul: İmge Kitabevi, 2000. First published 1989 by Arba Yayınları.

Koçunyan, Aylin. 'Long Live Sultan Abdülaziz, Long Live the Nation, Long Live the Constitution…'. In *Constitutionalism, Legitimacy, and Power:*

Nineteenth-Century Experiences, edited by Kelly L. Grotke and Markus J. Prutsch, 189–210. Oxford: Oxford University Press, 2014.

———. *Negotiating the Ottoman Constitution 1839–1876*. Paris: Peeters, 2018.

———. 'Nizâmnâme-i Millet-i Ermeniyân Anayasa Mıydı?' *Toplumsal Tarih* 216 (2011): 46–52.

Konortas, Paraskevas. 'From Tâ'ife to Millet: Ottoman Terms for the Ottoman Greek Orthodox Community'. In *Ottoman Greeks in the Age of Nationalism: Politics, Economy, and Society in the Nineteenth Century*, edited by Dimitri Gondicas and Charles Issawi, 169–79. Princeton: The Darwin Press, 1999.

Kostandyan, Ēmma. 'Mkrtich' A Vanets'i'. In *K'ristonya Hayastan Hanragitaran*, 745–7. Erevan: Haykakan Hanragitarani Glkhavor Khmbagrut'yun, 2002.

Kostopoulou, Elektra. 'Armed Negotiations: The Institutionalization of the Late Ottoman Locality'. *Comparative Studies of South Asia, Africa and the Middle East* 33, no. 3 (2013): 295–309.

Köksal, Yonca. 'Imperial Center and Local Groups: Tanzimat Reforms in the Provinces of Edirne and Ankara'. *New Perspectives on Turkey* 27 (2002): 107–38.

Köse, Ensar. 'Bir Hayalin Peşinde Yüz Yıl: Kudüs ve İstanbul Ermeni Patrikliğini Birleştirme Çabaları (1650–1750)'. *Tarih Dergisi* 63 (2016): 41–88.

———. 'İstanbul Ermeni Patrikliği'nin Osmanlı Hükümeti'yle Münasebetlerine Tesir Eden Dinamikler (18. Yüzyılın İlk Yarısı)'. *Osmanlı Medeniyeti Araştırmaları Dergisi* 3, no. 5 (2017): 1–24.

Kuran, Timur. *The Long Divergence: How Islamic Law Held Back the Middle East*. Princeton: Princeton University Press, 2011.

Kuroki, Hidemitsu. 'Neither "Western" nor "Orthodox": Establishing Greek Catholic Identity in the Ottoman Empire and Beyond'. In *Religious Interactions in Europe and the Mediterranean World: Coexistence and Dialogue from the Twelfth to the Twentieth Centuries*, edited by Katsumi Fukasawa, Benjamin J. Kaplan and Pierre-Yves Beaurepaire, 287–98. London: Routledge, 2017.

Kursar, Vjeran. 'Non-Muslim Communal Divisions and Identities in the Early Modern Ottoman Balkans and the *Millet* System Theory'. In *Power and Influence in South-Eastern Europe: 16th–19th Century*, edited by Maria Baramova, Plamen Mitev, Ivan Parvev and Vania Racheva, 97–108. Zürich: Lit, 2013.

Kurz, Marlene. *Ways to Heaven, Gates to Hell: Fażlīzāde ʿAli's Struggle with the Diversity of Ottoman Islam*. Berlin: EB-Verlag, 2011.

Küçük, Cevdet. 'Osmanlı İmparatorluğu'nda "Millet Sistemi" ve Tanzimat'. In *Mustafa Reşid Paşa ve Dönemi Semineri Bildiriler Ankara, 13–14 Mart 1985*, 13–23. Ankara: Türk Tarih Kurumu Basımevi, 1987.

———. 'Osmanlı Yönetiminde Gayrimüslimler ve "Millet Sistemi"'. In *Söğüt II Osmanlı Sempozyumu (Eylül 1985, Söğüt)*, 61–86. Ankara: Ertuğrul Gazi'yi Anma ve Söğüt Şenliği Vakfı, 1986.

Külekçi, Cahit. *İmtiyâzlar Bağlamında Osmanlı Devleti'nde Ermeniler*. Istanbul: Dün Bugün Yarın Yayınları, 2017.

Kymlicka, Will. *Multicultural Citizenship: A Liberal Theory of Minority Rights*. Oxford: Clarendon Press, 1995.

Laiou, Sophia. 'Christian Women in an Ottoman World: Interpersonal and Family Cases Brought Before the *Shari'a* Courts during the Seventeenth and Eighteenth Centuries (Cases Involving the Greek Community)'. In *Women in the Ottoman Balkans: Gender, Culture and History*, edited by Amila Buturović and İrvin Cemil Schick, 243–71. New York: Palgrave Macmillan, 2007.

Laqueur, Hans-Peter. *Hüve'l-Baki: İstanbul'da Osmanlı Mezarlıkları ve Mezar Taşları*, translated by Selahattin Dilidüzgün. Istanbul: Tarih Vakfı Yurt Yayınları, 1997.

Levy, Avigdor. 'Millet Politics: The Appointment of a Chief Rabbi in 1835'. In *The Jews of the Ottoman Empire*, edited by Avigdor Levy, 425–38. Princeton: Darwin Press, 1994.

Libaridian, Gerard. 'The Ideology of Armenian Liberation: The Development of Armenian Political Thought before the Revolutionary Movement (1639–1885)'. PhD diss., University of California Los Angeles, 1987.

Low, Michael Christopher. 'Unfurling the Flag of Extraterritoriality: Autonomy, Foreign Muslims, and the Capitulations in the Ottoman Hijaz'. *Journal of the Ottoman and Turkish Studies Association* 3, no. 2 (2016): 299–323.

Luke, Harry Charles. *Mosul and Its Minorities*. London: M. Hopkinson & Company, 1925.

Makdisi, Ussama. *The Culture of Sectarianism: Community, History, and Violence in Nineteenth-Century Ottoman Lebanon*. Berkeley: University of California Press, 2000.

Malkoç, Mustafa Numan. *İstanbul'daki Protestan Kiliseler*. Istanbul: Kaya Basım Yayın, 1999.

Mardin, Şerif. *The Genesis of Young Ottoman Thought: A Study in the Modernization of Turkish Political Ideas*. Princeton: Princeton University Press, 1962.

Masters, Bruce. *Christians and Jews in the Ottoman Arab World: The Roots of Sectarianism*. Cambridge: Cambridge University Press, 2001.

———. 'The Establishment of the Melkite Catholic *Millet* in 1848 and the Politics of Identity in Tanzimat Syria'. In *Syria and Bilad al-Sham under Ottoman Rule: Essays in Honour of Abdul-Karim Rafeq*, edited by Peter Sluglett and Stefan Weber, 455–73. Leiden: Brill, 2010.

———. 'The Millet Wars in Aleppo, 1726–1821: An Ottoman Perspective'. In *Aleppo and Its Hinterland in the Ottoman Period/Alep et sa province à l'époque ottomane*, edited by Stefan Winter and Mafalda Ade, 130–51. Leiden: Brill, 2019.

———. 'The Treaties of Erzurum (1823 and 1848) and the Changing Status of Iranians in the Ottoman Empire'. *Iranian Studies* 24, no. 1–4 (1991): 3–15.

Matsushima, Akio. *Reihai no Jiyu to Naporeon: Konin Shukyo Taisei no Seiritsu*. Tokyo: Yamakawa Shuppansha, 2010.

Miller, Owen. '"Back to the Homeland" (Tebi Yergir): Or, how Peasants Became Revolutionaries in Muş'. *Journal of the Ottoman and Turkish Studies Association* 4, no. 2 (2017): 287–308.

———. 'Sasun 1894: Mountains, Missionaries and Massacres at the End of the Ottoman Empire'. PhD diss., Columbia University, 2015.

Miller, Susan Gilson. 'Apportioning Sacred Space in a Moroccan City: The Case of Tangier, 1860–1912'. *City & Society* 13, no. 1 (2001): 57–83.

Miroğlu, Armaveni. 'Tarihi 16. Yüzyıla Uzanan Pangaltı Ermeni Mezarlığı (Surp Hagop Mezarlığı)'. *Toplumsal Tarih* 187 (2009): 34–8.

Mouffe, Chantal. *On the Political*. London: Routledge, 2005.

Mülayim, Ahmet. 'Rum Okulları'. In *Dünden Bugüne İstanbul Ansiklopedisi*, vol. 6, 347–9. Istanbul: Kültür Bakanlığı ve Tarih Vakfı, 1994.

Nalbandian, Louise. *The Armenian Revolutionary Movement: The Development of Armenian Political Parties through the Nineteenth Century*. Berkeley: University of California Press, 1963.

Nazikyan, G. A. *Arevmtahay Mankavarzhakan Mitk'n u Dprots'ě: 19-rd Dari Skzbits' Minch'ev 19-rd Dari 50–60akan T'vakannerě*. Erevan: Luys Hratarakch'ut'yun, 1969.

Ormanian, Malachia [Maghak'ia]. *Azkabadum: Hay Ughghap'aṛ Egeghets'ioy Ants'k'erě Sgizpēn Minch'ew Mer Ōrerě Haragits' Azkayin Barakanerov Badmuadz*, 3 vols. Istanbul: Hradaragut'iwn V. ew H. Nersesean, 1913–1927; repr. Beirut: Db. Sewan, 1959–1961.

———. *L'Église arménienne: Son histoire, sa doctrine, son régime, sa discipline, sa liturgie, sa littérature, son présent*. Paris: Ernest Leroux, 1910.

Ozil, Ayşe. *Orthodox Christians in the Late Ottoman Empire: A Study of Communal Relations*. London: Routledge, 2013.

Önderoğlu, Hediye. '154 Numaralı Manisa Şer'iyye Sicili'nin Transkripsiyon ve Değerlendirmesi (1095–1096/1684–1685)'. Master's thesis, Celal Bayar University, 2015.

Özbek, Nadir. 'Philanthropic Activity, Ottoman Patriotism, and the Hamidian Regime, 1876–1909'. *International Journal of Middle East Studies* 37, no. 1 (2005): 59–81.

———. 'The Politics of Taxation and "Armenian Question" during the Late Ottoman Empire, 1876–1908'. *Comparative Studies in Society and History* 54, no. 4 (2012): 770–97.

Özcoşar, İbrahim. 'Osmanlı Taşrasında Bir Patriklik: Yakubî Süryani Patrikliği'. *Avrasya İncelemeleri Dergisi* 7, no. 2 (2018): 154–81.

Özgüleş, Muzaffer. 'A Missing Royal Mosque in Istanbul that Islamized a Catholic Space: The Galata New Mosque'. *Muqarnas* 34 (2017): 157–95.

Özkan, Ayşe. '1587 Numaralı Rodoscuk (Tekfurdağı) Şer'iyye Sicilinin Transkripsiyonu ve Değerlendirilmesi'. Master's thesis, Sakarya University, 2019.

Özok-Gündoğan, Nilay. *The Kurdish Nobility in the Ottoman Empire: Loyalty, Autonomy and Privilege*. Edinburgh: Edinburgh University Press, 2022.

———. 'Ruling the Periphery, Governing the Land: The Making of the Modern Ottoman State in Kurdistan, 1840–70'. *Comparative Studies of South Asia, Africa and the Middle East* 34, no. 1 (2014): 160–75.

Özsu, Umut. *Formalizing Displacement: International Law and Population Transfers*. Oxford: Oxford University Press, 2015.

———. 'The Ottoman Empire, the Origins of Extraterritoriality, and International Legal Theory'. In *The Oxford Handbook of the Theory of International Law*, edited by Anne Orford and Florian Hoffmann, 123–37. Oxford: Oxford University Press, 2016.

Pamukciyan, Kevork. *Biyografileriyle Ermeniler*. Istanbul: Aras Yayıncılık, 2003.

Papademetriou, Tom. *Render unto the Sultan: Power, Authority, and the Greek Orthodox Church in the Early Ottoman Centuries*. Oxford: Oxford University Press, 2015.

Parla, Ayşe and Ceren Özgül. 'Property, Dispossession, and Citizenship in Turkey: Or, the History of the Gezi Uprising Starts in the Surp Hagop Armenian Cemetery'. *Public Culture* 28, no. 3 (2016): 617–53.

Paspatis, Aleksandros. *Balıklı Rum Hastanesi Kayıtlarına Göre İstanbul'un Ortodoks Esnafı, 1833–1860*, translated by Marianna Yerasimos. Istanbul: Kitap Yayınevi, 2014.

Peterson, Derek R. and Darren R. Walhof eds. *The Invention of Religion: Rethinking Belief in Politics and History*. New Brunswick, NJ: Rutgers University Press, 2002.

Petrov, Milen. 'Everyday Forms of Compliance: Subaltern Commentaries on Ottoman Reform, 1864–1868'. *Comparative Studies in Society and History* 46, no. 4 (2004): 730–59.

———. 'Tanzimat for the Countryside: Midhat Paşa and the Vilayet of Danube, 1864–1868'. PhD diss., Princeton University, 2006.

Philliou, Christine M. *Biography of an Empire: Governing Ottomans in an Age of Revolution*. Berkeley: University of California Press, 2011.

———. 'Communities on the Verge: Unraveling the Phanariot Ascendancy in Ottoman Governance'. *Comparative Studies in Society and History* 51, no. 1 (2009): 151–81.

al-Qattan, Najwa. '*Dhimmīs* in the Muslim Court: Legal Autonomy and Religious Discrimination'. *International Journal of Middle East Studies* 31, no. 3 (1999): 429–44.

———. 'Discriminating Texts: Orthographic Marking and Social Differentiation in the Court Record of Ottoman Damascus'. In *Arabic Sociolinguistics: Issues & Perspectives*, edited by Yasir Suleiman, 57–77. Richmond: Curzon Press, 1994.

Quataert, Donald. 'Clothing Laws, State, and Society in the Ottoman Empire, 1720–1829'. *International Journal of Middle East Studies* 29, no. 3 (1997): 403–25.

———. 'Labor Policies and Politics in the Ottoman Empire: Porters and the Sublime Porte, 1826–1896'. In *Humanist and Scholar: Essays in Honor of*

Andreas Tietze, edited by Heath W. Lowry and Donald Quataert, 59–69. Istanbul: The Isis Press, 1993.

———. *The Ottoman Empire 1700–1922*. 2nd edition. Cambridge: Cambridge University Press, 2005.

Rahn, Markus. *Die Entstehung des Armenischen Patriarchats von Konstantinopel*. Hamburg: Lit, 2002.

Riedler, Florian. 'Armenian Labor Migration to Istanbul and the Migration Crisis of the 1890s'. In *The City in the Ottoman Empire: Migration and the Making of Urban Modernity*, edited by Ulrike Freitag, Malte Fuhrmann, Nora Lafi and Florian Riedler, 160–176. London: Routledge, 2011.

Riegg, Stephan B. 'Imperial Challengers: Tsarist Responses to Armenian Raids into Anatolia, 1875–90'. *The Russian Review* 76, no. 2 (2017): 253–71.

Rodrigue, Aron. 'The Beginnings of Westernization and Community Reform Among Istanbul's Jewry, 1854–1865'. In *The Jews of the Ottoman Empire*, edited by Avigdor Levy, 439–56. Princeton: Darwin Press, 1994.

Rosenthal, Steven. *The Politics of Dependency: Urban Reform in Istanbul*. Westport, CT: Greenwood Press, 1980.

Rubin, Avi. *Ottoman* Nizamiye *Courts: Law and Modernity*. New York: Palgrave Macmillan, 2011.

Safrastjan, Ruben. 'Ottomanism in Turkey in the Epoch of Reforms in XIX C.: Ideology and Policy. I'. *Etudes balkaniques* 24 (1988): 72–86.

———. 'Ottomanism in Turkey in the Epoch of Reforms in XIX C.: Ideology and Policy. II'. *Etudes balkaniques* 25 (1989): 34–44.

Sahara, Tetsuya. *What Happened in Adana in April 1909? Conflicting Armenian and Turkish Views*. Istanbul: Isis Press, 2013.

Salt, Jeremy. *Imperialism, Evangelism and the Ottoman Armenians 1878–1896*. London: Frank Cass, 1993.

Sanjian, Avedis K. *The Armenian Communities in Syria under Ottoman Dominion*. Cambridge, MA: Harvard University Press, 1965.

Santus, Cesare. 'Sheikh ül-islam Feyzullah Efendi and the Armenian Patriarch Awetik': A Case of Entangled Confessional Disciplining?' In *Entangled Confessionalizations? Dialogic Perspectives on the Politics of Piety and Community-Building in the Ottoman Empire, 15th–18th Centuries*, edited by Tijana Krstić and Derin Terzioğlu, 233–54. Piscataway: Gorgias Press, 2022.

Sarıyıldız, Gülden. *Sicill-i Ahvâl Komisyonu'nun Kuruluşu ve İşlevi (1879–1909)*. Istanbul: Der Yayınları, 2004.

Seyfeli, Canan. *İstanbul Ermeni Patrikliği (Kuruluşu ve Tarihten Günümüze İdari Yapısı)*. Ankara: Aziz Andaç Yayınları, 2005.

Shapiro, Henry R. 'Falling Out of Love with the Franks: The Life and Writings of an Armenian Catholic Diplomat in the Service of Late Safavid Persia'. *Iranian Studies* 54, no. 3–4 (2021): 573–603.

———. *The Rise of the Western Armenian Diaspora in the Early Modern Ottoman Empire: From Refugee Crisis to Renaissance*. Edinburgh: Edinburgh University Press, 2022.

Sigalas, Nikos. '"And Every Language that Has Been Voiced Became a *Millet*": A Genealogy of the Late Ottoman *Millet*'. *Die Welt des Islams* 62, no. 3–4 (2022): 325–59.
Sipahi, Ali. 'At Arm's Length: Historical Ethnography of Proximity in Harput'. PhD diss., University of Michigan, 2015.
Somel, Selçuk Akşin. *The Modernization of Public Education in the Ottoman Empire 1839–1908: Islamization, Autocracy and Discipline*. Leiden: Brill, 2001.
———. 'Osmanlı Ermenilerinde Kültür Modernleşmesi, Cemaat Okulları ve Abdülhamid Rejimi'. *Tarih ve Toplum Yeni Yaklaşımlar* 5 (2007): 71–92.
———. 'Osmanlı Reform Çağında Osmanlıcılık Düşüncesi (1839–1913)'. In *Cumhuriyet'e Devreden Düşünce Mirası: Tanzimat ve Meşrutiyet'in Birikimi*, edited by Mehmet Ö. Alkan, vol. 1, 88–116. Istanbul: İletişim Yayınları, 2001.
Stamatopoulos, Dimitrios. 'The Bulgarian Schism Revisited'. *Modern Greek Studies Yearbook* 24–5 (2008–9): 105–25.
———. 'The Christian Orthodox Family in Crisis: The Ecumenical Patriarchate's Courts and the Reconstruction of the Private Sphere in Southeast Europe in the Nineteenth and Early Twentieth Centuries'. In *Problems of Crime and Violence in Europe, 1780–2000*, edited by Efi Avdela, Shani D'Cruze and Judith Rowbotham, 91–118. Lewiston: Edwin Mellen Press, 2010.
———. 'From Millets to Minorities in the 19th-Century Ottoman Empire: An Ambiguous Modernization'. In *Citizenship in Historical Perspective*, edited by Steven G. Ellis, Guðmundur Hálfdanarson and Ann Katherine Isaacs, 253–73. Pisa: Pisa University Press, 2006.
Stavrianos, Leften S. *The Balkans since 1453*. New York: Rinehart & Company, 1958.
Stein, Sarah Abrevaya. *Extraterritorial Dreams: European Citizenship, Sephardi Jews, and the Ottoman Twentieth Century*. Chicago: The University of Chicago Press, 2016.
Step'anyan, G. 'Hayatar̦ T'urk'eren Hay Mamulĕ'. In *Hay Parberakan Mamuli Patmut'yunits'*, edited by A. B. Karinyan, 239–74. Erevan: Haykakan SSR GA Hratarakch'ut'yun, 1963.
Strauss, Johann. 'A Constitution for a Multilingual Empire: Translations of *Kanun-i Esasi* and Other Official Texts into Minority Languages'. In *The First Ottoman Experiment in Democracy*, edited by Christoph Herzog and Malek Sharif, 21–51. Würzburg: Ergon in Kommission, 2010.
———. 'Ottomanisme et "ottomanité": Le témoignage linquistique'. In *Aspects of the Political Language in Turkey (19th–20th Centuries)*, edited by Hans-Lukas Kieser, 15–39. Istanbul: Isis Press, 2002.
Suciyan, Talin. *The Armenians in Modern Turkey: Post-Genocide Society, Politics and History*. London: I. B. Tauris, 2016.
———. *Outcasting Armenians: Tanzimat of the Provinces*. Syracuse: Syracuse University Press, 2023.

Suny, Ronald Grigor. *'They Can Live in the Desert but Nowhere Else': A History of the Armenian Genocide*. Princeton: Princeton University Press, 2015.

Şahiner, Araks. 'The Sarrafs of İstanbul: Financiers of the Empire'. Master's thesis, Boğaziçi University, 1995.

Tachjian, Vahé ed. *Ottoman Armenians: Life, Culture, Society* 1. Berlin: A Houshamadyan Publication, 2014.

Ter Minassian, Anahide. 'A Family of Armenian Amiras: The Dadians'. *Armenian Review* 45, no. 3 (1992): 1–16.

———. 'Sociétés de culture, écoles et presse arméniennes à l'époque d'Abd-ul-hamid II'. *Revue du monde arménien moderne et contemporain* 3 (1997): 7–30.

Tezcan, Baki. 'Ethnicity, Race, Religion and Social Class: Ottoman Markers of Difference'. In *The Ottoman World*, edited by Christine Woodhead, 159–70. London: Routledge, 2011.

———. *The Second Ottoman Empire: Political and Social Transformation in the Early Modern World*. Cambridge: Cambridge University Press, 2010.

T'orkomean, Vahram H. *Pzhishg Dōk't'. Servich'ēn Ēfēndi*. Vienna: Mkhit'arean Dbaran, 1893.

Toynbee, Arnold J. *Turkey*. New York: Scribner, 1927.

Tuğlacı, Pars. *İstanbul Ermeni Kiliseleri*. Istanbul: Pars Yayın, 1991.

———. *The Role of the Balian Family in Ottoman Architecture*. Istanbul: Yeni Çığır Bookstore, 1990.

———. *The Role of the Dadian Family in Ottoman Social, Economic and Political Life*. Istanbul: Pars Yayın, 1993.

———. *Tarih Boyunca Batı Ermenileri*, 4 vols. Istanbul: Pars Yayın, 2004–2009.

Tunaya, Tarık Zafer. 'Osmanlı Anayasacılık Hareketi ve "Hükumet-i Meşruta"'. *Boğaziçi Üniversitesi Dergisi* 6 (1978): 227–37.

Turna, Nalan. *19. Yüzyıldan 20. Yüzyıla Osmanlı Topraklarında Seyahat, Göç ve Asayiş Belgeleri: Mürûr Tezkereleri*. Istanbul: Kaknüs Yayınları, 2013.

Türesay, Özgür. '*Nizam*dan *Tanzimat*a, *Reaya*dan *Tebaa*ya Gidilirken: 1830'ların Başında Takvîm-i Vekayi'nin Siyasi Dili ve Söylemi'. *Tarih ve Toplum Yeni Yaklaşımlar* 20 (2022): 98–142.

———. 'Un nouveau type de sujets ottomans: l'apparition des *tebaa* au début du XIXe siècle'. In *Ethno-geópolitique des empires: de l'antiquité au monde contemporain*, edited by Yann Lignereux, Alain Messaoudi, Annick Peters-Custot and Jérôme Wilgaux, 181–202. Rennes: Presses universitaires de Rennes, 2021.

Ueno, Masayuki. 'Arumeniajin Osuman Kanryo no Kyoikuteki Haikei'. In *Kindai Isuramu no Kyoiku Shakaishi: Osuman Teikoku karano Tembo*, edited by Jun Akiba and Nobuya Hashimoto, 138–64. Kyoto: Syowado, 2014.

———. 'Empire as a Career: Hagop Grjigian or an Armenian in the Ottoman Bureaucracy'. *The Memoirs of the Toyo Bunko* 76 (2018): 57–80.

———. 'The First Draft of the Armenian Millet Constitution'. *Annals of Japan Association for Middle East Studies* 23 (2007): 213–51.

———. '"For the Fatherland and the State": Armenians Negotiate the Tanzimat Reforms'. *International Journal of Middle East Studies* 45, no. 1 (2013): 93–109.

———. 'In Pursuit of Laicized Urban Administration: The *Muhtar* System in Istanbul and Ottoman Attitudes toward Non-Muslim Religious Authorities in the Nineteenth Century'. *International Journal of Middle East Studies* 54, no. 2 (2022): 302–18.

———. 'One Script, Two Languages: Garabed Panosian and his Armeno-Turkish Newspapers in the Nineteenth-Century Ottoman Empire'. *Middle Eastern Studies* 52, no. 4 (2016): 605–22.

———. 'Religious in Form, Political in Content? Privileges of Ottoman Non-Muslims in the Nineteenth Century'. *Journal of the Economic and Social History of the Orient* 59, no. 3 (2016): 408–41.

———. 'Urban Politics in 19th-century Istanbul: The Case of the Armenian Cemetery in Beyoğlu'. In *Human Mobility and Multiethnic Coexistence in Middle Eastern Urban Societies 1: Tehran, Aleppo, Istanbul, and Beirut*, edited by Hidemitsu Kuroki, 85–102. Tokyo: ILCAA, 2015.

Verheij, Jelle. 'Diyarbekir and the Armenian Crisis of 1895'. In *Social Relations in Ottoman Diyarbekir, 1870–1915*, edited by Joost Jongerden and Jelle Verheij, 85–145. Leiden: Brill, 2012.

———. '"The Year of the Firman": The 1895 Massacres in Hizan and Şirvan (Bitlis Vilayet)'. *Études arméniennes contemporaines* 10 (2017): 125–59.

Vovchenko, Denis. *Containing Balkan Nationalism: Imperial Russia and Ottoman Christians, 1856–1914*. New York: Oxford University Press, 2016.

———. 'A Triumph of Orthodoxy in the Age of Nationalism: The Ecumenical Patriarchate, the Sublime Porte, Russia, and Greece (1856–1890)'. *Modern Greek Studies Yearbook* 28/29 (2012/2013): 255–66.

Werth, Paul W. 'Imperial Russia and the Armenian Catholicos at Home and Abroad'. In *Reconstruction and Interaction of Slavic Eurasia and Its Neighboring Worlds*, edited by Osamu Ieda and Tomohiko Uyama, 203–35. Sapporo: Slavic Research Center, Hokkaido University, 2006.

———. *The Tsar's Foreign Faiths: Toleration and the Fate of Religious Freedom in Imperial Russia*. Oxford: Oxford University Press, 2014.

Yaycioglu, Ali. *Partners of the Empire: The Crisis of the Ottoman Order in the Age of Revolutions*. Stanford: Stanford University Press, 2016.

Yi, Eunjeong. 'Interreligious Relations in 17th Century Istanbul in the Light of Immigration and Demographic Change'. *Radovi* 51, no. 1 (2019): 117–43.

Yılmaz, İlkay. *II. Abdülhamid Döneminde Güvenlik Politikaları, Mürur Tezkereleri, Pasaportlar ve Otel Kayıtları: Serseri, Anarşist ve Fesadın Peşinde*. Istanbul: Tarih Vakfı Yurt Yayınları, 2014.

Yoneoka, Daisuke. 'Hapusuburuku Teikokuka Bosunia niokeru Isuramu Tochi to sono Hanno: Reisu uru Urema Shoku wo Megutte'. *Shirin* 94, no. 2 (2011): 89–107.

Yosmaoğlu, İpek. *Blood Ties: Religion, Violence, and the Politics of Nationhood in Ottoman Macedonia, 1878–1908*. Ithaca: Cornell University Press, 2014.

Young, Pamela J. 'Knowledge, Nation, and the Curriculum: Ottoman Armenian Education (1853–1915)'. PhD diss., University of Michigan, 2001.

Yumul, Arus. 'Osmanlı'nın İlk Anayasası'. *Toplum ve Bilim* 83 (1999/2000): 338–51.

Zarinebaf, Fariba. *Mediterranean Encounters: Trade and Pluralism in Early Modern Galata*. Oakland: University of California Press, 2018.

Zürcher, Erik-Jan. 'Ottoman Sources of Kemalist Thought'. In *Late Ottoman Society: The Intellectual Legacy*, edited by Elisabeth Özdalga, 14–27. London: RoutledgeCurzon, 2005.

Index

EU Authorised Representative:
Easy Access System Europe Mustamäe tee 50, 10621 Tallinn, Estonia
gpsr.requests@easproject.com

Printed and bound by CPI Group (UK) Ltd, Croydon, CR0 4YY
29/09/2026
02224981-0012